BALANCING ANTI-MONEY LAUNDERING

Counter-Terrorist Financing Requirements and Financial Inclusion

The Case of Telecommunications Companies

EHI ERIC ESOIMEME

DSC Publications Ltd.

ISBN: 978-2787-89-2
ISBN 13: 978-978-2787-89-7
Published by DSC Publications Ltd.
No. 2, Dapo Bode Thomas Street,
Off Thorburn Street, Via Montgomery/Commercial Avenue.

To God Almighty for his sufficient grace and mercies throughout my life and for giving me the inspiration, strength, and motivation to write this excellent book

Acknowledgements

I take this opportunity to express my deep sense of gratitude to Mr. Ian Ross for his encouragement and support.

I would like to express my thanks to colleagues with whom I have had productive working relationships with over the years. I am grateful to Ian Ross, compliance, financial-crime specialist and trainer, Intersol Global (UK); Anatoly Yakorev, director, Center for Business Ethics & Compliance (Moscow, Russian Federation); Patricia Robertson, chartered FCSI, CDipAF, director, senior compliance and management consultant, Westport Global Ltd (United Kingdom); Daniel Rogers, managing director, AML360.com (Asia Pacific, United Kingdom, Middle East, and North America); Dr. Uju Ogubunka, FCIB, president, Bank Customers Association of Nigeria (BCAN); Mustapha Bouzizoua, compliance officer (financial crimes), HSBC Private Banking (France); Andrew Fleming, ICA AML Dip, global AML risk framework manager, HSBC Global Banking and Markets (London, United Kingdom); and Melissa Brown Levine, owner/senior editor at Brown Levine Productions (Hampton, Georgia).

I express my sincere appreciation to my mother, Dr. Angela Esoimeme, for her unwavering support, encouragement, and supreme patience. I consider myself particularly fortunate to have her as my mother. She created an environment of homely peace and tranquility while I strove to ensure that this publication was of unequaled excellence.

Table of Contents

PREFACE

Two billion people lack access to formal financial services. Approximately 90% of the unbanked live in developing countries. Greater financial inclusion can bring these people into the financial mainstream, with positive effects on economic growth, financial stability and social cohesion. Many of the smartest policies for increasing access to formal financial services have been innovated in developing countries—those who live with the challenges of financial exclusion every day.

In general terms, financial inclusion involves providing access to an adequate range of safe, convenient and affordable financial services to disadvantaged and other vulnerable groups, including low income, rural and undocumented persons, who have been underserved or excluded from the formal financial sector. Financial inclusion also involves making a broader range of financial products and services available to individuals who currently only have access to basic financial products. Financial inclusion can also be defined as ensuring access to appropriate financial products and services at an affordable cost in a fair and transparent manner.

It is acknowledged that financial exclusion works against effective anti-money laundering and combating the financing of terrorism (AML/CFT) policies. Indeed, the prevalence of a large informal, unregulated and undocumented economy negatively affects AML/CFT efforts and the integrity of the financial system. Informal, unregulated and undocumented financial services and a pervasive cash economy can generate significant money laundering and terrorist financing risks and negatively affect AML/CFT preventive, detection and investigation/prosecution efforts. Dependence on mainly informal financial services also limits access to reasonably priced credit and slows country's development. If the funds are kept outside the formal system, there is a limited multiplier effect in the economy.

Promoting formal financial systems and services is therefore central to any effective and comprehensive AML/CFT regime. Financial inclusion and an effective AML/CFT regime can and should be complementary national policy objectives with mutually supportive policy goals.

Accordingly, international AML/CFT standards have flexibility, enabling jurisdictions to craft effective and appropriate controls while taking into account the relevance of expanding access to financial services, as well as the diverse levels and types of risks posed by different products and supply channels. The challenge is finding the right level of protection for a particular financial environment.

As part of moves to further deepen financial inclusion in the country as well as ensuring improvement in the mobile money segment of Nigeria's information and communications technology sector, the Central Bank of Nigeria (CBN) and the Nigerian Communications Commission (NCC) signed a Memorandum of Understanding (MoU) on digital payment systems with both parties agreeing to jointly implement a payment systems framework. This MoU is coming after the CBN revealed that the financial inclusion rate remains below expectation. This is the case even when several initiatives have been introduced by the CBN (e.g., the introduction of microfinance banking, agent banking, tiered know-your-customer requirements and mobile money operations) in pursuit of its objective—that is, ensuring that over 80% of the bankable adults in Nigeria have access to financial services by 2020. In 2016, 58.4% of Nigeria's 96.4 million adults were financially served, leaving 41.6% financially excluded. The proportion of those who were banked was 38.3%, 10.3% were in the formal other category and 9.8% were served by the informal sector. This

shows that only 48.6% used formal services compared to 80% who are targeted in 2020.

In line with the MoU on digital payment systems, the CBN issued guidelines for licensing, regulation and operation of payment service banks (e.g., banking agents, telecommunications companies, retail chains and mobile money operators in the country). The focus of this book is on telecommunications companies. The director of the financial policy and regulation department of the regulatory body, Kevin Amuga, said the guidelines were in furtherance of the apex bank's effort to leverage technology to promote financial inclusion and enhance access to financial services for the rural poor, low-income earners and financially excluded in society.

The following research question explores how the right balance can be found:

How can telecommunications companies design AML/CFT measures that meet the goal of financial inclusion without compromising the measures that exist for combating money laundering, terrorist financing and other illicit transactions through the financial system?

THE OBJECTIVE(S)/PURPOSE OF THE BOOK:

This book will critically review the AML/CFT measures in the **Guidelines for Licensing, Regulation and Operation of Telecommunications Companies** issued by the CBN. The aim is to determine if the said guidelines adopt a balanced approach to financial inclusion, anti-money laundering measures and fundamental human rights.

RESEARCH METHODOLOGY

The research took the form of a desk study, which analyzed various documents and reports such as the **Revised Central Bank of Nigeria National Financial Inclusion Strategy 2018**, the **Guidelines for Licensing and Regulation of Payment Service Banks in Nigeria as issued by the Central Bank of Nigeria in October 2018**, the **Central Bank of Nigeria' Revised Assessment Criteria for Approved Persons' Regime for Financial Institutions 2015**, the **Central Bank of Nigeria Code of Corporate Governance for Banks and Discount Houses in Nigeria 2014**, the **Nigerian Money Laundering (Prohibition) Act, 2011 (as amended)**, the **Central Bank of Nigeria (Anti-Money Laundering and Combating the Financing of Terrorism in Banks and Other Financial Institutions in Nigeria) Regulations, 2013**, the **United Kingdom Payment Services Regulations 2017**, the **United Kingdom Payment Accounts Regulations 2015**, the **United Kingdom Electronic Money Regulations 2011**, the **Guidance on the Prevention of Money Laundering/Combating Terrorist Financing for the United Kingdom Financial Sector Part I as issued by the Joint Money Laundering Steering Group in June 2017 [Amended December 2017]**, the **United States Federal Financial Institutions Examination Council' Bank Secrecy Act/Anti-Money Laundering Examination Manual 2014**, the **Kenya Information and Communications (Amendment) Act 2013**, the **Kenya Information and Communications (Registration of SIM-cards) Regulations 2015**, the **Financial Action Task Force Guidance on the Risk-Based Approach to Combating Money Laundering and Terrorist Financing - High Level Principles and Procedures 2007**, the **Financial Action Task Force Guidance on Anti-Money Laundering and Terrorist Financing Measures and Financial Inclusion 2011**, the **International Standards on Combating Money Laundering and the Financing of Terrorism and Proliferation (The FATF**

Recommendations) 2012, the **Financial Action Task Force Guidance on Anti-Money Laundering and Terrorist Financing Measures and Financial Inclusion 2013 and** the **Financial Action Task Force Guidance for a Risk Based Approach: Prepaid Cards, Mobile Payments and Internet-Based Payment Services 2013.**

RESEARCH LIMITATIONS

Although the main focus of this book is on Nigeria, the measures and principles in it can be applied to any country that is faced with the challenge of designing AML/CFT measures for telecommunications companies.

Chapters 1 to 6 of this book will critically review the Regulatory Framework for Telecommunications Companies issued by the Nigerian Telecommunications Commission and the CBN to determine if the said regulations adopt a balanced approach to financial inclusion, anti-money laundering measures and fundamental human rights.

TARGET AUDIENCE:

The book focuses on telecommunications companies and financial institutions. It is also aimed at both undergraduate and postgraduate researchers.

CONTENT OF THE BOOK:

The first chapter begins with the analysis of the subject of financial inclusion in relation to its definition, its macroeconomic impact, its relationship with money laundering and mobile banking and its history. The chapter thereafter analyses the **Regulatory Framework for Telecommunications Companies** issued by the NCC to determine if the measures in the said regulations can effectively combat money laundering and terrorist financing in the new mobile banking regime.

Chapter 2 analyses **the Central Bank of Nigeria's Revised Assessment Criteria for Approved Persons' Regime for Financial Institutions 2015** to determine if the fit and proper test can effectively curb money laundering and terrorist financing in telecommunications companies. The chapter gives an explication of how telecommunications companies can assess the competence of candidates for board, top management and critical operational positions, and their integrity and suitability.

Chapter 3 analyses the **Anti-Money Laundering and Combating the Financing of Terrorism (AML/CFT) Policy of the Telecommunications Companies** that they must adapt to combat money laundering and terrorism financing. The chapter will determine if there is a need for reforms.

Chapter 4 analyses the whistle-blowing procedures of the **Central Bank of Nigeria Guidelines for Whistle-Blowing for Banks and Other Financial Institutions in Nigeria** to determine if the procedures can effectively curb money laundering and terrorist financing in telecommunications companies or if there is a need for reforms.

Chapter 5 expatiates on the **three-tiered know-your-customer requirements** that telecommunications companies with a payment service bank license are required to implement.

Chapter 6 critically analyses the **Telecommunications Regulatory Framework** to determine if it interferes with the fundamental human rights of Nigerians.

Each chapter of this book, from Chapters 2 to 6, has a discussion and conclusion section. The conclusion section provides recommendations for the policies that were analysed in the discussion section. No other book adopts this kind of approach.

THE INSPIRATION

I drew part of my inspiration to put together this outstanding book from one of my research papers: 'Enhancing Financial Inclusion: Telecoms and AML in Nigeria.' I wrote the paper for KYC360 (the global financial crime and compliance knowledge hub powered by RiskScreen).

The paper broadened my interest in the area of mobile banking. It also enabled me to really understand the connection between mobile banking and money laundering, and their importance for financial inclusion. The paper drove me to carry out more extensive research in this area.

Tom Brown (CAMS), tutor and lecturer in money laundering (LLM, master's degree level) at Cardiff University and senior consultant at Kaizen Compliance Solutions also inspired the writing of this book. Brown's lecture classes focused not only on the dissemination of credible information relating to money laundering rules and regulations but also on research development.

Brown encourages students to think out of the box and not limit their thoughts to issues predicated on the subject.

His teachings helped me to not only understand the anti-money laundering principles governing the financial sector but also to develop my research skills, and this has helped me to write this book on the subject of money laundering.

DETAILS OF COMPETING BOOKS, EITHER PUBLISHED OR IN PREPARATION, AND HOW THIS BOOK DISTINGUISHES ITSELF FROM THESE:

Several books have been published on mobile banking internationally. Notable among them are Pierre-Laurent Chatain, Andrew Zerzan, Wameek Noor, Najah Dannaoui, Louis de Koker and Bob Christen (2011), *Protecting Mobile Money against Financial Crimes: Global Policy Challenges and Solutions (English), Directions in Development; Finance.* Washington, DC: World Bank; Sunduzwayo Madise (2019), *The Regulation of Mobile Money: Law and Practice in Sub-Saharan Africa.* Palgrave Macmillan Studies in Banking and Financial Institutions; and Bernardo Nicoletti (2014), *Mobile Banking: Evolution or Revolution?* Palgrave Studies in Financial Services Technology.

The book by Chatain et al. (2011) dissected the various business models of m-money programs and provided an assessment of potential risks stemming from m-money services and the mitigation tools that can be applied. It did not critically review the AML/CFT measures in the **Guidelines for Licensing, Regulation and Operation of Telecommunications Companies** issued by the CBN.

The book by Madise (2019) did a comparative study of mobile money regimes in Kenya, Malaŵi, Tanzania and South Africa. It did not critically review the AML/CFT measures in the **Guidelines for Licensing, Regulation and Operation of Telecommunications Companies** issued by the CBN.

The book by Nicoletti (2014) analysed the application of mobile to the world of financial institutions. The author considered future developments and the possible use of mobile to help the transformation in products, processes, organizations and business models of financial institutions globally. The book did not analyse the **Regulatory Framework for Telecommunications Companies** issued by the NCC and the CBN.

This book by Ehi Eric Esoimeme analyses the Regulatory Framework for Telecommunications Companies issued by the NCC and the CBN to determine if the measures in the said regulations can effectively combat money laundering and terrorist financing in the new mobile banking regime.

Ehi Eric Esoimeme Esq., Llb (Unilag), Bl, Ica (Manchester), Llm (Cardiff), PhD (in View) (Unilag)

Managing Associate at Deji Sasegbon and Co.

Deputy Editor in Chief of Dsc Publications Ltd.

Editorial Board Member at the *International Journal of Law and Society*

Contributor at the *Journal of Money Laundering Control* (the world's only quarterly, peer-reviewed journal)

Contributor at the *Journal of Financial Crime*

Contributor at *Law Digest* (Africa's leading law journal)

Contributor at Kyc360 (the world's leading platform for anti-money laundering professionals)

Member of the Association of Certified Anti-Money Laundering Specialists (Acams)

Author of *Deterring and Detecting Money Laundering and Terrorist Financing*

Author of *The Risk-Based Approach to Combating Money Laundering and Terrorist Financing*

Author of *Banker-Customer Relationship: A Practical Legal Guide*

Author of approved scholarly papers (Ssrn) (Us)

Website: https://ehiericesoimeme.com/

ABOUT THE AUTHOR

Ehi Eric Esoimeme is the Deputy Editor in Chief of DSC Publications Ltd. His areas of expertise include, among others, comparative law, money laundering law and international banking law.

Ehi completed his undergraduate studies at the University of Lagos, postgraduate studies at Cardiff University and his professional course on Money Laundering Law at the University of Manchester.

Ehi has authored more than 30 publications, including three books on Money Laundering Law/Banking Law. Ehi's second book titled 'The Risk-Based Approach to Combating Money Laundering and Terrorist Financing' became a bestseller on Amazon for banking law. Ehi's fourth book titled 'Deterring and Detecting Money Laundering and Terrorist Financing: A Comparative Analysis of Anti–Money Laundering and Counterterrorism Financing Strategies' has received many commendations from both academic researchers and Anti-Money Laundering professionals.

Ehi was recently listed among the contributors for the new KYC360 website (the global financial crime and compliance knowledge hub powered by RiskScreen). Ehi Contributes articles, webinars and podcasts to the website. Ehi's most recent article titled "Using anti-money laundering measures to curb pension fraud in Nigeria" has been endorsed by professionals in the Anti-Money Laundering Industry.

Ehi is a member of the Industry's Largest International Network of Financial Crime Detection and Prevention Professionals (ACAMS). His Membership number is 1000157079. The Membership provides Ehi with access to exclusive anti money laundering publications, continuing education and training, networking and professional growth.

TABLE OF CASES

REFERENCES ARE TO PARAGRAPH NUMBERS

TABLES OF LEGISLATION

REFERENCES ARE TO PARAGRAPH NUMBERS

NIGERIA

PRIMARY LEGISLATION

Banks and Other Financial Institutions Act, 1991 (as amended)	2.0
Companies and Allied Matters Act, 1990 (as amended).	2.0
Constitution of the Federal Republic of Nigeria, 1999	6.1,6.2.2, 6.2.4
Economic and Financial Crimes Commission (Establishment) Act, 2004	1.5
Nigerian Communications Act, 2003	1.3
Nigerian Money Laundering Prohibition Act, 2011 (as amended)	1.5, 3.1, 3.3, 3.4, 3.5, 3.6, 6.1
Terrorism (Prevention) Act, 2011 (as amended)	1.5

SECONDARY LEGISLATION

Anti-Money Laundering/Combating the Financing of Terrorism (AML/CFT) Regulations for Designated non- Financial Businesses and Professions in Nigeria 2013	1.5
Central Bank of Nigeria (Anti-Money Laundering and Combating the Financing of Terrorism in Banks and other Financial Institutions in Nigeria) Regulations, 2013	1.5, 3.1.16, 3.4.1, 3.4.3, 3.7, 5.0,

TERTIARY LEGISLATION

KENYA

PRIMARY LEGISLATION

Kenya Information and Communications (Amendment) Act, 2013	1.4

SECONDARY LEGISLATION

Kenya Information and Communications (Registration of SIM-cards) Regulations, 2015	1.4

UNITED KINGDOM

SECONDARY LEGISLATION

Electronic Money Regulations, 2011	2.2
Payment Accounts Regulations, 2015	5.1,5.4
Payment Services Regulations, 2017	2.2

TERTIARY LEGISLATION

The Joint Money Laundering Steering Group JMLSG, Prevention of money laundering/combating terrorist financing 2017 Revised Version, Guidance for the UK financial sector Part I, June 2017 (Amended December 2017)	3.1.16, 3.5

UNITED STATES

PRIMARY LEGISLATION

Federal Deposit Insurance Act	3.7.1

TERTIARY LEGISLATION

Federal Financial Institutions Examination Council (2014), 'Bank Secrecy Act/Anti-Money Laundering Examination Manual', Available at: https://www.occ.treas.gov/publications/publications-by-type/other-publications-reports/ffiec-bsa-aml-examination-manual.pdf (accessed 10 January 2017)	3.1.16, 3.9

INTERNATIONAL GUIDELINES

Financial Action Task Force (2013), 'FATF Guidance: Anti-Money Laundering and Terrorist Financing Measures and Financial Inclusion', Available at: http://www.fatf-gafi.org/media/fatf/documents/reports/AML_CFT_Measures_and_Financial_Inclusion_2013.pdf (accessed 3 April 2018)	1.0,1.1, 1.2.
Financial Action Task Force (2013), 'Guidance for a Risk-Based Approach: Prepaid Cards, Mobile Payments and Internet-Based Payment Services', Available at: http://www.fatf-gafi.org/media/fatf/documents/recommendations/Guidance-RBA-NPPS.pdf (accessed 12 January 2017)	3.4
Financial Action Task Force (2012), 'International Standards on Combating Money Laundering and the Financing of Terrorism and Proliferation (The FATF Recommendations)', Available at: https://www.fatf-gafi.org/media/fatf/documents/recommendations/pdfs/FATF%20Recommendations%202012.pdf (accessed 18 April 2019)	1.2,2.1., 2.3,3.1, 3.3, 3.4, 3.5, 3.6, 3.8, 3.9.
Financial Action Task Force (2011), 'FATF Guidance: Anti-Money Laundering and Terrorist Financing Measures and Financial Inclusion', Available at: http://www.fatf-gafi.org/media/fatf/content/images/AML%20CFT%20measures%20and%20financial%20inclusion.pdf (accessed 4 April 2018)	1.2, 3.3.

Financial Action Task Force (2007), 'FATF Guidance on the Risk-Based Approach to Combating Money Laundering and Terrorist Financing - High Level Principles and Procedures', Available at: http://www.fatf-gafi.org/media/fatf/documents/reports/High%20Level%20Principles%20and%20Procedures.pdf (accessed 5 December, 2018) 3.9

LIST OF ABBREVIATIONS

ACAMS: Association of Certified Anti-Money Laundering Specialists (this is the largest international membership organization dedicated to enhancing the knowledge, skills and expertise of AML/CTF and financial crime detection and prevention professionals)

ACH: Automated Clearing House

ACSRT: African Centre for the Study and Research on Terrorism

AFF: Department of Justice's Assets Forfeiture Fund

AML: Anti-Money Laundering

APG: Asia Pacific Group

ARO: European Asset Recovery Office

ATM: Automated Teller Machine

AUSA: Assistant U.S. Attorney

BCCI: Bank of Credit and Commerce International

BED: Bank Examination Department

BNIs: Bearer Negotiable Instruments

BSA: Bank Secrecy Act

BVN: Bank Verification Number

CAC: Corporate Affairs Commission

CAFRA: Civil Asset Forfeiture Reform Act of 2000

CARIN: Camden Asset Recovery Inter-Agency Network

CBN: Central Bank of Nigeria

CBP: Cross Border Protection

CDD: Customer Due Diligence

CEMA: Customs & Excise Management Act

CEO: Chief Executive Officer

CFR: Code of Federal Regulations

CFRs: Consumer Fraud Reports

CFT: Combating the Financing of Terrorism

CFT: Countering the Financing of Terrorism (also used for combating the financing of terrorism)

CIP: Customer Identification Program

CPC: Criminal Procedure Code

CTF: Counter-Terrorist Financing

CTRs: Currency Transaction Reports

CVV/CVC code: Card Verification Value/Code

DFS: Department of Financial Services

DHL: Dalsey, Hillblom and Lynn (founders of DHL Worldwide Express)

DNFBPs: Designated non-financial businesses and professions

DNFIs: Designated non-financial institutions

DPA: Deferred Prosecution Agreement

DSS: Department of State Services

DVD: Digital Versatile Disc

DVSA: Driving Vehicle Standards Agency

EAG: Eurasian group on combating money laundering and financing of terrorism

ECHR: European Convention on Human Rights

EDD: Enhanced Due Diligence

EFCC: Economic and Financial Crimes Commission

EMIs: Electronic Money Institutions or E-Money Institutions

EO: Executive Order

FATF: Financial Action Task Force, an intergovernmental body whose purpose is to develop and promote broad AML/CTF standards, both at national and international levels

FBI: Federal Bureau of Investigation

FCA: Financial Conduct Authority, the UK regulator of the financial services industry

FCMB: First City Monument Bank

FCPA: Foreign Corrupt Practices Act

FCT: Federal Capital Territory, Abuja

FCUA: Federal Credit Union Act

FDIA: Federal Deposit Insurance Act

FDIC: Federal Deposit Insurance Corporation

FFIEC: Federal Financial Institutions Examination Council

FinCEN: Financial Crimes Enforcement Network, a bureau of the U.S. Department of the Treasury. The Director of FinCEN is appointed by the Secretary of the Treasury and reports to the Treasury Under Secretary for Terrorism and Financial Intelligence. FinCEN's mission is to safeguard the financial system from illicit use and combat money laundering and promote national security through the collection, analysis, and dissemination of financial intelligence and strategic use of financial authorities.

FINTECH: Financial Technology

FIU: Financial Intelligence Unit

FROs: Financial Reporting Orders

FSAPs: Financial Sector Assessment Programs

FSAs: Financial Stability Assessments

FSB: Financial Stability Board

FSMA: Financial Services and Markets Act 2000

FTC: Federal Trade Commission

FTOs: Foreign Terrorist Organizations

GIABA: Inter-Governmental Action Group against Money Laundering in West Africa

GSM: Global System for Mobile Communications

GTB: Guarantee Trust Bank

HIS: U.S. Immigration and Customs Enforcement's Homeland Security Investigations

HMRC: Her Majesty's Revenue and Customs

HMT: Her Majesty's Treasury

HNWI: High net worth individuals

IAIS: International Association of Insurance Supervisors

IBC: International Business Corporations

ICAEW: Institute of Chartered Accountants in England and Wales

ICPC: Independent Corrupt Practices and Other Related Offences Commission

ID: Identity Document

ILO: International Labour Organisation

IMF: International Monetary Fund

INCSR: International Narcotics Control Strategy Report

IOSCO: International Organization of Securities Commissions

IOTAs: Interest on Trust Accounts

IPOB: Indigenous People of Biafra

IRS: Internal Revenue Service

ISA: Investments and Securities Act

ISD: Insurance & Surveillance Department

JMLSG: Joint Money Laundering Steering Group

KYC: Know Your Customer

LCTR: Large Currency Transaction Report

ML: Money Laundering

MLPA: Money Laundering Prohibition Act

MMO: Mobile Money Operators

MONEYVAL: Committee of Experts on the Evaluation of Anti-Money Laundering Measures

MSB: Money Services Business

MSISDN: Mobile Station International Subscriber Directory Number and is the telephone number assigned to a SIM

MVTS: Money or Value Transfer Services

NAICOM: National Insurance Commission

NBFCs: Non-Banking Financial Companies

NCA: The National Crime Agency, the UK's financial intelligence unit

NCC: Nigeria Communications Commission with Regulatory powers over the telecommunication companies (Telcos)

NCS: Nigeria Customs Service

NCUA: National Credit Union Administration

NDIC: Nigeria Deposit Insurance Corporation

NDLEA: National Drug Law Enforcement Agency

NEFT: National Electronic Funds Transfer

NFIU: The Nigerian Financial Intelligence Unit (NFIU) is the central national agency in Nigeria responsible for the receipt and analysis of financial disclosures; currency transaction reports (CTR) and suspicious transaction reports (STR) on money laundering and terrorism financing. It also has the responsibility of disseminating intelligence generated there-from to competent authorities

NFM Council: National Frequency Management Council

NFP: National Focal Point

NFPT: National Focal Points on Terrorism

NGO: Nongovernmental Organization

NIA: National Intelligence Agency (this is a government division tasked with overseeing foreign intelligence and counterintelligence operations and has its headquarters in Abuja)

NIBSS: Nigeria Inter-Bank Settlement System;

NIP: NIBSS Instant Payments

NMLRA: National Money Laundering Risk Assessment

NOMS: National Offender Management Service

NPC: National Planning Commission

NPOs: Non-Profitable Organisations

NPPS: New Payment Products and Services

NRA: National Risk Assessment

NRAS: National Risk Assessment Secretariat

NSL: National Security Letter

NTFRA: National Terrorist Financing Risk Assessment

NUBAN: Nigeria Uniform Bank Account Number, this is a 10-digit Bank Account numbering system, used for all personal bank accounts i.e your account number

OCC: Office of the Comptroller of the Currency

OCP: Organised Crime Partnership

OFAC: Office of Foreign Assets Control

PEPs: Politically Exposed Persons

PHCN: Power Holding Company of Nigeria

PICs: Private Investment Companies

PIN: Personal Identification Number

PIs: Payment Institutions

PML: Prevention of Money Laundering Rules 2005

PND: Place No Debit

POCA: Proceeds of Crime Act 2002

POS: Point of Sale

PPIs: Pre-paid Payment Instruments

PSPs: Payment services providers

PUK: Personal Unblocking Key

PUPID: Payable upon Proper Identification

RBA: Risk-Based Approach

RBS: Risk Based Supervision

RCCs: Remotely Created Cheques

RRS: Rapid Response Squad

RUSI: Royal United Services Institute

RVs: Recreational Vehicles

SAN: Senior Advocate of Nigeria

SARs: Suspicious Activity Reports

SCIID: State Criminal Investigation and Intelligence Department, Yaba

SCPOs: Serious Crime Prevention Orders

SCUML: Special Control Unit against Money Laundering

SDGTs: Specially Designated Global Terrorists

SEC: Securities and Exchange Commission

SFO: Serious Fraud Office

SIID: Special Insured Institutions Department

SIM: Subscriber Identity Module, and includes Removable User Identity Module (RUIM).

SMS: Short Message Service

SROs: Self-Regulatory Organisations

SSS: The State Security Service (SSS) is also known as Department of State Services (DSS). This body is the main body responsible for intelligence gathering in Nigeria.

STRs: Suspicious Transaction Reports

SYSC: FCA Sourcebook: Senior Management Arrangements, Systems and Controls

TF: Terrorist Financing

TFI: Office of Terrorism and Financial Intelligence

TRO: Travel Restriction Order

TTF: Topical Trust Funds

U.S. Treasury: U.S. Department of the Treasury

UDHR: Universal Declaration of Human Rights

UHNWI: Ultra-High Net Worth Individuals

UKFIU: UK Financial Intelligence Unit

UNILAG: University of Lagos

UNODC: United Nations Office on Drugs and Crime

UNSC: United Nations Security Council

USA PATRIOT Act: Uniting and Strengthening America by Providing Appropriate Tools Required to Intercept and Obstruct Terrorism Act of 2001

USAO: United States Attorney's Office

USC: U.S. Code

USMS: U.S. Marshals Service

USSD: Unstructured Supplementary Service Data

VAT: Value Added Tax

Wi-Fi: Wireless Fidelity, meaning you can access or connect to a network using radio waves, without needing to use wires.

CHAPTER 1

INTRODUCTION TO FINANCIAL INCLUSION, MONEY LAUNDERING AND MOBILE BANKING – AN ANALYSIS OF THE REGULATORY FRAMEWORK FOR TELECOMMUNICATIONS COMPANIES

The rapid development of mobile money is creating unprecedented opportunities for poor people in developing countries to more actively participate in the economy. For millions of underserved individuals around the world, a mobile phone represents more than just a tool for communication; it has become a payment terminal in the pocket. Every day, the number of mobile device—and mobile money—users grows and offers hope to the billions of people without bank accounts.[1] Mobile banking could be defined as a facility which provides banking services such as

---

[1] Chatain, P. L., Zerzan, A., Noor, W., Dannaoui, N., and Koker, L. D. (2011), 'Protecting Mobile Money against Financial Crimes: Global Policy Challenges and Solutions', Available at: http://documents.worldbank.org/curated/en/854951468337169489/pdf/600600PUB0ID181Mobile09780821386699.pdf (accessed 17th of March, 2019).

balance enquiry, funds transfer, bill payment, and transaction history via a user's mobile phone.[2]

One of the biggest challenges to enabling the growth of mobile money and the digital finance ecosystem is designing cost-effective customer due diligence (CDD) procedures that enable universal access to mobile money services while preserving the integrity of the financial system. For the regulator, this means designing anti-money laundering and combating the financing of terrorism (AML/CFT) requirements that mitigate the risk of abuse of mobile money while still allowing customers to access and use these services safely and easily. Many low-income customers face barriers to financial services because they are unable to prove their identity through traditional means; they may live in a country that does not provide national identification documents (IDs), or they may be deprived of services where the costs of conducting CDD are too high, such as in remote areas where electricity is not available. Proportional controls are key to mitigating the risk of criminal activity on the mobile money platform while balancing the dual objectives of financial integrity and financial inclusion.[3]

1.1 FINANCIAL INCLUSION

Two billion people lack access to formal financial services. Approximately 90% of the unbanked live in developing countries.

---

[2] Dr. Agwu, E. M. & Dr. Carter, A. L. (2014), 'Mobile Phone Banking In Nigeria: Benefits, Problems and Prospects', International Journal of Business and Commerce, Vol. 3, No.6: Feb 2014[50-70].

[3] Castri, S. D., Grossman, J. and Sihin, R. (2015), 'Proportional risk-based AML/CFT regimes for mobile money: A framework for assessing risk factors and mitigation measures', Available at: https://www.gsma.com/mobilefordevelopment/wp-content/uploads/2015/10/Proportional-risk-based-AMLCFT-regimes-for-mobile-money.pdf (accessed 6 April, 2019). See also the Financial Action Task Force (2013), 'FATF Guidance: Anti-Money Laundering and Terrorist Financing Measures and Financial Inclusion', Available at: http://www.fatf-gafi.org/media/fatf/documents/reports/AML_CFT_Measures_and_Financial_Inclusion_2013.pdf (accessed 3 April 2018).

Greater financial inclusion can bring these people into the financial mainstream, with positive effects on economic growth, financial stability and social cohesion. Many of the smartest policies for increasing access to formal financial services have been innovated in developing countries—those who live with the challenges of financial exclusion every day.[4]

In general terms, financial inclusion involves providing access to an adequate range of safe, convenient and affordable financial services to disadvantaged and other vulnerable groups, including low income, rural and undocumented persons, who have been underserved or excluded from the formal financial sector. Financial inclusion also involves making a broader range of financial products and services available to individuals who currently only have access to basic financial products. Financial inclusion can also be defined as ensuring access to appropriate financial products and services at an affordable cost in a fair and transparent manner.[5]

Financial inclusion within the context of the **Central Bank of Nigeria' National Financial Inclusion Revised Strategy**, is achieved when adult Nigerians have easy access to a broad range of formal financial services that meet their needs and are provided at an affordable cost. The definition of financial inclusion used in the **Central Bank of Nigeria' Financial Inclusion Strategy** includes the following elements:

- Ease of access to financial products and services

[4] Alliance for Financial Inclusion (2017), 'AFI Members are Leaders in Financial Inclusion Policy', Available at: https://www.afi-global.org/policy-areas (accessed 2 April 2018).

[5] Financial Action Task Force (2013), 'FATF Guidance: Anti-Money Laundering and Terrorist Financing Measures and Financial Inclusion', Available at: http://www.fatf-gafi.org/media/fatf/documents/reports/AML_CFT_Measures_and_Financial_Inclusion_2013.pdf (accessed 3 April 2018).

  - Financial products must be within easy reach of all segments of the population and should not have onerous requirements.

- Use of a broad range of financial products and services
  - Financial inclusion implies not only access but usage of a full spectrum of financial services including, but not limited to payments, savings, credit, insurance, and pension products.
- Financial products designed according to need
  - Financial products must be designed to meet the needs of clients and should consider income levels, as well as access to distribution channels.
- Affordable –
  - Financial services should be affordable even for low-income groups.[6]

The major goal of the **Central Bank of Nigeria' National Financial Inclusion Revised Strategy** is to reduce the proportion of adult Nigerians that are financially excluded to 20% in year 2020 from its baseline figure of 46.3% in 2010. In other words, the strategy aims to promote a financial system that is accessible to all Nigerian adults, at an inclusion rate of 80%.[7]

[6] Central Bank of Nigeria (2018), 'National Financial Inclusion Strategy (Revised)', Available at: https://www.cbn.gov.ng/Out/2019/CCD/NATIONAL%20FINANCIAL%20INCLUSION%20STRATEGY.pdf (accessed 30 March, 2019).
[7] Central Bank of Nigeria (2018), 'National Financial Inclusion Strategy (Revised)', Available at: https://www.cbn.gov.ng/Out/2019/CCD/NATIONAL%20FINANCIAL%20INCLUSION%20STRATEGY.pdf (accessed 30 March, 2019).

1.2 FINANCIAL EXCLUSION AND ITS RELATIONSHIP WITH AML/CFT

Money laundering can be defined as the process of converting "black money" obtained from illicit sources such as narcotic trafficking, extortion, smuggling and the flesh trade, into legal money. Here, the original source of the money is concealed from the authorities.[8] Based on this definition, the overriding objective of money laundering is to allow criminals to access the profits of their illegal conduct by distancing themselves from it.[9] Terrorist financing is the financing of terrorist acts, and of terrorists and terrorist organisations.[10]

It is acknowledged that financial exclusion works against effective anti-money laundering and combating the financing of terrorism (AML/CFT) policies. Indeed, the prevalence of a large informal, unregulated and undocumented economy negatively affects AML/CFT efforts and the integrity of the financial system.

---

[8] Thanasegaran, H. and Shanmugam, B. (2007), 'International trade- based money laundering: the Malaysian perspective', Journal of Money Laundering Control, 10 (4), pp. 429-437; see also the following cases: R v. Nabil Zekari, [2010] EWCA Crim 1649, [2011] 1 Cr App R (S) 59 which is to the effect that: hiding proceeds of crime in your car comes within the meaning of concealing criminal property; Regina v. Fazal [2009] EWCA Crim 1697, [2010] 1 WLR 694 [22] which is to the effect that: where a person allows his account to be deposited and withdrawn with proceeds of fraud, such constitutes converting criminal property; R v. Christopher Smale and Ann Smale [2008] EWCA Crim 1235, [2009] 1 Cr App R (S) 25 which is to the effect that: entering into an arrangement could be by agreeing with someone to conceal money; Dare v. Crown Prosecution Service [2012] EWHC 2074 (Admin) (2013) 177 JP 37, [2012] Lloyd's Rep FC 718; Regina v. John Middleton, Veronica, Patricia Rourke [2008] EWCA Crim 233 which is to the effect that: holding a certain amount could amount to possessing criminal property.

[9] Alexander, K. (2001), 'The international anti-money- laundering regime: the role of the Financial Action Task Force', Journal of Money Laundering Control, 4(3), pp. 231-248.

[10] Financial Action Task Force (2012), 'International Standards on Combating Money Laundering and the Financing of Terrorism and Proliferation (The FATF Recommendations)', Available at: https://www.fatf-gafi.org/media/fatf/documents/recommendations/pdfs/FATF%20Recommendations%202012.pdf (accessed 18 April 2019).

Informal, unregulated and undocumented financial services and a pervasive cash economy can generate significant money laundering and terrorist financing risks and negatively affect AML/CFT preventive, detection and investigation/prosecution efforts. Dependence on mainly informal financial services also limits access to reasonably priced credit and slows a country's development. If the funds are kept outside the formal system, there is a limited multiplier effect in the economy.[11]

Promoting formal financial systems and services is therefore central to any effective and comprehensive AML/CFT regime. Financial inclusion and an effective AML/CFT regime can and should be complementary national policy objectives with mutually supportive policy goals.[12]

Accordingly, international AML/CFT standards have flexibility, enabling jurisdictions to craft effective and appropriate controls while taking into account the relevance of expanding access to financial services, as well as the diverse levels and types of risks posed by different products and supply channels. The challenge is finding the right level of protection for a particular financial environment.[13]

---

[11] Financial Action Task Force (2011), 'FATF Guidance: Anti-Money Laundering and Terrorist Financing Measures and Financial Inclusion', Available at: http://www.fatf-gafi.org/media/fatf/content/images/AML%20CFT%20measures%20and%20financial%20inclusion.pdf (accessed 4 April 2018).

[12] Financial Action Task Force (2013), 'FATF Guidance: Anti-Money Laundering and Terrorist Financing Measures and Financial Inclusion', Available at: http://www.fatf-gafi.org/media/fatf/documents/reports/AML_CFT_Measures_and_Financial_Inclusion_2013.pdf (accessed 3 April 2018).

[13] Financial Action Task Force (2011), 'FATF Guidance: Anti-Money Laundering and Terrorist Financing Measures and Financial Inclusion', Available at: http://www.fatf-gafi.org/media/fatf/content/images/AML%20CFT%20measures%20and%20financial%20inclusion.pdf (accessed 4 April 2018).

1.3 THE NIGERIAN TELECOMMUNICATIONS SECTOR: THE LAW ESTABLISHING IT AND THE LICENSING APPLICATION PROCESS

The telecom industry is a key enabler of productivity across economies and societies. It is not only a significant contributor to economic activities of a nation but also for growth of other sectors of the economy as well enhancing social lives of people. Disruptive innovations such as Mobile Broadband, internet of Things (IoT), Cloud Computing, Web Technologies, Artificial Intelligence which are all anchored on telecommunications are shaping the future of the world as these technologies enable users go about their daily routines with new ways of knowing, perceiving and even interacting with the physical world.[14]

The Nigerian Communications Commission is the independent National Regulatory Authority for the telecommunications industry in Nigeria. The Commission is responsible for creating an enabling environment for competition among operators in the industry as well as ensuring the provision of qualitative and efficient telecommunications services throughout the country.[15]

The mandate and authority of the Nigerian Communications Commission is derived from the **Nigerian Communications Act 2003 (NCA 2003)**, which was signed into law, after having been

[14] Nigerian Communications Commission (2018), 'NCC Collaborates with GSMA on Future of Industry Workshop - Driving Innovation and Growth', Available at: https://www.ncc.gov.ng/stakeholder/media-public/news-headlines/460-ncc-collaborates-with-gsma-on-future-of-industry-workshop-driving-innovation-and-growth (accessed 17 April 2019).

[15] Nigerian Communications Commission (2019), 'About the NCC', Available at: https://www.ncc.gov.ng/about-ncc/who-we-are (accessed 17 April 2019).

passed by both Houses of the National Assembly, by President Olusegun Obasanjo on July 8, 2003.

The **NCA 2003** applies to the provision and use of all communications services and networks, in whole or in part within Nigeria or on ships or aircraft registered in Nigeria, and was passed to meet the following objectives:

1. Promote the implementation of the national communications or, telecommunications policy as may from time to time be modified and amended;
2. Establish a regulatory framework for the Nigerian communications industry and for this purpose to create an effective, impartial and independent regulatory authority;
3. Promote the provision of modem, universal, efficient, reliable, affordable and easily accessible communications services and the widest range thereof throughout Nigeria;
4. Encourage local and foreign investments in the Nigerian communications industry and the introduction of innovative services and practices in the industry in accordance with international best practices and trends;
5. Ensure fair competition in all sectors of the Nigerian communications industry and also encourage participation of Nigerians in the ownership, control and management of communications companies and organisations;
6. Encourage the development of a communications manufacturing and supply sector within the Nigerian economy and also encourage effective research and development efforts by all communications industry practitioners;
7. Protect the rights and interest of service providers and consumers within Nigeria;

8. Ensure that the needs of the disabled and elderly persons are taken into consideration in the provision of communications services; and
9. Ensure an efficient management including planning, coordination, allocation, assignment, registration, monitoring and use of scarce national resources in the communications sub-sector, including but not limited to frequency spectrum, numbers and electronic addresses, and also promote and safeguard national interests, safety and security in the use of the said scarce national resources.[16]

By virtue of **section 31 (1) of the Nigerian Communications Act, 2003**, No person shall operate a communications system or facility nor provide a communications service in Nigeria unless authorised to do so under a communications licence or exempted under regulations made by the Nigerian Communications Commission under the Nigerian Communications Act, 2003.

Any person who acts in breach of **section 31 (1) of the Nigerian Communications Act, 2003** commits an offence and is liable on conviction to—

(*a*) a fine not less than the initial fee for the relevant licence;

(*b*) a fine not exceeding 10 (ten) times the initial fee for the relevant licence;

(c) imprisonment for a term not exceeding 1 (one) year; or

(*d*) both such fine and imprisonment;

Provided that upon conviction, the person shall also forfeit to the Nigerian Communications Commission the property, facilities;

[16] Nigerian Communications Act, 2003, s. 1.

installations and equipment used by him for the provision and operation of the unlicensed service.[17]

The Nigerian Communications Commission shall issue communications licences for the operation and provision of communications services or facilities by way of class or individual licences on such terms and conditions as the Commission may from time to time determine taking into consideration the objectives of the **Nigerian Communications Act, 2003** and the provisions of **section 33(3)** of the **Nigerian Communications Act, 2003.**[18]

An **Individual Licence** is a type of authorization in which the terms, conditions and obligations, scope and limitations are specific to the service being provided. Process of licensing can take the form of Auction, "First Come First Served", "Beauty Contest" or a standard administrative procedure, etc.

A **Class Licence** is a type of general authorization in which the terms and conditions/obligations are common to all license holders. It requires only registration with the **Nigerian Communications Commission** for applicants to commence operation.

The following describes the procedure and requirements toward applying for a license in both the Class and Individual categories from the Nigerian Communications Commission:

1.3.1 INDIVIDUAL LICENSE APPLICATION REQUIREMENTS

Application form for ₦1,000.00 payable to ***Nigerian Communications Commission***

---

[17] Nigerian Communications Act, 2003, s. 31(2).

[18] Nigerian Communications Act, 2003, s. 32(1).

- Fill the form and produce two copies of the form (2 copies).
- Also attach copies of relevant documents:
    - ***Certificate of Incorporation.***
    - ***Tax Clearance Certificate.***
    - ***Certified true copy of Articles & Memorandum of Association.***
    - ***Certified true copy of form CO7***
    - ***Feasibility report of proposed service applied for (where applicable).***
    - ***3 Passport photographs of authorized representative.***
    - ***Passport photographs of Directors of the company***
- Applications should be submitted in triplicates with all necessary documents attached, all spiral bound.
- Enquiries should be made to the Nigerian Communications Commission for the appropriate amount before payment.
- On submission of the form, a non-refundable administrative charge; which is 5% of the relevant license fee would be paid ₦...........
- License fee is payable on approval of application ₦...........
- ***All Automated Vehicle Tracking Service (AVTS) applicant must obtain a security clearance from the State Security Service (SSS). The Personal History Statement Forms (PHS) for the company and its Directors will be provided by the Commission for completion by applicant.***
- **All VAS (Content Service using Short Code) applicant (s) must present:**

1. Evidence of an Agreement or a Memorandum of Understanding (MOU) entered between the company and the Mobile Network Operator(s)

2. Alternatively, the company should provide a copy of License duly issued to it by the Central Bank of Nigeria for Mobile Money Services.

1.3.2 CLASS LICENSE APPLICATION REQUIREMENTS

- Obtain an application for One Thousand Naira (₦1,000.00) only payable to Nigerian Communications Commission
- Fill the form and produce one extra copy
- Also attach copies of relevant documents;
    - Certificate of Incorporation,
    - Tax Clearance Certificate.
    - Certified true copy of Articles & Memorandum of Association.
    - Certified true copy of form CO7
    - 2 Passport photographs of authorized representative.
    - Certificate of qualified technical staff
    - Brief on the proposed service
    - Passport photographs of Directors of the Company/Sole Proprietorship
- Application should be submitted in duplicates with all necessary documents attached, all spiral bound.
- Licence fee of Ten Thousand Naira (₦10,000.00) only, is payable on submission of application.[19]

[19] Nigerian Communications Commission (2019), 'Licensing Application Process', Available at: https://www.ncc.gov.ng/licensing-regulatory/licensing/licensing-procedures#class-license (accessed 18 April 2019).

1.4 THE CURRENT REGULATORY FRAMEWORK FOR THE TELECOMMUNICATIONS INDUSTRY

In order to achieve its mandate, the Nigerian Communications Commission has put in place the necessary licensing and regulatory framework for the supply of telecommunications services. This section will focus on the Regulations and Guidelines that can help curb fraud, money laundering and terrorist financing in mobile banking:

A. Nigerian Communications Commission (Registration of Telephone Subscribers) Regulations, 2011.

The objective of the **Nigerian Communications Commission (Registration of Telephone Subscribers) Regulations, 2011** is to provide a regulatory framework for the registration of subscribers to Mobile Telephone Services utilising subscription medium in the Federal Republic of Nigeria; and for the establishment, control, administration and management of the Central Database.[20]

The **Nigerian Communications Commission (Registration of Telephone Subscribers) Regulations, 2011** applies to all persons and licensees including corporate, private and commercial subscribers to Mobile Telephone Services utilising Subscription Medium in the Federal Republic of Nigeria; and subscribers of foreign licensees who are roaming on the network of a licensee in Nigeria; Provided that subscribers of foreign licensees shall not be required to register where they have registered their subscriber information in the jurisdiction of the relevant foreign licensee and there exists necessary arrangements between the Nigerian Communications Commission and the relevant regulatory

[20] Nigerian Communications Commission (Registration of Telephone Subscribers) Regulations, 2011, regulation 2.

authority of the foreign licensee to access such subscriber information.[21]

The **Nigerian Communications Commission** shall establish and maintain a database of all registered subscribers' information to be known as "the Central Database". The Central Database shall be domiciled within the Commission and shall provide a platform for the central processing and storage of subscribers' information. The Central Database shall be segregated across Network Services in such a manner as to ensure easy access to data by authorised persons in respect of subscribers' information of the different licensees.[22] The Central Database shall be the property of the Government of the Federal Republic of Nigeria; the management, care and control of the Central Database shall be vested in the Nigerian Communications Commission subject to the provisions of these Regulations.[23]

Licensees and independent registration agents shall, on a monthly basis or at such regular intervals as the Nigerian Communications Commission may from time to time specify, transmit all subscriber Information captured and registered within the preceding month or such other period as may be stipulated by the Nigerian Communications Commission, to the Central Database. The Administration of the Central Database shall be in accordance with the latest standards issued from time to time by the International Organisation for Standardization in relation to security and management of electronics and personal data.[24] A licensee shall have the right to retain and use its subscribers information on its

---

[21] Nigerian Communications Commission (Registration of Telephone Subscribers) Regulations, 2011, regulation 3.
[22] Nigerian Communications Commission (Registration of Telephone Subscribers) Regulations, 2011, regulation 4.
[23] Nigerian Communications Commission (Registration of Telephone Subscribers) Regulations, 2011, regulation 5.
[24] Nigerian Communications Commission (Registration of Telephone Subscribers) Regulations, 2011, regulation 6.

network in accordance with the provisions of Part VI of the **General Consumer Code of Practice for Telecommunications Services and any other instrument** issued from time to time by the Nigerian Communications Commission.[25]

In furtherance of the rights guaranteed **by section 37 of the Constitution of the Federal Republic of Nigeria, 1999** and subject to any guidelines issued by the **Nigerian Communications Commission** including terms and conditions that may from time to time be issued either by the **Nigerian Communications Commission** or a licensee, any subscriber whose personal information is stored in the Central Database or a licensee's database, shall be entitled to view the said information and to request updates and amendments thereto. The subscriber information contained in the Central Database shall be held on a strictly confidential basis and no person or entity shall be allowed access to any subscriber information on the Central Database except as provided in the **Nigerian Communications Commission (Registration of Telephone Subscribers) Regulations, 2011**. Licensees, Independent Registration Agents and Subscriber Registration Solution Providers shall not under any circumstances retain, duplicate, deal in or make copies of any Subscriber Information or store in whatever form any copies of the subscriber information for any purpose other than as stipulated in the **Nigerian Communications Commission (Registration of Telephone Subscribers) Regulations, 2011** or in an Act of the National Assembly. Licensees, Independent Registration Agents, Subscriber Registration Solution Providers and the **Nigerian Communications Commission** shall each take all reasonable precautions in accordance with international practices to preserve the integrity and prevent any corruption, loss or unauthorised

---

[25] Nigerian Communications Commission (Registration of Telephone Subscribers) Regulations, 2011, regulation 7.

disclosure of subscriber information obtained pursuant to these Regulations and shall take steps to restrict unauthorized use of the Subscriber Information by their employees who may be involved in the capturing or processing of such subscriber information. Licensees shall utilise personal information retained pursuant to the **Nigerian Communications Commission (Registration of Telephone Subscribers) Regulations, 2011**, solely for their operations and in accordance with the provisions of **Part VI of the General Consumer Code of Practice for Telecommunications Services** and any other instruments of the **Nigerian Communications Commission** or any Act of the National Assembly regulating the specific purposes for which the personal information may be used. Licensees, Independent Registration Agents and Subscriber Registration Solution Providers shall not retain the Biometrics of any subscriber after transmission thereof to the Central Database.[26]

Notwithstanding the provisions of the **Nigerian Communications Commission (Registration of Telephone Subscribers) Regulations, 2011** restricting access to Subscriber Information on the Central Database and subject to the provisions of any Act of the National Assembly, subscriber information on the Central Database shall be provided only to Security Agencies; provided that a prior written request is received by the **Nigerian Communications Commission** from an official of the requesting Security Agency who is not below the rank of an Assistant Commissioner of Police or a co-ordinate rank in any other Security Agency. The written notice by the Security Agency shall indicate

[26] Nigerian Communications Commission (Registration of Telephone Subscribers) Regulations, 2011, regulation 9.

the rank of the official of the requesting Security Agency and the purpose for which the information is required.[27]

Release of Personal Information to Security Agents shall be in accordance with the provisions of the **Nigerian Communications Act 2003**, the **Nigerian Communications Commission (Registration of Telephone Subscribers) Regulations, 2011** and any guidelines or instrument issued from time to time by the **Nigerian Communications Commission** and in a format to be determined by the **Nigerian Communications Commission.** Subscriber information shall not be released to a licensee, Security Agency or any other person, where such release of Subscriber Information would constitute a breach of the **Constitution** or any other Act of the National Assembly, for the time being in force in Nigeria or where such release of subscriber information would constitute a threat to national security. Licensees shall not release personal information of a subscriber to any third party without obtaining the prior written consent of the subscriber. No subscriber information shall be transferred outside the Federal Republic of Nigeria without the prior written consent of the **Nigerian Communications Commission.** For the purpose of sub-regulation (3) of the **Nigerian Communications Commission (Registration of Telephone Subscribers) Regulations, 2011**, the term "third party" shall exclude Security Agencies as defined in the Regulations.[28]

Licensees, Independent Registration Agents and Subscriber Registration Solution Providers shall in accordance with registration specifications and at no cost to the **Nigerian**

[27] Nigerian Communications Commission (Registration of Telephone Subscribers) Regulations, 2011, regulation 8.

[28] Nigerian Communications Commission (Registration of Telephone Subscribers) Regulations, 2011, regulation 10.

Communications Commission or the subscriber capture, register and transmit to the Central Database the—

(*a*) biometrics and other personal information of subscribers who requests for the activation of the licensee's subscription medium; and

(*b*) in the case of a corporate body or other juristic person, the biometrics and other personal information of the authorised representative of the corporate body or other juristic person and the name, address and where applicable, the registration number of the juristic person issued by the Corporate Affairs Commission.[29]

Licensees shall only provide new subscribers with subscription mediums enabled for limited access to their network services and such limited access shall last for the duration of the activation window. It shall be the responsibility of a new subscriber to, at any time within the activation window, present personal information to the licensee from whom the subscription medium is obtained for registration in accordance with the requirements of the **Nigerian Communications Commission (Registration of Telephone Subscribers) Regulations, 2011**. Upon the capturing and registration of the biometrics and the personal information of a new subscriber, the licensee shall activate the subscription medium on its network service and transmit the subscriber's information to the Central Database.[30]

Subject to the terms of any contractual arrangement with the **Nigerian Communications Commission,** the Licensees, Independent Registration Agents and Subscriber Registration Solution Providers shall carry out the capturing and registration of

---

[29] Nigerian Communications Commission (Registration of Telephone Subscribers) Regulations, 2011, regulation 11.

[30] Nigerian Communications Commission (Registration of Telephone Subscribers) Regulations, 2011, regulation 12.

the biometrics and other personal information of existing subscribers within the subscribers' registration period in accordance with the provisions of **regulation 11(2)** of the **Nigerian Communications Commission (Registration of Telephone Subscribers) Regulations, 2011** and the registration specifications. Where the **Nigerian Communications Commission** deems it necessary, it may authorise the licensees to undertake the registration of existing subscribers on their respective networks and upon the issuance of any directive authorising such registration, the **Nigerian Communications Commission (Registration of Telephone Subscribers) Regulations, 2011** shall apply with necessary modifications to such registration, as if reference to new subscriber means existing subscriber. Licensees shall support and promote the registration of existing subscribers by the Independent Registration Agents and shall promptly, upon being notified by the **Nigerian Communications Commission**, deactivate any subscription where the Personal Information of the Subscriber has not been entered into the Central Database by the end of the Subscriber registration period or such extensions thereof as the **Nigerian Communications Commission** may prescribe. A deactivated subscription shall be reactivated upon the registration of the Biometric Information and other personal information of the relevant subscriber in accordance with the relevant provisions of the **Nigerian Communications Commission (Registration of Telephone Subscribers) Regulations, 2011** and confirmation by the **Nigerian Communications Commission** of the entry thereof into the Central Database.[31]

Subject to the provisions to Regulation 3 of the **Nigerian Communications Commission (Registration of Telephone Subscribers) Regulations, 2011** and any instrument or guidelines

[31] Nigerian Communications Commission (Registration of Telephone Subscribers) Regulations, 2011, regulation 13.

issued from time to time by the **Nigerian Communications Commission**, a licensee who is providing roaming services in Nigeria to a subscriber of a foreign licensee shall register the personal information of such subscriber in accordance with the provisions of the **Nigerian Communications Commission (Registration of Telephone Subscribers) Regulations, 2011** before providing such subscriber with roaming services. The activation window shall be a period of 48 hours.[32]

A licensee may deactivate and deregister a subscription medium upon a request by a subscriber after verification and confirmation of the subscriber information on the subscription medium. Records on any deactivation or deregistration shall be transmitted to the Central Database by the licensee in accordance with specifications issued by the **Nigerian Communications Commission**.[33] There shall be no proxy registration of any subscription medium.[34] A person may register any number of Subscription Mediums with any Licensee.[35] A subscriber shall be liable for activities carried out using a Subscription Medium registered with that subscriber's personal information.[36]

By virtue of **regulation 19(1) of the Nigerian Communications Commission (Registration of Telephone Subscribers) Regulations, 2011**, any licensee who fails to capture, register, deregister or transmit the details of any individual or corporate subscribers to the Central Database as specified in the **Nigerian**

---

[32] Nigerian Communications Commission (Registration of Telephone Subscribers) Regulations, 2011, regulation 14.
[33] Nigerian Communications Commission (Registration of Telephone Subscribers) Regulations, 2011, regulation 15.
[34] Nigerian Communications Commission (Registration of Telephone Subscribers) Regulations, 2011, regulation 16.
[35] Nigerian Communications Commission (Registration of Telephone Subscribers) Regulations, 2011, regulation 17.
[36] Nigerian Communications Commission (Registration of Telephone Subscribers) Regulations, 2011, regulation 18.

Communications Commission (Registration of Telephone Subscribers) Regulations, 2011 or as may be stipulated from time to time by the **Nigerian Communications Commission** is liable to a penalty of N200,000.00 for each subscription medium.

A licensee who activates any Subscription Medium without capturing, registering and transmitting the personal information to the Central Database commits an offence and shall on conviction be liable to a fine of N200,000.00 for each unregistered activated Subscription Medium.[37]

By virtue of **regulation 20(1) of the Nigerian Communications Commission (Registration of Telephone Subscribers) Regulations, 2011,** any licensee who activates or fails to deactivate a subscription medium in violation of any provision of the **Nigerian Communications Commission (Registration of Telephone Subscribers) Regulations, 2011** is liable to a penalty of N200,000.00 for each unregistered but activated subscription medium.

Where the **Nigerian Communications Commission** is satisfied that a body corporate is culpable, the Director, Chief Executive Officer, Manager or Secretary shall also be liable to pay a fine of N200,000 unless, having regard to the nature of his functions in that capacity and to all the surrounding circumstances, he proves that—

(*i*) the offence was committed without his knowledge, consent or connivance; and

(*ii*) he took all reasonable precautions and exercised due diligence to prevent the commission of the breach.[38]

---

[37] Nigerian Communications Commission (Registration of Telephone Subscribers) Regulations, 2011, regulation 19(2).

[38] Nigerian Communications Commission (Registration of Telephone Subscribers) Regulations, 2011, regulation 20(2).

By virtue of **regulation 21(1) of the Nigerian Communications Commission (Registration of Telephone Subscribers) Regulations, 2011,** any entity including licensees, independent registration agents or subscriber registration solution providers who retains, duplicates or deals with Subscriber's information in contravention of any of the provisions of the **Nigerian Communications Commission (Registration of Telephone Subscribers) Regulations, 2011** is liable to a penalty of N200,000.00 per Subscription Medium.

Where an entity, including licensees, independent registration agents or subscriber registration solution providers is found to have utilised a subscriber's information in any business, commercial or other transactions, such entity is liable to a penalty of N1,000,000.00 per Subscription Medium.[39]

Without prejudice to any specific provision that relates to criminal proceedings, the **Nigerian Communications Commission** may, in the exercise of its enforcement powers, institute civil proceedings in Court against any person for any remedy including injunctive relief, recovery of administrative fines, specific performance or pecuniary awards or damages. The **Nigerian Communications Commission** may issue directions in writing to any person or licensee and the **Nigerian Communications Commission** may seek the assistance of any law enforcement agency to enforce compliance with any directions' issues.[40]

On the 12th of April, 2019, the Nigerian Communications Commission restated that appropriate registration of Subscriber Identity Module (SIM) numbers by operators and telecom consumers in Nigeria is mandatory.

---

[39] Nigerian Communications Commission (Registration of Telephone Subscribers) Regulations, 2011, regulation 21(2).

[40] Nigerian Communications (Enforcement Processes, etc.) Regulations, regulation 4.

According to Efosa Idehen, the Nigerian Communications Commission Director for Compliance Monitoring and Enforcement who spoke on behalf of Sunday Dare, it is illegal to buy or use SIM cards that have been previously registered by a different, usually fictitious names and identities because this will make it difficult to trace users of such SIM cards when the cards are used for crimes. By implication, anyone who bought or sell SIM cards that have been pre-registered will be arrested and prosecuted by appropriate agencies of government.

"This explained why the **Nigerian Communications Commission** issued directions to telecom operators to deactivate all illegal SIM cards and also instructed that any registered and activated Mobile Station International Subscriber Directory Number (MSISDN) with no Revenue Generating Event (RGE) within 48 hours should automatically be returned to one way service" Idehen stated and added that this means a subscriber so circumstanced can only receive call on the SIM but will not be able to initiate a call. He noted that the directive to registration agents and citizens to register SIM cards only in "controlled environments" (within a permanent structure or facility), and traceable to a specific agent, is still in force.

Finally, Idehen recalled that concerns about infractions connected to SIM cards was the reason the **Nigerian Communications Commission** sanctioned some operators, arrested and prosecuted some registration agents, and confiscated both their equipment as well as the improperly activated SIM cards found with them.[41]

The Republic of Kenya also adopts the Sim Registration policy measure.

[41] Nigerian Communications Commission (2019), 'NCC Reiterates, "SIM Registration is Compulsory", Available at: https://www.ncc.gov.ng/stakeholder/media-public/news-headlines/512-ncc-reiterates-sim-registration-is-compulsory (accessed 17 April 2019).

Section 27 of the Kenya Information and Communications (Amendment) Act 2013 and **regulations 4 to 18 of the Kenya Information and Communications (Registration of SIM-cards) Regulations, 2015** require companies and individual subscribers – including minors – to register their Sim cards.

A person who intends to register a SIM-card in Kenya is required to provide the following particulars to the telecommunications operator or agent—

(a) full names;

(b) identity card, service card, passport or alien card number;

(c) date of birth;

(d) gender;

(e) physical address;

(f) postal address, where available;

(g) any other registered subscriber number associated with the subscriber;

(h) an original and a copy of the national identity card, service card, passport or alien card;

(i) an original and a copy of the birth certificate, in respect of registration of minors;

(j) subscriber number in respect to existing subscribers;

(k) a certified copy of the certificate of registration or incorporation and a copy of the national identity card or passport of at least one director, where relevant; and

(l) a letter duly sealed by the chief executive officer or the person responsible for the day to day management of the statutory body.[42]

Where there is a change in any of the details provided by a subscriber above, the subscriber shall within thirty days of the change taking place inform the telecommunications operator or an agent of the change.[43] The telecommunications operator shall then amend the relevant registration particulars of the subscriber within seven days upon receipt of the notice.[44]

A person, who knowingly provides false information to a telecommunications operator or an agent during the registration process, commits an offence.[45]

A telecommunications operator or an agent shall when registering a person, verify the information provided by the subscriber.[46]

A telecommunications operator or an agent shall require the following documents to verify the registration particulars of a subscriber—

(a) for a Kenyan citizen—

(i) an original identity card;

[42] The Kenya Information and Communications (Registration of SIM-cards) Regulations 2015, regulation 5(1).
[43] The Kenya Information and Communications (Registration of SIM-cards) Regulations 2015, regulation 5(2).
[44] The Kenya Information and Communications (Registration of SIM-cards) Regulations 2015, regulation 5(3).
[45] The Kenya Information and Communications (Registration of SIM-cards) Regulations 2015, regulation 5(4).
[46] The Kenya Information and Communications (Registration of SIM-cards) Regulations 2015, regulation 6(1).

(ii) an original and valid passport;

(iii) an original service card for a member of the Kenya Defence Forces; or

(iv) an original birth certificate;

where a person who is a Kenyan citizen but is not in possession of original identification documents, desires to register as a subscriber, he or she shall produce—

(i) a waiting card; or

(ii) a police abstract and a certified copy of an identification document;

(b) for East African residents—

(i) an original national identity card;

(ii) an original national passport;

(iii) an original East African passport; or

(iv) any other original and valid registration documents acceptable as national identification documents in the country of domicile, which registration documents shall be published by the Authority from time to time;

(c) for a foreign national—

(i) an original and valid passport; or

(ii) an original alien card.

(d) for a corporate person or a statutory body, certified copies of the following documents —

(i) certificate of incorporation and an original national identity card or passport of at least one director;

(ii) certificate of registration and original national identity card or passport of the proprietor or at least one partner as the case may be; or

(iii) the relevant legislation or Gazette Notice establishing the statutory body.[47]

A telecommunications operator shall verify the registration particulars of subscribers provided by a telecommunications operator's agents.[48]

By virtue of **Regulation 8 of the Kenya Information and Communications (Registration of SIM-cards) Regulations 2015**, a telecommunications operator or agent shall—

(a) enter the registration particulars provided by a person in an electronic or physical form;

(b) require a person to appear before the telecommunications operator or agent in person;

(c) update the information obtained pursuant to regulation 5 to the telecommunications operator's database; and

(d) maintain the registration particulars obtained in a secure and confidential manner.[49]

A minor who wishes to register a SIM-card shall be accompanied by his or her guardian possessing relevant identification particulars as provided for under **regulations 5 and 6** of the **Kenya**

---

[47] The Kenya Information and Communications (Registration of SIM-cards) Regulations 2015, regulation 6(2).

[48] The Kenya Information and Communications (Registration of SIM-cards) Regulations 2015, regulation 6(3).

[49] The Kenya Information and Communications (Registration of SIM-cards) Regulations 2015, regulation 7(2).

Information and Communications (Registration of SIM-cards) Regulations, 2015.[50] The telecommunications operator or agent shall record the date of birth of the minor on registration of the minor's SIM-card.[51] A guardian accompanying a minor for purposes of registering a minor's SIM-card shall be registered as the subscriber of that particular SIM-card until the minor attains the age of majority.[52]

Upon the minor attaining the age of majority, a telecommunications operator shall advise a minor registered as a user under the **Kenya Information and Communications (Registration of SIM-cards) Regulations, 2015** to register his or her personal identification details according to **regulations 5 and 6** within a period of ninety days on attainment of the age of majority and the telecommunications operator shall inform the minor that his or her telecommunications services shall be suspended if he or she fails to comply with these Regulations.[53] Where, within ninety days a person fails to register identification particulars, the SIM-card shall be suspended and deactivated in the manner provided for under the **Kenya Information and Communications (Registration of SIM-cards) Regulations, 2015.**[54]

Where an adult has no legal capacity to transact on his or her own behalf, the requirements of the **Kenya Information and**

[50] The Kenya Information and Communications (Registration of SIM-cards) Regulations 2015, regulation 8(1).
[51] The Kenya Information and Communications (Registration of SIM-cards) Regulations 2015, regulation 8(2).
[52] The Kenya Information and Communications (Registration of SIM-cards) Regulations 2015, regulation 8(3).
[53] The Kenya Information and Communications (Registration of SIM-cards) Regulations 2015, regulation 8(4).
[54] The Kenya Information and Communications (Registration of SIM-cards) Regulations 2015, regulation 8(5).

Communications (Registration of SIM-cards) Regulations, 2015 shall apply with necessary modifications.[55]

There shall be no proxy registration of any SIM-card, except as otherwise permitted under **regulation 8** of **the Kenya Information and Communications (Registration of SIM-cards) Regulations, 2015.**[56]

A person shall transfer a SIM-Card registered in his or her name by making an application to the relevant telecommunications operator informing the telecommunications operator of his or her wish to discontinue the use of the SIM-Card and to transfer the benefits, use and liability of the SIM-card to a particular person.[57] When considering such an application, the telecommunications operator shall abide by the requirements of **regulation 6 and regulation** 7 of the **Kenya Information and Communications (Registration of SIM-cards) Regulations, 2015** as though the transfer was a new application.[58]

A telecommunications operator shall grant the Authority's officers access to its systems, premises, facilities, files, records and other data to enable the Authority inspect such systems, premises,

---

[55] The Kenya Information and Communications (Registration of SIM-cards) Regulations 2015, regulation 8(6).
[56] The Kenya Information and Communications (Registration of SIM-cards) Regulations 2015, regulation 9(1).
[57] The Kenya Information and Communications (Registration of SIM-cards) Regulations 2015, regulation 10(1).
[58] The Kenya Information and Communications (Registration of SIM-cards) Regulations 2015, regulation 10(2).

facilities, files, records and other data for purposes of ensuring compliance with the Act and these Regulations.[59]

A person who commits an offence under **the Kenya Information and Communications (Registration of SIM-cards) Regulations, 2015** for which no specific penalty has been provided in the Kenya Information and Communications Act shall, on conviction, be liable to a fine not exceeding three hundred thousand shillings or to imprisonment for a term not exceeding six months or to both.[60]

In a press release by the **Communications Authority of Kenya (CA)**, the Telecommunications Regulator warned that Mobile users providing false information to register SIM-card risks six months imprisonment or a fine of Ksh100,000 if found guilty.

The warning by **Communications Authority of Kenya (CA)** comes in the wake of a crackdown that has so far seen 62 SIM card hawkers apprehended and convicted in courts of law. Thirty-four (34) of them have been slapped with penalties, while warrants of arrests have been issued against the others. SIM-card registration regulations also outlaw the hawking of SIM cards, which offence attracts a fine of up to Ksh.500,000 or 12 months imprisonment or both.[61]

---

[59] The Kenya Information and Communications (Registration of SIM-cards) Regulations 2015, regulation 11.

[60] The Kenya Information and Communications (Registration of SIM-cards) Regulations 2015, regulation 1

[61] Communications Authority of Kenya (2018), 'Mobile Subscribers Providing False Information in SIM Card Registration Risk Six Months In Jail', Available at: https://ca.go.ke/mobile-subscribers-providing-false-information-in-sim-card-registration-risk-six-months-in-jail/ (accessed 8 May 2019).

Francis Wangusi, Director General, Communications Authority of Kenya CA, on the 4th of June 2018, in a media briefing said the continued use of unregistered SIM cards is not only criminal but also a threat to national security. "Unregistered SIM cards are misused to perpetuate crime, including money laundering, kidnapping, malicious calls, cybercrime and mobile money fraud," Mr Wangusi said.[62]

The SIM Registration exercise will assist in easy identification of mobile telephone users and for the detection of crimes perpetrated by deviant users of mobile phones. The information collected and verified by Mobile Banking Operators will help telecommunications companies determine the risk(s) posed by a particular customer's account, allowing the institution to ensure that it has the proper controls in place, including suspicious activity monitoring procedures, and to monitor and report on the risks of a particular client. Customer identification and verification can reduce the risk of impersonation fraud that go with the use of pre-registered SIM cards; it will prevent a situation where a criminal impersonates a telecommunications customer by using the identity of the said customer to perpetrate fraud and money laundering.

The prohibition of the use of pre-registered SIM cards will help prevent a situation where High-risk customers like Politically Exposed Persons (PEPs) make use of the SIM cards of low-risk customers (e.g. pensioners) to operate a mobile banking account. Corrupt PEPs could use pre-registered SIM cards to conceal the origins of criminal funds by investing large sums of money in the new mobile banking scheme; the money comes back as clean

[62] Communications Authority of Kenya (2018), 'Mobile Subscribers Providing False Information in SIM Card Registration Risk Six Months In Jail', Available at: https://ca.go.ke/mobile-subscribers-providing-false-information-in-sim-card-registration-risk-six-months-in-jail/ (accessed 8 May 2019).

money once the corrupt PEP makes a withdrawal and purchases properties with the illicit funds by using shell companies.

Sim card registration is aimed at enhancing national security by making it possible to trace details of subscribers engaged in criminal activities such as spreading hate speech, mobile money conman ship, extortion or demanding for ransom in kidnapping cases.

B. NIGERIAN COMMUNICATIONS COMMISSION GUIDELINES ON SIM REPLACEMENT

The Objectives of these Guidelines are to:

I. Prescribe a regulatory framework and provide a procedure for network providers to effect a SIM Replacement for subscribers.

II. To stipulate the minimum standard of care which operators shall exercise in order to prevent unauthorised replacements of SIMs.

III. Provide guidance on the standard and procedure which Network Service Providers are expected to adhere to in the process of conducting a SIM Replacement.[63]

These Guidelines shall apply to all Network Service Providers that provide service using SIMs and R-UIMs. The Guidelines apply to all subscribers including postpaid and prepaid subscribers.[64]

By virtue of **paragraph 4** of the **Nigerian Communications Commission Guidelines on Sim Replacement**, a SIM can be replaced if it is faulty, damaged, stolen, lost, obsolete (but eligible for replacement or an upgrade), and any other reasonable legitimate reason or condition necessitating a SIM replacement; Provided that an operator may refuse a SIM Replacement request

[63] Nigerian Communications Commission Guidelines on Sim Replacement, para. 2.
[64] Nigerian Communications Commission Guidelines on Sim Replacement, para. 3.

where there are reasonable grounds to believe that the replacement ought not to be carried out and the **Nigerian Communications Commission** is notified within 24 hours of such a decision.

The medium of reporting rejected SIM Replacements would be in the same data dump format utilized for submission of SIM registration details, subject to any modifications the **Nigerian Communications Commission** may make from time to time.[65]

All SIM Replacements shall be undertaken by Network Service Providers or their licensed agents/dealers.[66] Below are the requirements for Sim Replacement:

1. The request for SIM Replacement can be made by a Subscriber.

2. The SIM must have been registered in accordance with the **Registration of Telephone Subscribers Regulations** issued by the **Nigerian Communications Commission.**

3. The subscriber requesting for the replacement must provide the following:

a. Information about the three (3) most frequently called numbers from that SIM which must be verified by the Network Service Provider. The frequently called numbers must have been dialed at least five times over a 30 days period.

b. Where the SIM to be replaced is a data SIM, the subscriber will be required to provide any two of the following:

i. Last recharge amount and date;

ii. Name of internet bundle value activated and data allowance allocated;

iii. Last three (3) sites visited.

---

[65] Nigerian Communications Commission Guidelines on Sim Replacement, para. 4.
[66] Nigerian Communications Commission Guidelines on Sim Replacement, para. 5.

c. An affidavit signed by the subscriber and a passport photograph of the subscriber where the replacement is to be done by a proxy.

d. Details of the last recharge on the SIM.

e. Details of the last paid invoice for post-paid subscribers.

4. The SIM must be active on the network of the operator.

5. A person requesting a replacement must fill a Standard Form as provided in the Schedule to the **Nigerian Communications Commission Guidelines on Sim Replacement for SIM Replacement.**

6. A valid photo identification of the Subscriber must be provided.

7. The SIM pack or other evidence of direct purchase/ownership of the SIM must be provided and where it is unavailable, an affidavit attesting to the ownership and loss of the SIM must be provided.

8. The Network Service Provider must capture a facial image of the subscriber which must be kept for twelve (12) months.

9. All completed SIM Replacement Forms and other requirements as stated in the **Nigerian Communications Commission Guidelines on Sim Replacement** must be verified and approved by the Network Service Provider before carrying out the SIM Replacement.

10. Upon satisfactory receipt of validated information the Network Service Provider may execute the replacement and provide the person requesting the replacement with a new SIM.[67]

The Network Service Provider must carry out a quarterly audit of SIM Replacement transactions carried out by both its staff and agents to ensure the integrity of its Replacement processes and that appropriate documentation was in all cases provided that

[67] Nigerian Communications Commission Guidelines on Sim Replacement, para. 6.

appropriate documentation was in all cases provided prior to Replacement. A Report on the audit in Paragraph 8.1 must be forwarded to the **Nigerian Communications Commission** in Microsoft Excel format as provided in Schedule 2 of the **Nigerian Communications Commission Guidelines on Sim Replacement** for SIM Replacement. All Network Service Providers must keep a register of all SIM Replacements undertaken by it for not less than twelve (12) months.[68]

Online SIM Replacement can only be carried out either through the Network Service Provider's secured website or self-service terminal:

1. The Network Service Provider shall create on its secured website a platform where Subscribers can carry out SIM Replacement using the unique Identification and PIN issued by the Network Service Provider.

2. The Network Service Provider shall issue interested Subscribers with a unique Identification and PIN.

3. The Subscriber is required to purchase a new SIM Card to which the MSISDN of the old SIM Card would be transferred.

4. The Subscriber can login to the portal through the Network Service Provider's secured website using the unique Identification and Personal Information Number (PIN) issued to the Subscriber.

5. The Subscriber will input the following information;

a. Date of Birth

b. Mother's Maiden Name

c. Place of Birth

d. Three frequently called numbers

---

[68] Nigerian Communications Commission Guidelines on Sim Replacement, para. 8.

e. The MSISDN of the SIM to be replaced.

6. Where the information provided matches the record on the Network Service Provider's system, the Subscriber will be prompted to enter the MSISDN of the new SIM purchased and the operator would then the carry out the SIM replacement by transferring the old MSISDN to the new SIM.

7. No Network Service Provider is allowed to carry out SIM Replacement over the phone.[69]

A replacement SIM shall be activated within two (2) hours once the verification of Subscriber information has been carried out.[70]

With regards to penalties for violating certain provisions of the **Nigerian Communications Commission Guidelines on Sim Replacement**, paragraph 11 provides as follows:

I. Any SIM Replacement done in violation of these Guidelines shall be sanctioned in accordance with the **Nigerian Communications (Enforcement Processes, Etc.) Regulations 2005**.

II. A Network Service Provider shall be held liable for any SIM Replacement carried out in violation of **the Nigerian Communications Commission Guidelines on Sim Replacement** or done fraudulently by its agent or dealer.

III. The subscriber can pursue any other remedies against a Network Service Provider for any SIM Replacement done fraudulently by such Network Service Provider or its agent or dealer.[71]

The measures provided in the Nigerian Communications Commission Guidelines on Sim Replacement can help guard

---

[69] Nigerian Communications Commission Guidelines on Sim Replacement, para. 9.

[70] Nigerian Communications Commission Guidelines on Sim Replacement, para. 10.

[71] Nigerian Communications Commission Guidelines on Sim Replacement, para. 11

against Sim Swap Fraud. Sim Swap Fraud is a new and little-reported scam which overrides the additional security introduced by banks to protect customer transactions. Fraudsters can complete cash transfers from a stranger's account by accessing one-time Personal Identification Number (PIN) codes and Short Message Service (SMS) notifications. Criminal gangs obtain an individual's bank details by bamboozling them with a phishing email, or by purchasing them from organised crime networks. They then open a parallel business account with the same bank, in the customer's name, since this involves fewer security checks if the account holder is already a customer. Having worked out possible answers to security questions from the victim's social media accounts, they call the victim's mobile phone provider, posing as the customer, to report that their phone is lost or damaged.

Provided they can answer basic security questions, the old sim is cancelled and a new one activated. From then on, they can commandeer their victim's mobile account, intercepting or initiating calls, texts and authorisations such as those used for cash transfers. They can also request that security settings are changed to stop the victim gaining access to their account.

The first the victim will know of a problem is when their mobile stops working and they report it to their provider. In the meantime, their bank account may have been emptied.[72]

[72] The Guardian (2015), 'Sim swap' gives fraudsters access-all-areas via your mobile phone', Available at: https://www.theguardian.com/money/2015/sep/26/sim-swap-fraud-mobile-phone-vodafone-customer (accessed 23 August 2017).

1.5 ENHANCING FINANCIAL INCLUSION USING TELECOMMUNICATIONS COMPANIES AND AML MEASURES

Over the years, financial institutions in Nigeria have utilized the mobile network to drive financial inclusion - through approval of telecommunications companies. One example is **First Bank of Nigeria.**

The FirstBank Unstructured Supplementary Service Data (USSD) Code *894# allows you to do Quick Banking. **894** is a quick, convenient, secure and easy way to perform your banking transactions (transfer money, check balance, buy airtime, pay bills and lots more) anytime and anywhere, using any type of phone without need for internet connectivity or data.

Once you have a FirstBank account with a linked debit card, a phone number profiled for SMS alert and a mobile phone, you are just one dial away from enjoying the unbeatable 894 experience. Simply dial *894*0# to get started! Customers can also dial *894# and get access to Quick Banking services in a menu-based layout without having to dial the codes.

When dialed, two options are displayed for the customer to choose from:

- Quick Banking- Follow prompts to access the listed services for FirstBank account holders ONLY.
- Firstmonie- For electronic wallet-based transactions. This product is available to both account holders and non-account holders.[73]

Zenith Bank also has this similar feature. You can open an Account in Zenith Bank by simply dialing *966*0# and following the

[73] FirstBank (2019), 'Quick Banking with FirstBank USSD Code *894#', Available at: https://www.firstbanknigeria.com/894-2/ (accessed 22 April 2019).

onscreen prompts. An account number will be created automatically and sent to you via Short Message Service (SMS). Account opening forms are NOT required for the signup process. Once you sign up, look out for your ten-digit account number (NUBAN):

- To check for balances on any of your accounts, all you need to do is simply dial; ***966*00#** on your mobile phone and follow the on-screen prompts.
- To load airtime and data for self and others Simply dial ***966*Amount*Mobile Number#** on your phone (e.g. *966*1000*0803456789#) to buy airtime.
- To transfer funds conveniently Dial *966*Amount*Account Number# (e.g. *966*1000*1234567890#) from the phone number you registered with Zenith Bank, then follow the on-screen prompts.
- To pay your Digital Satellite Television (DStv) and Power Holding Company of Nigeria (PHCN) bills, simply dial; ***966*7*Amount*Customer ID#** on your mobile phone and follow the on-screen prompts. To pay other **Zenith Billers**, simply dial; ***966*6*Biller code*Amount#** on your mobile phone and follow the on-screen prompts.
- To update your Bank Verification Number (BVN) Simply dial ***966*BVN#** using the number associated with your Zenith Bank account.[74]

Mobile Banking can also be done through the use of a Mobile Banking App. One example is **GTBank** Mobile App.

---

[74] Zenith Bank (2019), 'EazyBanking', Available at: https://www.zenithbank.com/966/#what-is-star966-eazybanking (accessed 22 April 2019).

A quick download of the GTBank mobile banking app can transform your smartphone into a powerful banking tool. With the GTBank Mobile Banking App, a customer can perform transactions and manage his or her bank account(s) from his or her mobile device. On the Mobile Banking App, All GTBank customers who are eligible and profiled for Mobile Banking can:

- Check balance;
- Stop and confirm cheques;
- Purchase airtime (Airtel, 9Mobile, Glo, MTN, Visafone);
- Purchase both domestic and international flight tickets;
- Pay bills (DStv, Lekki Concession Commission (LCC) toll, PHCN, Swift Networks;
- Transfer money – Own account, other GTBank accounts, NIP & NEFT to other banks.

To obtain log in details for Mobile Banking, you can visit any GTBank branch.

The hardware token is required for all transactions on Mobile Banking. Personal Identification Number (PIN) authentication will suffice.[75]

WEMA Bank allows for Mobile Banking with ALAT. ALAT is Nigeria's first fully functional digital bank. With ALAT, you can do all your banking transactions without being physically present at a bank.

ALAT will save you time with a simple account opening process that takes less than five minutes, help you put money away easily by automating your saving, make sure your bills are paid on time

[75] GTBank (2019), 'Mobile Banking', Available at: https://www.gtbank.com/personal-banking/ways-to-bank/mobile-app (accessed 22 April, 2019).

with its scheduled payments feature and deliver a free debit card you can activate, lock and unlock from your phone to you anywhere in Nigeria. You can use ALAT on iOS and Android devices.

You can open an ALAT account easily on from your phone. Install ALAT from the Apple App Store or the Google Play Store, open the app and sign up with your Bank Verification Number and a valid phone number. Opening an ALAT account from your phone takes about five minutes, a lot quicker than going to a regular bank to open an account.

With photos of your face and signature, you can open a basic ALAT account. This account is restricted to a balance of 300,000 naira, a single deposit limit of 50,000 naira, and a daily transaction limit of 30,000 naira. When you upload photos of your government-approved ID card and a utility bill, your account will be upgraded to a standard savings account without these restrictions.

To open a basic ALAT account, you'll need to upload a photo of your face and a photo of your signature (sign on a plain piece of white paper). For a full ALAT account, you'll also need to upload a photo of your government-approved ID card (your international passport, driver's license, national ID card or voter card) and a photo of a utility bill (not older than 3 months). Your ALAT account number will be emailed to you. It will also be displayed on your dashboard each time you log in to ALAT.

Although ALAT claims to be different from other Mobile Banking Apps as it states in its website that a customer will not need to go to a physical bank to get a debit card and activate it, submit documents and often, to get some kinds of customer support, an ALAT account can only be funded with the funds deposited in another Bank Account.

For example, a newly opened ALAT account can be funded:

1. By direct debit from your Wema Bank account to your ALAT account: a. Log in to the ALAT app and click **Fund My Account**. b. Click the **From Wema Account** menu option. Both the ALAT and Wema accounts will be displayed with their account balances. c. Type the amount you want to fund your ALAT account with. d. Type the six-digit code sent to your registered phone number by SMS. e. Click **Fund Account** to complete.

2. With a bank card from any Nigerian bank: a. Log in to the ALAT app and Click **Fund My Account**. b. Click the **From Other Bank Card** menu option and type the debit card details (card number, expiry date and Card Verification Value/Code, CVV) in the fields provided. c. Authenticate with the card PIN and type the token sent to your phone number by SMS to add the card. d. Type the amount to be transferred from the added debit card to your ALAT account and authenticate with the card PIN and the six-digit code sent to your phone number by SMS.

3. With a foreign bank card: a. Log in to the ALAT app and Click **Fund My Account**. b. Click the **From Foreign Card** menu option and type the debit card details (card number, expiry date and CVV) in the fields provided. c. Authenticate with the card PIN and type the token sent to your phone number by SMS to add the card. d. Type the amount to be transferred from the added debit card to your ALAT account and authenticate with the card PIN and the six-digit code sent to your phone number by SMS.

4. By transferring money from another bank's online banking platform.[76]

[76] ALAT BY WEMA (2019), 'Frequently Asked Questions', Available at: http://www.alat.ng/faq (accessed 22 April 2019).

Aside from Banks in Nigeria, other platforms have utilized the mobile banking technology in Nigeria. Only 9 years ago, Paga was the first licensed mobile money platform to exist in Nigeria. While other platforms such as Teasy, PayAttitude, Cellulant, Etranzact/Pocketmoni, FETS and Readycash have emerged in the market, Paga has made the most impressive progress, recording a milestone of 8,000,000+ users at the end of 2017 and a sum total of 42.7 million transactions till date, with a total value of over N660 billion, largely due to their 15,000+ growing agent network.[77]

Despite the recorded success of the Mobile Banking scheme by financial institutions and other Mobile Money Operators in Urban Areas in Nigeria, the Central Bank of Nigeria is yet to be convinced that the scheme is making measurable impact on financial inclusion, especially for rural and remote areas around Nigeria.[78]

Currently, there is an estimate of 21 licensed mobile money operators operating to varying degrees of success, but the telecommunications companies are beginning to push to be licensed, citing the success of MPesa, the most successful mobile money operators in Kenya.[79]

As part of moves to further deepen financial inclusion in the country as well as ensuring improvement in the mobile money segment of Nigeria's information and communications technology

---

[77] E Abiodun (2018), 'What's the future of mobile payments in Nigeria?', Available at: https://guardian.ng/business-services/whats-the-future-of-mobile-payments-in-nigeria/ (accessed 22 April 2019).

[78] Central Bank of Nigeria (2018), 'National Financial Inclusion Strategy (Revised)', Available at: https://www.cbn.gov.ng/Out/2019/CCD/NATIONAL%20FINANCIAL%20INCLUSION%20STRATEGY.pdf (accessed 30 March, 2019).

[79] Vanguard (2018), 'MOBILE MONEY: Telcos push aggressively for payment banking services license', Available at: https://www.vanguardngr.com/2018/10/mobile-money-telcos-push-aggressively-for-payment-banking-services-license/ (accessed 22 April 2019).

(ICT) sector, the Nigerian Communications Commission (NCC), and the Central Bank of Nigeria, signed a Memorandum of Understanding (MoU) on digital payment systems with both parties agreeing to jointly implement a payment systems framework.[80] This MoU is coming after the Central Bank of Nigeria revealed that the financial inclusion rate remains below expectation. This is the case even when several initiatives have been introduced by the Central Bank of Nigeria (e.g., the introduction of microfinance banking, agent banking, tiered know-your-customer requirements and mobile money operations) in pursuit of its objective—that is, ensuring that over 80% of the bankable adults in Nigeria have access to financial services by 2020.[81] In 2016, 58.4% of Nigeria's 96.4 million adults were financially served, leaving 41.6% financially excluded. The proportion of those who were banked was 38.3%, 10.3% were in the formal other category and 9.8% were served by the informal sector. This shows that only 48.6% used formal services compared to 80% who are targeted in 2020.[82]

In line with the MoU on digital payment systems, the Central Bank of Nigeria issued guidelines for licensing, regulation and operation of payment service banks (e.g., banking agents, telecommunications companies, retail chains and mobile money operators in the country). The focus of this book is on telecommunications companies. The director of the financial

80 The Guardian (2018), 'NCC, CBN sign MoU on mobile money, financial inclusion', Available at: https://guardian.ng/business-services/ncc-cbn-sign-mou-on-mobile-money-financial-inclusion/ (accessed 30 March, 2019).

81 Central Bank of Nigeria (2018), 'National Financial Inclusion Strategy (Revised)', Available at: https://www.cbn.gov.ng/Out/2019/CCD/NATIONAL%20FINANCIAL%20INCLUSION%20STRATEGY.pdf (accessed 30 March, 2019).

82 Central Bank of Nigeria (2018), 'National Financial Inclusion Strategy (Revised)', Available at: https://www.cbn.gov.ng/Out/2019/CCD/NATIONAL%20FINANCIAL%20INCLUSION%20STRATEGY.pdf (accessed 30 March, 2019).

policy and regulation department of the regulatory body, Kevin Amuga, said the guidelines were in furtherance of the apex bank's effort to leverage technology to promote financial inclusion and enhance access to financial services for the rural poor, low-income earners and financially excluded in society.[83]

Presently, the major telecommunication companies operating in Nigeria are Airtel, 9mobile, Globacom and MTN. Airtel has 44,970,973 subscribers in Nigeria, 9mobile has 16,385,317 subscribers, Globacom has 45,603,638 subscribers and MTN has 66,665,378 subscribers.[84]

This book seeks to explore the following research question:

How can telecommunications companies design AML/CFT measures that meet the goal of financial inclusion without compromising the measures that exist for combating money laundering, terrorist financing and other illicit transactions through the financial system?

Chapters 2 to 6 of this book will critically review the AML/CFT measures in the **Guidelines for Licensing, Regulation and Operation of Telecommunications Companies** issued by the Central Bank of Nigeria. The aim is to determine if the said Guidelines adopt a balanced approach to financial inclusion and anti-money laundering measures.

By virtue of the Central Bank of Nigeria's guidelines for licensing, regulation and operation of telecommunications companies, the current anti-money laundering laws and regulations will now apply

---

[83] Premium Times (2018), 'CBN issues guidelines for licensing, regulation of payment service banks', Available at: https://www.premiumtimesng.com/business/business-news/293746-cbn-issues-guidelines-for-licensing-regulation-of-payment-service-banks.html (accessed 30 March, 2019).

[84] Nigerian Communications Commission (2019), 'Market Share by Operator (GSM) (January 2019)', Available at: https://www.ncc.gov.ng/stakeholder/statistics-reports/industry-overview#view-graphs-tables-2 (accessed 7 April 2019).

to telecommunications companies who are given a payment service bank license.

The laws enacted to combat money laundering and terrorist financing in Nigeria include: the **Money Laundering Prohibition Act 2011 (as amended), Terrorism (Prevention) Act, 2011 (as amended), Economic and Financial Crimes Commission (Establishment) Act, 2004, Central Bank of Nigeria (Anti-Money Laundering and Combating the Financing of Terrorism in Banks and other Financial Institutions in Nigeria) Regulations 2013, Anti-Money Laundering/Combating the Financing of Terrorism (AML/CFT) Regulations for Designated non- Financial Businesses and Professions in Nigeria 2013** and the **Anti-Money Laundering/Combating the Financing of Terrorism (AML/CFT) Reporting Guidelines 2012.**

The **Money Laundering Prohibition Act 2011 (as amended) (MLPA)**, **Terrorism (Prevention) Act, 2011 (as amended), Central Bank of Nigeria (Anti-Money Laundering and Combating the Financing of Terrorism in Banks and other Financial Institutions in Nigeria) Regulations 2013** and other AML/CFT Guidelines provide guidance to telecommunications companies to carry out AML/CFT under the regulatory purview of the CBN.

The **Money Laundering Prohibition Act 2011 (as amended)** and the **Central Bank of Nigeria (Anti-Money Laundering and Combating the Financing of Terrorism in Banks and other Financial Institutions in Nigeria) Regulations 2013** establish the requirements for record-keeping and reporting by designated non-financial institutions, businesses and professions, banks and other financial institutions. Relevant provisions of the law and regulation above were designed to help identify the source, volume and movement of currency and other monetary instruments transported or transmitted into or out of Nigeria, or deposited in financial institutions in the country.

The enabling Act and Regulation under reference seek to achieve the above objective by requiring individuals, banks and other financial institutions to render suspicious transaction reports (STRs) to Nigerian Financial Intelligence Unit (NFIU) only, properly identify persons conducting transactions and maintain a paper trail by keeping appropriate records of their financial transactions. Should the need arise, these records will enable law enforcement and regulatory agencies to pursue investigations of criminal, tax & regulatory violations, and provide useful evidence in prosecuting money laundering and other financial crimes.

The **Money Laundering Prohibition Act 2011 (as amended)** and the **Central Bank of Nigeria (Anti-Money Laundering and Combating the Financing of Terrorism in Banks and other Financial Institutions in Nigeria) Regulations 2013** apply equally to all banks, other financial institutions and persons that are under the regulatory purview of the CBN. The law also imposes criminal liability on a person or financial institution that knowingly assists in the laundering of money or fails to report suspicious transactions conducted through it. The CBN Regulation also directs financial institutions to establish and maintain procedures reasonably designed to ensure and monitor compliance with the reporting and record-keeping requirements of the MLPA, 2011.

A financial institution is required to render a Suspicious Transaction Report (STR) to NFIU only and inform the Unit of same whenever it detects a known or suspected criminal violation of MLPA or a suspicious transaction related to money laundering and terrorism financing activities or a violation of other laws and regulations.

The **Economic and Financial Crimes Commission (Establishment) Act, 2004** and the **Terrorism (Prevention) Act, 2011 (as amended)** criminalize the financing of terrorism. The **Central Bank of Nigeria (Anti-Money Laundering and Combating the Financing of Terrorism in Banks and other Financial Institutions in Nigeria) Regulations 2013** has also augmented the existing AML/CFT legal framework by strengthening customer identification procedures, prohibiting financial institutions from engaging in business with foreign shell banks, requiring financial institutions to have due diligence procedures, (in some cases) have Enhanced Due Diligence (EDD) Procedures for foreign correspondent and private banking accounts and improve information sharing between financial institutions on one hand, and the law enforcement agencies (LEAs) and regulators on the other.

Provisions of the Money Laundering Prohibition Act 2011 (as amended) and the Central Bank of Nigeria (Anti-Money Laundering and Combating the Financing of Terrorism in Banks and other Financial Institutions in Nigeria) Regulations 2013:

(*i*) Require financial institutions to have AML/CFT Program;

(*ii*) Provide the CBN with the authority to impose sanctions for AML/CFT infractions committed by institutions and persons in the course of transactions;

(*iii*) Facilitate access to records and require financial institutions to give prompt response to regulatory requests for information; and

(i*v*) Require financial institutions to consider their AML/CFT records when reviewing mergers, acquisitions and other applications for business combinations.

(*v*) Provide for civil and criminal penalties for money laundering;

Section 15 (2) of the Money Laundering Prohibition Act, 2011 (as amended) clearly stipulates the offence of money laundering as thus:

"Any person or body corporate, in or outside Nigeria, who directly or indirectly—

(a) conceals or disguises the origin of;

(b) converts or transfers;

(c) removes from the jurisdiction; or

(d) acquires, uses, retains or takes possession or control of any fund or property, knowingly or reasonably ought to have known that such fund or property is, or forms part of the proceeds of an unlawful act; commits an offence of money laundering under this Act."

It also stipulates amongst others, the following penalty for contravention: "A person who contravenes the provisions of subsection (2) of this section is liable on conviction to a term of not less than 7 years but not more than 14 years imprisonment.

a) A body corporate who contravenes the provisions of subsection (2) of this section is liable on conviction to a fine of not less than 100% of the funds and properties acquired as a result of the offence committed; and

b) Withdrawal of license.

c) Where the body corporate persists in the commission of the offence for which it was convicted in the first instance, the Regulators may withdraw or revoke the certificate or license of the body corporate."

Money laundering involves three independent stages namely Placement, Layering and Integration.

Placement - This is the stage where the funds from the illicit activities are physically placed into the economy. It may include the co-mingling of funds from legitimate sources and illegitimate sources. Examples of this stage include direct deposit of funds into Bank accounts, purchase of luxury goods such as cars and artworks, etc.

Layering - This involves the creation of complex transactions in order to distance the funds from the original source and also to obliterate the audit trail, (e.g. wire transfers, letter of credit, purchase of financial instruments, transfer to offshore accounts, re-sale of assets, etc.)

Integration - It is the stage at which the money is integrated into the legitimate economic and financial system and is assimilated with all the other assets in the system. Integration of the 'cleaned' money into the economy is accomplished by the launderer making it appear to have been legally earned. At this stage, it is exceedingly difficult to distinguish legal and illegal wealth, e.g. Inflow from offshore for investments, funds from sale of real estate.

Terrorism financing involves three stages namely Sourcing, Moving and Executing.

Sourcing (raise) - this stage involves raising funds by terrorists through donations, self-funding and criminal activities such as proceeds of drug trafficking, extortion, cheque fraud, credit card fraud, legitimate business, use of charitable organizations, sham charities, etc.

Moving (transfer) - this involves use of charities and non-profit organizations, use of Alternative Remittance Systems (ARS), use of cash couriers, use of gold to move value, wire transfers to move money across borders and the formal financial sector.

Executing (use) - in this stage funds are required to promote a militant ideology, pay operatives and their families, arrange for travel, train new members, forge documents, pay bribes, acquire weapons, and stage attacks.

Funds used to support terrorism may originate from legitimate sources, criminal activities or both. Nonetheless, disguising the source of terrorist financing, regardless of whether the source is of legitimate or illicit origin is key. Thus, if the source can be concealed, it remains available for future terrorist financing activities. Similarly, it is important for terrorists to conceal the use of the funds so that the financed activity goes undetected.[85]

---

[85] Central Bank of Nigeria (2018), 'Anti-Money Laundering/Combating the Financing of Terrorism (AML/CFT) Policy and Procedure Manual', Available at: https://www.cbn.gov.ng/Out/2019/CCD/CBN%20Anti-money%20laundering%20_combating%20the%20financing%20of%20terrorism%20_Manual%20(2).pdf (accessed 21 April, 2019).

CHAPTER 2

THE FIT AND PROPER TEST

Knowing your employees is as important as knowing your customers. An insider can pose the same fraud/money laundering threat as a customer and a criminally co-opted telecommunications employee might facilitate fraud and money laundering.[86]

By virtue of **Paragraph 7.2 of the Central Bank of Nigeria Guidelines for Licensing and Regulation of Payment Service Banks, the Central Bank of Nigeria' Revised Assessment Criteria for Approved Persons' Regime for Financial Institutions 2015** will now apply to telecommunications companies who are seeking a Payment Service Bank license.

The **Revised Assessment Criteria for Approved Persons' Regime for Financial Institutions** ensures that only "fit and proper persons" are approved for appointment to board and top management positions in banks and other financial institutions. The conditions specified in **the Revised Assessment Criteria for Approved Persons' Regime for Financial Institutions** are minimum requirements for candidates occupying or intending to occupy the under-listed board and senior/top management positions in Nigerian banks, discount houses, development finance and other financial institutions.

---

[86] SSA ZAIDI (2015), 'Banks need to follow Know Your Employees norms for robust internal AML control systems', Available at: https://www.moneylife.in/article/banks-need-to-follow-know-your-employees-norms-for-robust-internal-aml-control-systems/44095.html (accessed 15 February 2018).

Fitness tests assess the competence of candidates for board, top management and critical operational positions and their capacity to fulfill the responsibilities of their positions while propriety tests assess their integrity and suitability.

In assessing a candidate's integrity and suitability, elements to be considered include:

1. Breach of **Sections 19 (1)(a)** and **44 (now 48)** of **Banks and Other Financial Institutions Act (BOFIA) Cap. B3, Laws of the Federation of Nigeria 2004**, where such a candidate is or has been:

a. of unsound mind or as a result of ill- health is incapable of carrying out his duties; or

b. declared bankrupt or suspends payments or compounds with his creditors including his bankers; or

c. convicted of any offence involving dishonesty or fraud; or

d. guilty of serious misconduct in relation to his duties; or

e. disqualified or suspended from practicing his profession; or

f. a director of a financial institution or any candidate directly involved in the management of a financial institution under the purview of the **Central Bank of Nigeria** which has been wound up by the Federal High Court;

And whether:

2. the candidate is or has been the subject of any proceedings of a disciplinary or criminal nature, or has been notified of any impending proceedings or any investigation, which might lead to such proceedings. However, this provision will not apply where a person involved in such proceedings has been exonerated;

3. such appointment would result in conflict of interest thus contravening the provisions of **section 19 (2) and (3) of BOFIA Cap. B3, Laws of the Federation of Nigeria 2004**;

4. the candidate, or any business in which he has controlling interest or exercises significant influence, has been investigated, disciplined, suspended or criticized by a regulatory or professional body, a court or tribunal, whether publicly or privately;

5. the candidate has been the subject of any justified complaint relating to regulated activities;

6. the candidate has been dismissed, asked to resign from employment or from a position of trust, fiduciary appointment or similar position because of questions about his honesty and integrity;

7. the candidate has ever been disqualified under **BOFIA** or the **Companies and Allied Matters Act (CAMA)** or any other legislation or regulation, from acting as a director or serving in a managerial capacity;

8. the candidate deliberately misled (or attempts to mislead) by act or omission, a client, the institution and/or the regulators;

9. the candidate deliberately falsified documents to mislead a client, the institution and/or regulators;

10. the candidate has deliberately failed to inform the client, institution and/or regulator, without reasonable cause, of the fact that their understanding of a material issue is incorrect, despite being aware of their misunderstanding;

11. the candidate had deliberately failed to disclose the existence of falsified documents;

12. the candidate has deliberately prepared inaccurate or inappropriate records or returns.[87]

---

[87] Central Bank of Nigeria' Revised Assessment Criteria for Approved Persons' Regime for Financial Institutions 2015, section 2.0.

To assess the competence of candidates for board and top management positions, their capacity to fulfill the responsibilities of their positions and their ability to understand the technical requirements of the business, the Central Bank of Nigeria (CBN) shall take into account all relevant considerations, including but not limited to factors listed against each of the positions.

Furthermore, the financial institution shall conduct an assessment of the fitness and propriety of its board/top management staff biennially or any other period as may be specified by the CBN. Performance on the job shall be an integral part of this assessment.

Candidates will be expected to meet the general guidelines under **section 4.0** of **the Revised Assessment Criteria for Approved Persons' Regime for Financial Institutions 2015** as well as the relevant fitness requirements specified either under any of the sub-sections of **section 5.0 or 6.0**.

Where candidates are deficient or fail the fitness test, they will be allowed a period of two years within which to undergo training to remedy the deficiency. However, if the candidate is unable to fulfill the requirements under these guidelines after two years of failing the test, he/she may be required to relinquish his/her board/top management appointment.[88]

2.1 FITNESS REQUIREMENTS FOR BANKS, DISCOUNT HOUSES AND TELECOMMUNICATIONS COMPANIES

The fitness requirements for appointment to board and top management positions in the above financial institutions/ telecommunications companies are as stated below:

[88] Central Bank of Nigeria' Revised Assessment Criteria for Approved Persons' Regime for Financial Institutions 2015, section 3.0.

2.1.1 MANAGING DIRECTOR

- A minimum of first degree or its equivalent in any discipline plus a higher degree or professional qualification in any business-related discipline.
- Candidates must also have a minimum of 20 years postgraduation experience, out of which at least 15 must have been in the banking industry and, at least 2 as Deputy Managing Director (DMD)/Executive Director (ED), with responsibility in several areas of banking operations including business development and customer relationship management.

For Non-interest banks, the candidates should in addition to the above possess requisite knowledge and experience/training in Islamic banking and finance.[89]

2.1.2 DEPUTY MANAGING DIRECTOR/EXECUTIVE DIRECTORS

- A minimum of first degree or its equivalent in any discipline plus a higher degree or professional qualification in any business-related discipline.
- Candidates must also have a minimum of 18 years postgraduation experience, out of which at least 13 must have been in the banking industry and, at least 2 as General Manager. Evidence of experience in several areas of banking operations including business development and customer services management.
- A Deputy Managing Director/Executive Director must have served for a minimum of two (2) years for him/her to be qualified for appointment as a Managing Director.

---

[89] Central Bank of Nigeria' Revised Assessment Criteria for Approved Persons' Regime for Financial Institutions 2015, section, 5.1.

For Non-interest banks, the candidates should in addition to the above possess requisite knowledge and experience/training in Islamic banking and finance.[90]

2.1.3 GENERAL MANAGER

- A minimum of first degree or its equivalent in any discipline plus a relevant higher degree or professional qualification.
- Candidates must also have a minimum of 15 years postgraduation experience, out of which at least 12 must have been in the banking industry and at least 2 as Deputy General Manager. Evidence of experience in at least three (3) major areas of banking operations.

For Non-interest banks, the candidates should in addition to the above possess requisite knowledge and experience/training in Islamic banking and finance.[91]

2.1.4 DEPUTY GENERAL MANAGER

- A minimum of first degree or its equivalent in any discipline plus a relevant higher degree or professional qualification.
- Candidates must also have a minimum of 15 years postgraduation experience, out of which at least 10 must have been in the banking industry and at least 2 as Assistant General Manager. Evidence of experience in at least three (3) major areas of banking operations.

[90] Central Bank of Nigeria' Revised Assessment Criteria for Approved Persons' Regime for Financial Institutions 2015, section, 5.2.
[91] Central Bank of Nigeria' Revised Assessment Criteria for Approved Persons' Regime for Financial Institutions 2015, section, 5.3.

For Non-interest banks, the candidates should in addition to the above possess requisite knowledge and experience/training in Islamic banking and finance.[92]

2.1.5 ASSISTANT GENERAL MANAGER

- A minimum of first degree or its equivalent in any discipline plus a relevant higher degree or professional qualification.
- A minimum of 15 years post-graduation experience, out of which at least 10 must have been in the banking industry, and at least 3 years on senior manager or equivalent position.
- Evidence of experience in at least three (3) major areas of banking operations.

For Non-interest banks, the candidates should in addition to the above possess requisite knowledge and experience/training in Islamic banking and finance.[93]

2.1.6 NON-EXECUTIVE DIRECTORS

Without prejudice to the provisions of the **Code of Corporate Governance**, candidates must possess:

a. A first degree or its equivalent in any discipline plus membership of any other relevant and recognized professional institute;

b. A minimum of eight (8) years post- graduation experience;

c. Proven skills and competencies in their fields;

d. Knowledge of the operations of banks/development finance institutions/discount houses and relevant laws and regulations guiding the financial services industry; and

---

[92] Central Bank of Nigeria' Revised Assessment Criteria for Approved Persons' Regime for Financial Institutions 2015, section, 5.4.

[93] Central Bank of Nigeria' Revised Assessment Criteria for Approved Persons' Regime for Financial Institutions 2015, section, 5.5.

e. Ability to interpret financial statements and make meaningful contributions to board deliberations;

In considering nominees with limited academic/professional qualifications and industry experience, the CBN shall take into account the following:

i. Direct involvement of the nominee in an established business enterprise with total assets of not less than N300million.

ii. The quality of courses and seminars attended in the last five (5) years prior to his nomination.

iii. The size, scope and complexity of the institution;

iv. The relevant experience and qualifications of other Board members;

v. The existence and number of Independent Directors on the Board;

vi. An assurance that the proposed director(s) would be exposed to accelerated training over a short period of time; and

vii. Assignment of responsibilities commensurate with their experiences.[94]

2.1.7 INDEPENDENT DIRECTORS

a. Independent Directors shall be appointed in accordance with:

i. The CBN's Circular of October 26, 2007 titled "**Guidelines for the Appointment of Independent Directors**";

ii. The "**Revised Code of Corporate Governance for Banks and Discount Houses in Nigeria**" of May 25, 2014;

[94] Central Bank of Nigeria' Revised Assessment Criteria for Approved Persons' Regime for Financial Institutions 2015, section, 5.6.

iii. Section 257(1) of the **Companies and Allied Matters Act (CAMA), 1990 as amended**;

iv. Any other relevant law, rules and regulations issued from time to time by the CBN.

b. In particular, an Independent Director shall be a member of the Board of Directors who has no direct material relationship with the financial institution or any of its officers, major shareholders, subsidiaries and affiliates; a relationship which may impair the director's ability to make independent judgments or compromise the director's objectivity in line with Corporate Governance best practices.

c. An Independent Director shall not:

i. beyond his services on the Board of a financial institution, provide financial, legal and/or consulting services to the institution or its subsidiaries/affiliates or had done so in the preceding 5 years;

ii. be a current or former employee who had served in the financial institution in the past and none of his immediate family members should be an employee or former staff of the financial institution at the top management level in the preceding 5 years;

iii. borrow funds from the financial institution, its officers, subsidiaries and affiliates;

iv. be part of management, executive committee or board of trustees of an entity, charity or otherwise, supported by the financial institution;

v. serve on the Board of a subsidiary or affiliate of the financial institution.

d. An Independent Director shall have:

i. sound knowledge of the operations of listed companies, the relevant laws and regulations guiding the industry,

ii. a minimum academic qualification of first degree or its equivalent with not less than 10 years of relevant working experience.

iii. proven skills and competencies in their fields.

e. In addition, the requirements for Non-Executive Directors stated above shall apply.

f. For Non-interest banks, at least one of the independent directors should preferably be an expert in Islamic Commercial Jurisprudence (Fiqh Mu'amalat)

Notwithstanding the requirements stated above, the CBN may at its discretion, approve or disapprove the appointments of candidates under special circumstances.[95]

2.1.8 CHIEF COMPLIANCE OFFICER

A compliance officer is responsible for the oversight of the firm's anti–money laundering (AML) systems and controls, which include appropriate training for the firm's employees in relation to money laundering and considering each report received from staff to determine whether it gives rise to knowledge, suspicion or reasonable grounds for knowledge or suspicion that another person is engaged in money laundering.[96]

The institution's board of directors is required to designate a qualified individual to serve as the Chief Compliance Officer (CCO). The CCO is responsible for the coordinating and

---

[95] Central Bank of Nigeria' Revised Assessment Criteria for Approved Persons' Regime for Financial Institutions 2015, section, 5.7.

[96] Money Laundering Prohibition Act 2011 (as amended), s. 9 (1); Federal Financial Institutions Examination Council (2014), 'Bank Secrecy Act/Anti-Money Laundering Examination Manual', Available at: https://www.occ.treas.gov/publications/publications-by-type/other-publications-reports/ffiec-bsa-aml-examination-manual.pdf (accessed 10 January 2017); Senior Management Arrangements, Systems and Controls (SYSC), 6.3.9 (1) R, see also SYSC, 6.3.7 G.

monitoring of day-to-day anti-money laundering and combating the financing of terrorism (AML/CFT) compliance by the institution. The CCO is also charged with managing all aspects of the AML/CFT Compliance Programme and with managing the institution's adherence to the **Money Laundering Prohibition Act 2011 as amended (MLPA)**, **AML/CFT Regulation** and other **AML/CFT Requirements**. However, it is the board of directors that is ultimately responsible for the institution's AML/CFT compliance.

As the title of the individual responsible for overall AML/CFT compliance is of importance, his/her level of authority and responsibility within the financial institution is also critical. Though the CCO may delegate the AML/CFT duties to other employees, he/she will be held responsible for the overall AML/CFT compliance by the institution. The board of directors is responsible for ensuring that the CCO has sufficient authority and resources (monetary, physical and personnel) to administer an effective AML/CFT Compliance Programme based on the institution's risk profile.

The CCO should be fully knowledgeable of the MLPA, AML/CFT Regulation and all related requirements. The CCO should also understand the institution's products, services, customers, entities, geographic locations and the potential money laundering and terrorist financing risks associated with these activities. The appointment of a CCO is not sufficient to meet the regulatory requirement if that person does not have the expertise, authority or time to satisfactorily carry out the job efficiently and effectively.

The telecommunications company must confirm that the line of communication allows the CCO to regularly apprise the board of directors and senior management of ongoing compliance with AML/CFT regime of the institution, and ensure that pertinent

MLPA-related information, including the reporting of suspicious transaction reports (STRs) rendered to the Nigerian Financial Intelligence Unit (NFIU) are reported to the board of directors or an appropriate board committee so that these individuals can make informed decisions about the overall AML/CFT compliance of the institution.

Telecommunications companies must ensure also that the CCO is responsible for carrying out the directives of the board and ensuring that employees adhere to the institution's AML/CFT policies, procedures and processes.[97]

The Financial Action Task Force (FATF) has advised countries to enact laws that require financial institutions to implement programmes against money laundering and terrorist financing. These programmes should include the appointment of a compliance officer at the management level.[98]

In its attempt to ensure strict compliance with all extant regulations; particularly those relating to foreign exchange transactions, Financial Action Task Force (FATF) and Anti-Money Laundering/ Combating the Financing of Terrorism (AML/CFT), the CBN via a circular dated September 28, 2016, decided to enhance the minimum qualifications for the position of the Chief Compliance Officers (CCOs) of Deposit Money Banks (DMBs).

Going forward, DMBs are required to appoint not only a CCO who must not be below the rank of a General Manager regardless

---

[97] Central Bank of Nigeria (2011), 'Central Bank of Nigeria's Anti-Money Laundering/Combating the Financing of Terrorism (AML/CFT) Risk Based Supervision (RBS) Framework, 2011', Available at: https://www.cbn.gov.ng/out/2012/ccd/cbn%20approved%20framework.pdf (accessed 16th April, 2019).

[98] The Financial Action Task Force (FATF): International Standards on Combating Money Laundering and the financing of terrorism and proliferation, (The FATF Recommendations) 2012, Recommendation 18

of the category of institution but also an Executive Compliance Officer (ECO) who should not be below the rank of an Executive Director. The CCO will report to the ECO while the ECO will in turn report directly to the Board of Directors.

The CBN will hold the Executive Compliance Officer responsible and accountable for any breach of any extant regulation in the DMBs. For avoidance of doubt, the CBN shall suspend/dismiss any ECO and CCO found wanting in the discharge of his/her responsibility.

DMBs are required to forward the names of their ECO and CCO together with their curriculum vitae to the CBN for approval. The ECOs are however allowed to combine the responsibility with other functions while CCOs will focus ONLY on compliance matters in the bank.[99]

The fitness requirements for appointment to the office of Chief Compliance Officer and Executive Compliance Officer is as provided in the Fit and Proper (Approved Persons) Framework for General Managers and Executive Directors; this has been explained in great detail in sections 2.1.3 and 2.1.2 of this chapter.

The Recommended Additional Certification for the office of Chief Compliance Officer and Executive Compliance Officer is the International Compliance Association Certificate (ICA). or Certified Anti Money Laundering Specialists (CAMS), or Certified Fraud Examiner (CFE).[100]

---

[99] Central Bank of Nigeria (2016), 'Circular to All Deposit Money Banks (DMBs)', Available at: https://www.cbn.gov.ng/out/2016/fprd/aml%20september%202016%20circular%20to%20banks%20on%20ccos%20(2).pdf (accessed 15 April, 2019).

[100] Central Bank of Nigeria (2014), 'Circular to Banks, Discount Houses and Other Financial Institutions: Status and Reporting Line of Chief Compliance Officers', Available at: https://www.cbn.gov.ng/out/2014/fprd/status%20and%20reporting%20line%20of%20chief%20compliance%20officers.pdf (accessed 15 April, 2019).

The CBN, via a circular to Banks, Discount Houses and other Financial Institutions dated the 17th of November, 2014, had noted the onerous challenge of having dedicated Compliance Officers (CO) at each branch of a bank and has given dispensation that banks may elect to operate a *cluster structure, whereby a designated CO would be responsible for a cluster of branches instead of having a CO at each branch, as earlier advised in the circular under reference.* Consequently, the CBN has approved the establishment of Zonal Compliance Officers for banks, who must at a minimum, be on the same level with the management of the Zones where they work. Branch /Cash Centres, therefore, need not have Compliance Officers, provided the Compliance Officer at the Zone that controls the Branch/Cash Centre, effectively performs compliance functions at the Branch/Cash Centre. **Where a bank or a financial institution decides to operate the cluster arrangement, details of such arrangement must be sent to the Director, Banking Supervision Department, or Director, Other Financial Institutions Department CBN, as the case may be, for prior approval.**

The cluster structure must however take into cognisance, the size, number and proximity to each branch as well as the level of automation of the compliance function, without compromising compliance. **It is important to note that the function of Compliance Office(r) must be clearly separated from that of internal Control/Audit.** Compliance Officers of Banks, Discount Houses and Other Financial Institutions should meet the criteria specified for the category of their institutions.

All banks and other financial institutions are hereby enjoined to comply strictly with the requirements of this circular.[101]

---

[101] Central Bank of Nigeria (2014), 'Circular to Banks, Discount Houses and Other Financial Institutions: Status and Reporting Line of Chief Compliance Officers', Available at:

2.2 DISCUSSION

By virtue of **Paragraph 7.2 of the Central Bank of Nigeria Guidelines for Licensing and Regulation of Payment Service Banks**, any investor with a shareholding of 5% and above, a Managing Director, Deputy Managing Director/Executive Directors, General Manager, Deputy General Manager, Assistant General Manager, Non-Executive Directors and Independent Directors of Telecommunications companies must pass the fit and proper test before they can be granted a Payment Service Bank license.

This measure is in line with the approach adopted by the United Kingdom in the **Payment Services Regulations 2017** and the **Electronic Money Regulations 2011**.

A condition for authorisation under both the **United Kingdom Payment Services Regulations 2017** and the **Electronic Money Regulations 2011** is that the applicant must satisfy the Financial Conduct Authority that any persons having a qualifying holding in it are fit and proper persons having regard to the need to ensure the sound and prudent conduct of the affairs of the applicant. This comprises two elements: first, the applicant will need to assess whether any persons (or entities) have a qualifying holding in the applicant and notify the Financial Conduct Authority of their identity; and secondly, the Financial Conduct Authority will assess the fitness and propriety of any such persons (or entities).[102]

A 'qualifying holding' is defined by reference to article 4(1)(36) of Regulation (EU) 575/2013 on prudential requirements for credit institutions and investment firms. The United Kingdom' Financial

---

https://www.cbn.gov.ng/out/2014/fprd/status%20and%20reporting%20line%20of%20chief%20compliance%20officers.pdf (accessed 15 April, 2019).

[102] United Kingdom Payment Services Regulations 2017, regulation 6(7) (a) and paragraph 13 Schedule 2; Electronic Money Regulations 2011, regulation 6(6)(a) and paragraph 8 Schedule 1.

Conduct Authority refers to people with a qualifying holding as 'controllers'.

A controller is an individual or firm that does one of the following:

- holds 10% or more of the shares in the applicant firm (including through a parent);
- is able to exercise significant influence over the management of the applicant firm through their holding in the applicant firm or a parent;
- is entitled to control or exercise control of 10% or more of the voting power in the applicant firm (including through a parent); or
- is able to exercise significant influence over the management of the applicant firm through their voting power in it or a parent.[103]

Whilst it is impossible to list every fact or matter that would be relevant to the fitness and propriety of a controller, the following are examples of factors that the Financial Conduct Authority will consider. Whether:

- the person has been convicted of any criminal offence particularly of dishonesty, fraud, or financial crime;
- the person is currently being investigated for any criminal offence. This would include where an individual has been arrested or charged;
- the person has been the subject of any adverse finding or any settlement in civil proceedings, particularly in connection with investment or other financial business, misconduct, fraud or the formation or management of a firm, particularly a payment institution (PI) or an electronic

---

103 United Kingdom Payment Services Regulations 2017, regulation 6(7) (a) and paragraph 13 Schedule 2; Electronic Money Regulations 2011, regulation 6(6)(a) and paragraph 8 Schedule 1.

money institution (EMI). This would include any findings by the Financial Conduct Authority, by other regulatory authorities (including a previous regulator), clearing houses and exchanges, professional bodies, or government bodies or agencies (such as HMRC, the Serious Organised Crime Agency, the Serious Fraud Office, etc.) that the individual has breached or contravened any financial services legislation. The regulatory history of the firm or individual is therefore likely to be relevant;

- the person has been the subject of any existing investigation or disciplinary proceedings, by us, by other regulatory authorities (including a previous regulator), clearing houses and exchanges, professional bodies, or government bodies or agencies (such as HMRC, the Serious Organised Crime Agency, the Serious Fraud Office, etc.);
- the person has been refused membership, registration or authorisation of a professional organisation or has had that registration, authorisation, membership or licence revoked, withdrawn or terminated, or has been expelled by a regulatory or government body;
- the person has been a director, partner, or concerned in the management, of a business that has gone into insolvency, liquidation or administration while the person has been connected with that organisation;
- in the past, the person has been candid and truthful in all their dealings with any regulatory body and whether the person demonstrates a readiness and willingness to comply with the requirements and standards of the regulatory system and with other legal, regulatory and professional requirements and standards.[104]

---

[104] Financial Conduct Authority (2017), 'Payment Services and Electronic Money – Our Approach:

In determining the honesty, integrity and reputation of an individual, the matters that the Financial Conduct Authority will have regard to include, but are not limited to:

- relevant convictions or involvement in relevant criminal proceedings or ongoing investigations;
- relevant civil or administrative cases;
- relevant disciplinary action (including disqualification as company director; and;
- whether an assessment of the reputation of the individual has already been conducted by a competent authority.[105]

In determining an individual's competence, capability and experience, the Financial Conduct Authority will have regard to whether the individual has the:

- knowledge
- experience
- training

to be able to perform the activity of providing payment services.[106]

Background screening of candidates occupying or intending to occupy the under-listed board and senior/top management positions, especially for criminal history, is essential to keeping out unwanted employees and identifying those to be removed. This process can be an effective risk-management tool by providing the Central Bank of Nigeria with a degree of certainty that the information provided by the applicant is true and correct, and that the potential employee does not have a criminal record.

The FCA's role under the Payment Services Regulations 2017 and the Electronic Money Regulations 2011', para. 3.98.

105 Financial Conduct Authority (2017), 'Payment Services and Electronic Money – Our Approach: The FCA's role under the Payment Services Regulations 2017 and the Electronic Money Regulations 2011', para. 3.107.

106 Financial Conduct Authority (2017), 'Payment Services and Electronic Money – Our Approach: The FCA's role under the Payment Services Regulations 2017 and the Electronic Money Regulations 2011', para. 3.112.

Used effectively, the pre-employment background screening process may reduce turnover by verifying that the potential employee has the requisite skills, certification, license or degree for the position; deter theft and embezzlement; and prevent litigation over hiring practices.

Despite the advantages of the fit and proper test, there have been damning reports that some politicians are using fraudsters working in banks to launder public funds. According to the Chairman of the **Economic and Financial Crimes Commission**, **Ibrahim Magu**, fraudsters have been aiding politically exposed and other persons to commit various financial crimes.[107] This revelation epitomises systemic failure aggravated by the Central Bank of Nigeria's weak regulation.

The **Financial Conduct Authority** (the conduct regulator for 56,000 financial services firms and financial markets in the United Kingdom and the prudential regulator for over 18,000 of those firms), on the other hand, has taken action against firms for violating anti-money laundering laws. On the **31st of January, 2017**, the **Financial Conduct Authority** (FCA) fined Deutsche Bank AG (Deutsche Bank) £163,076,224 for failing to maintain an adequate anti-money laundering (AML) control framework during the period between 1 January 2012 and 31 December 2015. This is the largest financial penalty for AML controls failings ever imposed by the FCA, or its predecessor the Financial Services Authority (FSA).

According to the **Financial Conduct Authority**, Deutsche Bank exposed the UK financial system to the risks of financial crime by failing to properly oversee the formation of new customer relationships and the booking of global business in the UK. As a

---

[107] The Punch (2019), 'Fraudsters working in banks, aiding corrupt politicians – EFCC', Available at: https://punchng.com/fraudsters-working-in-banks-aiding-corrupt-politicians-efcc/ (accessed 6 April, 2019).

consequence of its inadequate AML control framework, Deutsche Bank was used by unidentified customers to transfer approximately $10 billion, of unknown origin, from Russia to offshore bank accounts in a manner that is highly suggestive of financial crime.

Mark Steward, Director of Enforcement and Market Oversight at the FCA, said:

"Financial crime is a risk to the UK financial system. Deutsche Bank was obliged to establish and maintain an effective AML control framework. By failing to do so, Deutsche Bank put itself at risk of being used to facilitate financial crime and exposed the UK to the risk of financial crime."

"The size of the fine reflects the seriousness of Deutsche Bank's failings. We have repeatedly told firms how to comply with our AML requirements and the failings of Deutsche Bank are simply unacceptable. Other firms should take notice of today's fine and look again at their own AML procedures to ensure they do not face similar action."

The FCA found significant deficiencies throughout Deutsche Bank's AML control framework. The FCA specifically found that, during the relevant period, Deutsche Bank's Corporate Banking and Securities division (CB&S) in the UK:

- performed inadequate customer due diligence
- failed to ensure that its front office took responsibility for the CB&S division's Know Your Customer obligations
- used flawed customer and country risk rating methodologies
- had deficient AML policies and procedures
- had an inadequate AML IT infrastructure

- lacked automated AML systems for detecting suspicious trades
- failed to provide adequate oversight of trades booked in the UK by traders in non-UK jurisdictions

As a result of these failings Deutsche Bank failed to obtain sufficient information about its customers to inform the risk assessment process and to provide a basis for transaction monitoring. The failings allowed the front office of Deutsche Bank's Russia-based subsidiary (DB Moscow) to execute more than 2,400 pairs of trades that mirrored each other (mirror trades) between April 2012 and October 2014.

The mirror trades were used by customers of Deutsche Bank and DB Moscow to transfer more than $6 billion from Russia, through Deutsche Bank in the UK, to overseas bank accounts, including in Cyprus, Estonia, and Latvia. The orders for both sides of the mirror trades were received by DB Moscow, which executed both sides at the same time.

The customers on the Moscow and London sides of the mirror trades were connected to each other and the volume and value of the securities was the same on both sides. The purpose of the mirror trades was the conversion of Roubles into US Dollars and the covert transfer of those funds out of Russia, which is highly suggestive of financial crime.

A further $3.8 billion in suspicious "one-sided trades" also occurred. The FCA believes that some, if not all, of an additional 3,400 trades formed one side of mirror trades and were often conducted by the same customers involved in the mirror trading.

As a result, Deutsche Bank breached Principle 3 (taking reasonable steps to organise its affairs responsibly and effectively, with adequate risk management systems) of the FCA's Principles for

Businesses. In addition, Deutsche Bank also breached Senior Management Arrangements, Systems and Controls (SYSC) rules 6.1.1 R and 6.3.1 R.

The FCA emphasises the importance of having a strong AML control framework through its proactive supervisory programmes on AML. Firms are regularly reminded of the importance of safeguarding the UK financial system from financial crime and how to comply with AML requirements.

Deutsche Bank agreed to settle at an early stage of the FCA's investigation and therefore qualified for a 30% (stage 1) discount. This discount does not apply to the £9.1 million in commission that Deutsche Bank generated from the suspicious trading, which has been disgorged as part of the overall penalty meaning that the firm has received no financial benefit from the breach. Were it not for the 30% discount the financial penalty would have been £229,076,224.[108]

On the **6th day of June, 2018**, the Financial Conduct Authority fined Canara Bank £896,100 for anti-money laundering systems failings and imposed a restriction, preventing it from accepting deposits from new customers for 147 days. According to the Financial Conduct Authority, Between 26 November 2012 and 29 January 2016, Canara failed to maintain adequate anti-money laundering systems and failed to take sufficient steps to remedy identified weaknesses, despite having been notified of shortcomings in its anti-money laundering systems and controls. Mark Steward, Executive Director of Enforcement and Market Oversight at the Financial Conduct Authority, said:

---

[108] Financial Conduct Authority (2017), 'FCA fines Deutsche Bank £163 million for serious anti-money laundering controls failings', Available at: https://www.fca.org.uk/news/press-releases/fca-fines-deutsche-bank-163-million-anti-money-laundering-controls-failure (accessed 6 April 2019).

"Financial crime and money–laundering failures are areas of focused priority for us. Canara was warned its money laundering controls were inadequate and so its failure to remediate them properly is at the more serious end of the range of sanctions."

The Final Notice highlights the importance of branches of overseas banks and their senior management having sufficient understanding of their regulatory responsibilities and ensuring those obligations are met with appropriate resources. Specifically, the Financial Conduct Authority found that Canara failed to maintain adequate systems and controls to manage the risk of money laundering. These failures were systemic and affected almost all levels of its business and governance structure including: (1) Senior Management; (2) Governance/Oversight; (3) three Lines of Defence; (4) Money laundering reporting function; and (5) AML systems and controls. As a result, Canara breached Principle 3 (taking reasonable steps to organise its affairs responsibly and effectively, with adequate risk management systems) of the FCA's Principles for Businesses.

Canara agreed to resolve the case and qualified for a 30% discount.[109]

On the **19th day of March, 2019**, UBS AG (UBS) was fined £27,599,400 by the Financial Conduct Authority (FCA) for failings relating to 135.8 million transaction reports between November 2007 and May 2017.

Mark Steward, FCA Executive Director of Enforcement and Market Oversight said:

[109] Financial Conduct Authority (2018), 'FCA fines and imposes a restriction on Canara Bank for anti-money laundering systems failings', Available at: https://www.fca.org.uk/news/press-releases/fca-fines-and-imposes-restriction-canara-bank-anti-money-laundering-systems-failings (accessed 6 April 2019).

'Firms must have proper systems and controls to identify what transactions they have carried out, on what markets, at what price, in what quantity and with whom. If firms cannot report their transactions accurately, fundamental risks arise, including the risk that market abuse may be hidden.'

Effective market oversight relies on the complete, accurate and timely reporting of transactions. This information helps the FCA to effectively supervise firms and markets. In particular, transaction reports help the FCA identify potential instances of market abuse and combat financial crime.

UBS failed to ensure it provided complete and accurate information in relation to approximately 86.67m reportable transactions. It also erroneously reported 49.1m transactions to the FCA, which were not, in fact, reportable. Altogether, over a period of 9 and a half years, UBS made 135.8m errors in its transaction reporting, breaching FCA rules.

The FCA also found that UBS failed to take reasonable care to organise and control its affairs responsibly and effectively in respect of its transaction reporting. These failings related to aspects of UBS's change management processes, its maintenance of the reference data used in its reporting and how it tested whether all the transactions it reported to the FCA were accurate and complete.

UBS agreed to resolve the case and so qualified for a 30% discount in the overall penalty. Without this discount, the FCA would have imposed a financial penalty of £39,427,795.[110]

---

110 Financial Conduct Authority (2019), 'FCA fines UBS AG £27.6 million for transaction reporting failures', Available at: https://www.fca.org.uk/news/press-releases/fca-fines-ubs-ag-276-million-transaction-reporting-failures (accessed 6 April 2019).

On the **28th day of March, 2019,** Goldman Sachs International (GSI) was fined £34,344,700 by the Financial Conduct Authority (FCA) for failing to provide accurate and timely reporting relating to 220.2 million transaction reports between November 2007 and March 2017. Mark Steward, FCA Executive Director of Enforcement and Market Oversight said:

'The failings in this case demonstrate a failure over an extended period to manage and test controls that are vitally important to the integrity of our markets. These were serious and prolonged failures. We expect all firms will take this opportunity to ensure they can fully detail their activity and are regularly checking their systems so any problems are detected and remedied promptly, unlike in this case.'

Accurate and complete transaction reporting helps underwrite market integrity and supervise firms and markets. In particular, transaction reports help the FCA identify potential instances of market abuse and combat financial crime. GSI failed to ensure it provided complete, accurate and timely information in relation to approximately 213.6m reportable transactions. It also erroneously reported 6.6m transactions to the FCA, which were not, in fact, reportable. Altogether, over a period of 9 and a half years, GSI made 220.2m errors in its transaction reporting, breaching FCA rules.

The FCA also found that GSI failed to take reasonable care to organise and control its affairs responsibly and effectively in respect of its transaction reporting. These failings related to aspects of GSI's change management processes, its maintenance of the counterparty reference data used in its reporting and how it tested whether all the transactions it reported to the FCA were accurate and complete.

GSI agreed to resolve the case and so qualified for a 30% discount in the overall penalty. Without this discount, the FCA would have imposed a financial penalty of £49,063,900.[111]

The **Central Bank of Nigeria** is yet to bring any enforcement action against any financial institution in Nigeria despite disturbing revelations from the Economic and Financial Crimes Commission and the media.

2.3 CONCLUSION

This chapter critically analysed the Fit and Proper Test as contained in the **Central Bank of Nigeria's Guidelines for Licensing, Regulation and Operation of Telecommunications Companies** to determine that the Fit and Proper Test could achieve its desired objective of a balanced approach to financial inclusion and anti-money laundering measures if the following recommendations are implemented:

I. The **Central Bank of Nigeria' Revised Assessment Criteria for Approved Persons' Regime for Financial Institutions 2015** should be further revised to allow for on-going screening for specific positions in telecommunications companies, as circumstances change, or for a comprehensive review of departmental staff over a period of time. Telecommunications companies should have a policy that mandates that the lie detector test should be taken once in 5 years by all staff of the company. For Staff in very sensitive positions, the lie detector test should be taken every three years. This will enable the lie detector policy to

[111] Financial Conduct Authority (2019), 'FCA fines Goldman Sachs International £34.3 million for transaction reporting failures', Available at: https://www.fca.org.uk/news/press-releases/fca-fines-goldman-sachs-international-transaction-reporting-failures (accessed 6 April 2019).

be more effective. Let us take for example, a person passes the fit and proper test genuinely without any influence of fraud and corruption; there is still a possibility that the person may change over time. The temptation to follow current employees to collect bribes is very high. But if the telecommunications company put a policy in place that mandates every staff to take the lie detector test every five years starting from the first five years after recruitment, the cankerworm called fraud and corruption may be curbed effectively. Imagine if every staff knew that they were going to be asked by an examiner, 5 years after working, to confirm if they ever collected bribe during the time, they served in the company, most employees will desist from taking bribes or engaging in corrupt acts. The fit and proper test of the Central Bank of Nigeria applies to prospective employees wishing to occupy senior positions in banks and telecommunications companies but the lie detector test will apply to all employees in the company.

II. The Central Bank of Nigeria should ensure that telecommunications companies are subject to adequate regulation and supervision and are effectively implementing the **Financial Action Task Force (FATF) Recommendations**. Available evidence suggests that the Economic and Financial Crimes Commission has recovered more than two trillion dollars in 12 years, as of February 2016. The money passed through the banks; much of it ended up in safe havens in Europe and other parts of the world. But delinquent banks pay a heavy price abroad when caught in such a labyrinth.[112] For instance, the Financial

[112] The Punch (2017), 'Court BVN ruling: Saving genuine account owners', Available at: http://punchng.com/court-bvn-ruling-saving-genuine-account-owners/ (accessed 8 April 2018).

Crimes Enforcement Network (FinCEN), in coordination with the Office of the Comptroller of the Currency, and the United States Department of Justice, had on February 15, 2018, assessed a one hundred and eighty five million dollars civil money penalty against U.S. Bank National Association for willful violations of several provisions of the Bank Secrecy Act (BSA).[113] The Central Bank of Nigeria is strongly advised to enforce its regulations and punish errant banks/telecommunications companies so as to discourage their serial abuse of guidelines for the financial sector. This approach will strengthen Know Your Customer policies, aimed at reducing fraud and money laundering. **This measure is in line with the Financial Action Task Force Recommendations (Recommendation 26).**

[113] Financial Crimes Enforcement Network (2018), 'FinCEN Penalizes U.S. Bank National Association for Violations of Anti-Money Laundering Laws', Available at: https://www.fincen.gov/news/news-releases/fincen-penalizes-us-bank-national-association-violations-anti-money-laundering (accessed 9 April 2018).

CHAPTER 3

ANTI-MONEY LAUNDERING AND COMBATING THE FINANCING OF TERRORISM POLICY

Telecommunications companies are required to submit a formal application for the grant of a Payment Service Bank licence addressed to the Governor of the **Central Bank of Nigeria.**[114] The application is to be accompanied with Detailed Manuals and Policies, particularly a Financial Management Policy that highlights the bank's financial management policies and procedures, and system of internal controls. The Policy should include, at a minimum:

a) **Anti-Money Laundering and Combating Financing of Terrorism (AML/CFT) Policy;**

b) Enterprise-Wide Risk Management Framework;

c) Code of Ethics and Business Conduct that specifies high standards for honesty, integrity, and impartiality for the bank's employees, officers, and directors and provides guidance on avoiding conflicts of interest, self-dealing, and other types of impropriety as specified in the BOFIA or by the Bank. Every director and officer of the bank shall be required to sign the Code of Ethics and Business Conduct.[115]

---

[114] The Central Bank of Nigeria Guidelines for Licensing and Regulation of Payment Service Banks 2018, para. 6.1.

[115] The Central Bank of Nigeria Guidelines for Licensing and Regulation of Payment Service Banks 2018, para. 6.1.

The focus of this chapter is on the Anti-Money Laundering and Combating the Financing of Terrorism (AML/CFT) Policy of Telecommunications Companies.

The Board of Directors is responsible for providing leadership and direction in the management of the firm's AML/CFT compliance risk. The Board will approve the firm's AML/CFT Compliance Manual and it will periodically assess the extent to which the firm manages its Money Laundering/Financing Terrorism (ML/FT) risks. The Board will oversee the implementation of the policies contained in the compliance manual through its Audit Committee.

The Chief Compliance Officer (CCO) is responsible for coordinating the identification, management of compliance risks and the supervision of other compliance functions of the company. The CCO responsibilities amongst others include:

- Coordinate and implement the firm's AML/CFT compliance initiatives.
- Develop the compliance strategy, policy, structure and processes.
- Report periodically on AML/CFT compliance related matter to the Management and Audit Committee of the Board.
- Report non-compliance and other potential exposures to the management immediately and establish prompt mechanisms for the resolution thereof.
- Collaborate with internal stakeholders and other Regulators.
- Ensure continuous training of AML/CFT compliance officers to ensure that they have required technical knowledge and regulatory framework that applies to the firm.

- Establish and inculcate an AML/CFT compliance culture in the firm through the development of an appropriate compliance awareness programme.
- Ensure that management incorporates AML/CFT regulatory requirements into operations manual.
- Collaborate with Capacity Development Department in the training of staff in AML/CFT awareness, detection methods and reporting requirements.
- Ensure that all new and old AML/CFT regulatory directives are communicated to staff.
- Assist Departments and Branches to identify and resolve issues related to AML/CFT non-compliance risk.
- Develop formal arrangements to help the company and its Officers to become more mindful, knowledgeable and capable of responding to those ML/FT risks that can affect the firm's reputation and legal exposure.

The specific duties of compliance officers are:

- Co-ordinate and monitor day to day compliance with applicable Money Laundering laws and regulations.
- Receive and vet suspicious transaction reports from staff.
- Assist the CCO in organizing AML/CFT programmes for employees of the company,
- Ensure timely rendition of AML/CFT regulatory reports.

Employees are expected to be familiar and comply with applicable laws and regulations:

- Employees are to adhere to the AML/CFT compliance Policy Manual of the firm;
- Employees should conduct business in accordance with applicable anti-money laundering, counter-terrorist financing laws and regulations, corporate policies, and maintain the highest ethical standards;

- Employees must not provide advice or other assistance to individuals or groups who attempt to violate or evade anti-money laundering, counter-terrorist financing laws and regulations or corporate policies;
- Employees should refrain from willfully ignoring indications that a customer seeks to engage in a relationship or transaction other than for a lawful purpose;
- Employees should avoid establishing relationships with individuals or entities who may pose undue reputational risk to the firm; and
- Employees should protect the firm's reputation for integrity and fair dealing, by ensuring that the firm's customers and the transactions engaged in on its behalf are legitimate.[116]

3.1. CUSTOMER IDENTIFICATION PROGRAM

Telecommunications companies are required to implement a written Customer Identification Program ("CIP") appropriate for its size and type of business. The program must include procedures to identify and verify the true identity of the legal beneficiaries to the customer's account and to take appropriate follow-up action where necessary. This measure is in line with the **Financial Action Task Force Recommendations (Recommendation 10)** and the **Nigerian Money Laundering Prohibition Act 2011 (as amended) (Section 3).**

3.1.1 ORDINARY ACCOUNTS

Telecommunications companies are required to obtain the following information in relation to private individuals' resident in Nigeria (Ordinary Accounts):

- Duly completed account opening form.

[116] Central Bank of Nigeria' Anti-Money Laundering/Combating the Financing of Terrorism (AML/CFT) Policy and Procedure Manual' 2018, para. 9.0.

- Valid means of identification (ID) of signatory or person introducing another customer.
- Residence permit (for expatriates).
- Passport photographs.
- Birth certificate of a minor and 2 passport photographs of the trustee (applicable to savings account for children).
- Tax Identification Number (applicable to residents of Abuja).
- Proof of residence.
- Duly registered Power of Attorney, where an individual appoints another person to be a signatory to his personal account.
- Bank Verification Number.

3.1.2 TIER 1 ACCOUNTS

Telecommunications companies are required to obtain the following information in relation to Individual (Tier 1 Accounts):

- Duly completed account opening form.
- Bank verification Number
- One passport photograph.

These accounts can only permit single deposit amount of N50,000 and a maximum cumulative balance of N300,000.[117]

Mobile Money wallet holders on Tiered Know Your Customer (KYC) Level 1 are not required to provide Bank Verification Number as part of the KYC documentation, while BVN is

---

[117] Central Bank of Nigeria (2016), 'Circular to Banks and Other Financial Institutions: Review of Restrictions and Limits on Levels I and II of the Tiered KYC Accounts', Available at: https://www.cbn.gov.ng/out/2016/fprd/july%202016%20circular%20tkyc%20review.pdf (accessed 6 May 2019).

mandatory for Mobile Money wallet holders on KYC levels 2 and 3.[118]

3.1.3 A PRIVATE INDIVIDUAL NOT RESIDENT IN NIGERIA

Telecommunications companies are required to obtain the following information in relation to a Private Individual not resident in Nigeria:

For this category of customers who cannot make face-to- face contact, any of the following would suffice as evidence of the name of the customer:

- Notarized International passports;
- Notarized National identity cards; or
- Notarized International driver's license.

Reference numbers, date and country of issue should be obtained and the information recorded in the customer's file as part of the identification evidence.

Separate evidence is required to be obtained with respect to the applicant's permanent residential address from the best available evidence, preferably from an official source. The address must be verifiable by way of a recorded description or other means. "P.O. Box number" alone should not be accepted as evidence of address.

The above should be verified through a reputable credit or financial institution in the applicant's home country or country of residence. However, particular care must be taken when relying on

[118] Central Bank of Nigeria (2017), 'Review of Daily Mobile Money Wallet Transaction and Balance Limit and Bank Verification Numbers (BVN) Requirement for Mobile Money Wallet Holders', Available at: https://www.cbn.gov.ng/out/2017/bpsd/review%20of%20daily%20mm%20wallet%20transaction%20&%20bvn%20requirement%20for%20mobile%20money%20wallet%20holders.pdf (accessed 6 May 2019).

identification evidence provided from other countries, such evidence must be duly confirmed.

3.1.4 SALARY SAVINGS ACCOUNT

Telecommunications companies are required to obtain the following information in relation to Salary Savings Account:

- Duly completed account opening form.
- Letter of introduction from the company/appropriate authority (for individual current and savings salary account holders who do not have acceptable means of identification.
- Means of ID (secondary IDs approved by the bank).
- Bank Verification Number.

3.1.5 CORPORATE ACCOUNTS

Telecommunications companies are required to obtain the following information in relation to Corporate Accounts:

- Duly completed account opening form.
- Certified True Copy (CTC) of Form CAC 2/ CAC1.1.
- CTC of Form CAC7/CAC 1.1.
- Certificate of incorporation.
- CTC of Memorandum and Articles of Association.
- Tax Identification Number (TIN).
- Valid means of ID of each signatory and Directors.
- Residence Permit (foreigners).
- Passport photograph of each signatory.
- Nigeria Investment Promotion Commission (NIPC) certificate (for corporate entities incorporated in Nigeria with foreign ownership).
- Executed and sealed Board resolution.
- Current proof of residence/address.
- Bank Verification Number.

- CBN licence for finance companies and international money transfer operators as well as the Special Control Unit against Money Laundering (SCUML) certificate for designated non-financial businesses and professions.

3.1.6 ENTERPRISE ACCOUNTS

Telecommunications companies are required to obtain the following information in relation to Enterprise Accounts:

- Duly completed account opening form.
- Certificate of registration of business name.
- Form of application of registration of business name.
- Tax Identification Number (TIN).
- Passport photographs of each signatory.
- Valid means of ID of each signatory.
- Current proof of residence/address.
- Residence permit (foreigners).
- Bank Verification Number.
- SCUML certificate as applicable.

3.1.7 PARTNERSHIP ACCOUNTS

Telecommunications companies are required to obtain the following information in relation to Partnership Accounts:

- Duly completed account opening form.
- Partnership resolution.
- Certificate of registration of business name.
- Form of application of registration of business name.
- Tax Identification Number (TIN).
- Letter of appointment as bankers.
- Residence Permit (foreigners).
- Valid means of ID of each signatory.
- Proof of address.

- Partnership deed or agreement.
- Passport photographs of each signatory.
- Bank Verification Number.

3.1.8 CLUBS, SOCIETIES, ASSOCIATIONS AND UNINCORPORATED SOCIETIES

Telecommunications companies are required to obtain the following information in relation to Clubs, Societies, Associations and Unincorporated Societies:

- Duly completed account opening package.
- Constitution, rules and regulations.
- CTC of certificate of registration.
- Passport photograph for each signatory.
- Society/Club/Association's resolution to open account.
- Form of identification for each signatory.
- Tax Identification Number (TIN).
- Residence permit (foreigners).
- Utility receipt.
- Bank Verification Number.

3.1.9 MINISTRIES, PARASTATALS AND OTHER GOVERNMENT BODIES

Telecommunications companies are required to obtain the following information in relation to Ministries, Parastatals and other Government Bodies:

- Duly completed account opening form.
- Copy of gazette or Act establishing the parastatal (if applicable).
- Board resolution authorizing the opening of the account (if incorporated or has a duly constituted Board).

- Copy of certificate of incorporation (if an incorporated parastatal).
- Copy of MEMART (if incorporated or has a duly constituted Board).
- Valid means of ID of each signatory.
- Authorisation of Accountant General of the Federation/State or relevant Local Government Council.

3.1.10 EXECUTORS/ADMINISTRATORS

Telecommunications companies are required to obtain the following information in relation to Executors/Administrators:

- Duly completed account opening form.
- Passport photograph.
- Letter of Administration or Probate.
- Valid ID for each signatory.
- Current proof of residence/address for each signatory.
- Banker's confirmation and letter of indemnity
- Bank Verification Number.

3.1.11 NGOS AND MULTILATERAL AGENCIES

Telecommunications companies are required to obtain the following information in relation to NGOs and Multilateral Agencies:

- Duly completed account opening form.
- Passport photograph for each signatory.
- Valid Id for each signatory.
- References (two) for each signatory.
- Valid ID for each signatory.
- Registration certificate (If applicable).
- Tax Identification Number (TIN).
- Passport photographs for each signatory.

- Proof of address.
- Copy of Rules/Constitution.
- Bank Verification Number.
- SCUML certificate where applicable.

3.1.12 TRUSTEES

Telecommunications companies are required to obtain the following information in relation to Trustees:

- Duly completed account opening form.
- Passport photograph for each signatory.
- Valid Id for each signatory.
- References (two) for each signatory.
- Registration certificate (If applicable).
- Proof of residence/ address.
- Deed of appointment as trustees.
- Executed and sealed Board resolution.
- Bank Verification Number.

3.1.13 RELIGIOUS BODIES/ORGANISATIONS

Telecommunications companies are required to obtain the following information in relation to Religious Bodies/Organisations:

- Duly completed account opening form.
- Certified True Copy of registration certificate or document establishing the organization.
- Constitution/document guiding their operations.
- Letter of introduction of the signatories to the account.
- Valid means of identification of the signatory(ies).
- Two (2) references.

3.1.14 EMBASSIES, CONSULATES AND HIGH COMMISSIONS OF FOREIGN COUNTRIES

Telecommunications companies are required to obtain the following information in relation to Embassies, Consulates and High Commissions of Foreign Countries:

- Duly completed account opening form.
- Letter of credence of the ambassador from the home country.
- Copy of current international passport of signatories.
- Letter of reference from the Ministry of External Affairs.
- Official document from home country establishing the authority of the embassy to open the account and how the account is to be operated.

3.1.15 PARTNERSHIP ACCOUNTS

Telecommunications companies are required to obtain the following information in relation to Partnership Accounts:

- Duly completed account opening form.
- Partnership resolution.
- Certificate of registration of business name.
- Form of Application for registration of business name.
- Tax Identification Number (TIN).
- Letter of appointment as bankers.
- Residence permit (foreigners).
- Valid ID of each of the signatories.
- Proof of address.
- Partnership deed.

3.1.16 STAFF ACCOUNTS

Telecommunications companies are required to obtain the following information in relation to Staff Accounts:

- Two recent passport photographs.
- Valid ID.
- Bank Verification Number.

The above listed customer due diligence information should be verified by at least one of the following methods:

- For established corporate entities - reviewing a copy of the latest report and accounts (audited, if available);
- Conducting an enquiry by a business information service, or an undertaking from a reputable and known firm of lawyers or accountants confirming the documents submitted;
- Undertaking a company search and/or other commercial enquiries to see that the institution has not been, or is not in the process of being dissolved, struck off, wound up or terminated;
- Utilizing an independent information verification process, such as accessing public and private databases;
- Obtaining satisfactory prior bank references;
- Physical visitation to the corporate entity place of business; and
- Contacting the corporate entity by telephone, mail or e-mail.

When using an electronic/digital source to verify a customer's identity, telecommunications companies should ensure that they are able to demonstrate that they have both verified that the customer exists, and satisfied themselves that the individual seeking the business relationship is, in fact, that customer (or beneficial owner).[119]

---

[119] The Joint Money Laundering Steering Group JMLSG, *Prevention of money laundering/ combating terrorist financing* 2017 Revised Version, Guidance for the UK financial sector Part I, June 2017 (Amended December 2017), para. 5.3.79

Electronic verification may be carried out by the telecommunications company either direct, using as its basis the customer's full name, address and date of birth, or through an organisation which meets the criteria in paragraphs 5.3.51 and 5.3.52 of the JMLSG Guidance for the UK financial sector Part I, June 2017 (Amended December 2017).[120]

A number of commercial agencies which access many data sources are accessible online by firms, and may provide telecommunications companies with a composite and comprehensive level of electronic verification through a single interface. Such agencies use databases of both positive and negative information, and many also access high-risk alerts that utilise specific data sources to identify high-risk conditions, for example, known identity frauds or inclusion on a sanctions list. Some of these sources are, however, only available to closed user groups.[121]

Positive information (relating to full name, current address, date of birth) can prove that an individual exists, but some can offer a higher degree of confidence than others. Such information should include data from more robust sources - where an individual has to prove their identity, or address, in some way in order to be included, as opposed to others, where no such proof is required.[122]

Negative information includes lists of individuals known to have committed fraud, including identity fraud, and registers of

[120] The Joint Money Laundering Steering Group JMLSG, *Prevention of money laundering/ combating terrorist financing* 2017 Revised Version, Guidance for the UK financial sector Part I, June 2017 (Amended December 2017), para. 5.3.80

[121] The Joint Money Laundering Steering Group JMLSG, *Prevention of money laundering/ combating terrorist financing* 2017 Revised Version, Guidance for the UK financial sector Part I, June 2017 (Amended December 2017), para. 5.3.46

[122] The Joint Money Laundering Steering Group JMLSG, *Prevention of money laundering/ combating terrorist financing* 2017 Revised Version, Guidance for the UK financial sector Part I, June 2017 (Amended December 2017), para. 5.3.47

deceased persons. Checking against such information may be necessary to mitigate against impersonation fraud.[123]

For an electronic check to provide satisfactory evidence of identity on its own, it must use data from multiple sources, and across time, or incorporate qualitative checks that assess the strength of the information supplied. An electronic check that accesses data from a single source (e.g., a single check against the Electoral Roll) is not normally enough on its own to verify identity.[124]

Before using a commercial agency for electronic verification, telecommunications companies should be satisfied that information supplied by the data provider is considered to be sufficiently extensive, reliable and accurate. This judgement may be assisted by considering whether the provider meets all the following criteria:

- **i. it is recognised, through registration with the Information Commissioner's Office, to store personal data;**
- **ii. it uses a range of positive information sources that can be called upon to link an applicant to both current and previous circumstances;**
- **iii. it accesses negative information sources, such as databases relating to identity fraud and deceased persons;**
- **iv. it accesses a wide range of alert data sources; and**
- **v. it has transparent processes that enable the telecommunications company to know what checks were carried out, what the results of these checks were, and**

[123] The Joint Money Laundering Steering Group JMLSG, *Prevention of money laundering/ combating terrorist financing* 2017 Revised Version, Guidance for the UK financial sector Part I, June 2017 (Amended December 2017), para. 5.3.49

[124] The Joint Money Laundering Steering Group JMLSG, *Prevention of money laundering/ combating terrorist financing* 2017 Revised Version, Guidance for the UK financial sector Part I, June 2017 (Amended December 2017), para. 5.3.50

what they mean in terms of how much certainty they give as to the identity of the subject.[125]

In addition, a commercial agency should have processes that allow the enquirer to capture and store the information they used to verify an identity.[126]

A telecommunications company shall make an initial assessment of a customer's risk profile from the information provided and verified and particular attention shall be focused on those customers identified as having a higher risk profile and any additional inquiries made or information obtained in respect of those customers shall include:

i. Evidence of an individual's permanent address sought through a credit reference agency search, or through independent verification by home visits;

ii. Personal reference by an existing customer of the same institution;

iii. Prior bank reference and contact with the bank regarding the customer;

iv. Source of wealth; and

v. Verification of employment and public position held where appropriate.[127]

Customers that pose higher money laundering or terrorist financing risks present increased exposure to telecommunications

---

[125] The Joint Money Laundering Steering Group JMLSG, *Prevention of money laundering/ combating terrorist financing* 2017 Revised Version, Guidance for the UK financial sector Part I, June 2017 (Amended December 2017), para. 5.3.52

[126] The Joint Money Laundering Steering Group JMLSG, *Prevention of money laundering/ combating terrorist financing* 2017 Revised Version, Guidance for the UK financial sector Part I, June 2017 (Amended December 2017), para. 5.3.53.

[127] CBN (Anti-Money Laundering and Combating the Financing of Terrorism in Banks and Other Financial Institutions in Nigeria) Regulations, 2013, Schedule II Paragraph 1(5).

companies; due diligence policies, procedures, and processes should be enhanced as a result. Enhanced due diligence (EDD) for higher-risk customers like politically exposed persons is especially critical in understanding their anticipated transactions and implementing a suspicious activity monitoring system that reduces the firm's reputation, compliance, and transaction risks. Higher-risk customers and their transactions should be reviewed more closely at account opening and more frequently throughout the term of their relationship with the firm.

The firm may determine that a customer poses a higher risk because of the customer's business activity, ownership structure, anticipated or actual volume and types of transactions, including those transactions involving higher-risk jurisdictions. If so, the firm should consider obtaining, both at account opening and throughout the relationship, the following information on the customer:

i. Purpose of the account;

ii. Source of funds and wealth;

iii. Individuals with ownership or control over the account, such as beneficial owners, signatories or guarantors;

iv. Occupation or type of business (of customer or other individuals with ownership or control over the account);

v. Financial statements;

vi. Banking references;

vii. Domicile (where the business is organized);

viii. Proximity of the customer's residence, place of employment, or place of business to the firm;

ix. Description of the customer's primary trade area and whether international transactions are expected to be routine;

x. Description of the business operations, the anticipated volume of currency and total sales, and a list of major customers and suppliers;

xi. Explanations for changes in account activity.[128]

3.2 ACCOUNT MONITORING

Occasionally customers may seek to deliberately build up a degree of trust before they use their account for criminal or/and terrorist financing purposes. Customers may be involved in money laundering and terrorist financing, therefore any product or service offered by the telecommunications company is a potential medium for either activity.

The nature of business must be recorded when the account is opened and that is the initial yardstick by which staff will measure whether the account is being conducted in line with the expectations or whether suspicious transactions are being passed through. It is the early period of a new customer relationship that represents the greatest vulnerability and warrants close attention.

It is also vital that telecommunications companies accept every opportunity to update information on customers in order to maintain a high standard of monitoring. Attention should also be given to ensuring that documentation is reviewed on a regular basis and is automatically updated when events such as change of address or change of signatories occurs.

---

[128] Federal Financial Institutions Examination Council (2014), 'Bank Secrecy Act/Anti-Money Laundering Examination Manual', Available at: https://www.occ.treas.gov/publications/publications-by-type/other-publications-reports/ffiec-bsa-aml-examination-manual.pdf (accessed 10 January 2017).

Identification of any of the types of transaction does not automatically establish suspicion, but should arouse prompt enquiry and consideration of the circumstance. Hence, there is need for good Know Your Customer (KYC)/Know Your Customer's Business (KYCB) knowledge and records.

Whereas the primary responsibility for identifying suspicious transactions lies with the staff processing or checking items, Telecommunications companies, as an additional safeguard, should deploy appropriate software/technology that will generate report for suspicious transactions that are scrutinized by the Chief Compliance Officer.

On risk assessment basis, customer information must be updated during general communication with customers. This information must include but is not limited to the names of current directors (if applicable), type of business and volume to be expected over the account. It also gives the customer the opportunity to inform the telecommunications company of any new areas of business intended.

Consequently, the telecommunications company will be able to see if there are any material changes to the organization. Such information is an integral part of the KYC process and must be kept up to date.

When a transaction or suspicious transaction whether or not it relates to the laundering of the proceeds of a crime or an illegal act-

- Involves a frequency which is unjustifiable or unreasonable,
- Is surrounded by conditions of unusual or unjustified complexity; or
- Appears to have no economic justification or lawful objective,

The telecommunications company shall obtain information from the customer as to the origin and destination of the funds, the aim of the transaction and the identity of the beneficiary. All transactions falling into this category shall be reported to the AML/CFT Office within 7 days after the occurrence of the transaction using the template provided.

The telecommunications company will acquire an AML Software, for the purpose of identifying potential suspicion in customers' activities and for filtering transactions.

Notwithstanding the software in place at the telecommunications company, it is still the responsibility of every branch operatives to file any unusual transaction that may be grounds for suspicion of Money Laundering and Terrorist Financing which might not adequately be captured by the software.[129]

When a transaction falls within the definition covered by this Compliance Manual, the authorized Staff of the Branch where the transaction occurs shall immediately follow the procedure below:

- Seek information from the customer as to the source of the funds, the purpose of the transaction and the identity of the beneficiary.
- The Branch Controller shall make a formal report to the AML/CFT Compliance Office within 2 days of the determination of the occurrence of the suspicious transaction.
- Upon receipt of the report, the AML/CFT Compliance Office shall carry out a careful check on the transaction to enable it form an opinion whether it falls within the definition given above.

---

[129] Central Bank of Nigeria' Anti-Money Laundering/Combating the Financing of Terrorism (AML/CFT) Policy and Procedure Manual' 2018, para. 29.0.

- The CCO shall designate an Officer to promptly review account/transactions in conjunction with the compliance officer in the Branch. Every action taken shall be recorded.
- The CCO shall carry out further evaluation and form final opinion on whether the transaction qualifies to be lodged as Special Reports on Funds Transactions (SRFT) or not.
- Once this is established, the CCO will cause a detailed report on the matter containing all relevant information on the matter.
- The Chief Compliance Officer (CCO) shall promptly process the reports and escalate it to the Nigerian Financial Intelligence Unit (NFIU).[130]

3.3 RECORD KEEPING

Telecommunications companies should keep all records of the identification data obtained through the customer due diligence process (*e.g.*, copies or records of official identification documents such as passports, identity cards, driver's licenses and similar documents, account files and business correspondence, including the results of any analysis undertaken such as inquiries to establish the background and purpose of complex and unusual large transactions), for at least five years after the business relationship is ended, or after the date of the occasional transaction. This measure is in line with the **Financial Action Task Force Recommendations (Recommendation 11)** and the **Nigerian Money Laundering Prohibition Act 2011 (as amended) (Section 7).**

[130] Central Bank of Nigeria' Anti-Money Laundering/Combating the Financing of Terrorism (AML/CFT) Policy and Procedure Manual' 2018, para. 30.0.

The rationale for record keeping is to facilitate the reconstruction of individual transactions and provide, if necessary, evidence for the prosecution of criminal activity.[131]

3.3.1 PRESERVATION OF RECORDS

The records related to the transactions discussed below must be retained by a financial institution/telecommunications company for at least five years. However, as noted below, the records related to the identity of a telecommunications company's customer must be maintained for five years after the account (e.g., loan, deposit or trust) is closed. Additionally, on a case-by-case basis, a telecommunications company may be ordered or requested to maintain some of these records for longer periods.

1. International Transactions in Excess of the Designated Threshold

Telecommunications companies are required to maintain records of requests made or instructions received or given regarding transfers of currency or other monetary instruments, cheques, funds, investment securities or credit greater than the designated threshold to or from any person, account or place outside the country concerned.

2. Signature Cards

Telecommunications companies are required to keep records of each grant of signature authority over each deposit account.

---

131 Financial Action Task Force (2011), 'FATF GUIDANCE: Anti-Money Laundering and Terrorist Financing Measures and Financial Inclusion', Available at: http://www.fatf-gafi.org/media/fatf/content/images/AML%20CFT%20measures%20and%20financial%20inclusion.pdf (accessed 13 January 2017).

3. Account Statements

Telecommunications companies are also required to keep statements, ledger cards or other records on each deposit account showing each transaction in or with respect to that account.

4. Cheques

Each cheque, draft or money order drawn on the telecommunications company or issued and payable by it must be kept.

5. Deposits

Each deposit slip or credit ticket reflecting a transaction, record for direct deposit or other funds transfer deposit transactions are required to be kept. The slip or ticket must record the amount of any currency involved.

6. Records to Reconstruct Demand Deposit Accounts

To be kept are the records prepared or received by the telecommunications company in the ordinary course of business which would be needed to reconstruct a transaction account and to trace a cheque deposited in a demand deposit account through its domestic processing system or to supply a description of a deposited cheque.

7. Certificates of Deposit Purchased or Presented

This record which contained the following will be kept:

(i) Name of customer (purchaser or presenter).

(ii) Address of customer.

(iii) Tax Identification Number (TIN) of customer.

(iv) Description of the certificate of deposit.

(v) Notation of the method of payment if purchased.

(vi) Date of transaction.

8. Purchase of Monetary Instruments

A telecommunications company must maintain records of each of its cheques/draft, cashier's cheque, money order or traveler's cheque.

If the purchaser has a deposit account with the telecommunications company, this record shall contain:

(i) Name of purchaser.

(ii) Date of purchase

(iii) Type(s) of instrument purchased.

(iv) Amount of each of the instrument(s) purchased.

(v) Serial number(s) of the instrument(s) purchased.

If the purchaser does not have a deposit account with the Telecommunications Company, this record shall contain:

(i) Name of purchaser.

(ii) Address of purchasers.

(iii) Social security number of purchaser or alien identification number.

(iv) Date of birth of purchaser.

(v) Date of purchase

(vi) Type(s) of instrument purchased.

(vii) Amount of each of the instrument(s) purchased.

(viii) Serial number(s) of the instrument(s) purchased.

(ix) Description of document or method used to verify the name and address of the purchaser (e.g., state of issuance and number driver's licence).

9. Funds Transfers

A telecommunications company's AML/CFT record-keeping requirements with respect to funds transfer vary based upon its role with respect to the funds transfer.

10. Telecommunications Company acting as an originator

For each payment order that the Telecommunications Company accepts as the originator, it must obtain and retain records of the following information:

(i) Name and address of originator.

(ii) Amount of the payment order.

(iii) Execution date of the payment order.

(iv) Any payment instruction received from the originator with the payment order.

(v) Identity of the beneficiary's financial institution.

(vi) As many of the following items as are received with the payment order:

(a) Name and address of the beneficiary

(b) Account number of the beneficiary.

(c) Any other specific identifier of the beneficiary.

(d) For each payment order that a telecommunications company accepts for an originator that is not its established customer, it (in addition to the information listed above) must obtain appropriate extra information as may be required.

11. A Telecommunications Company acting as an intermediary or a beneficiary's bank

For each payment order that a telecommunications company accepts as an intermediary bank or a beneficiary's financial institution, it must retain a record of the payment order.

For each payment order that a telecommunications company accepts for a beneficiary that is not its established customer, the institution must also obtain additional information as required.

12. Tax Identification Number (TIN)

The institution is required to keep the record of the TIN of any customer opening an account.

In cases of joint accounts, information on a person with a financial interest must be maintained.

13. Exceptions in respect of TIN

A telecommunications company does not need to maintain TIN for accounts or transactions with the following:

(i) Agencies and instrumentalities of federal, state, local or foreign governments.

(ii) Judges, public officials or clerks of courts of record as custodians of funds in controversy or under the control of the court.

(iii) Certain aliens.

(iv) Certain tax-exempt organizations and units of tax-exempt organizations.

(v) A person under 18 years of age with respect to an account opened as a part of a school thrift savings Programme.

14. Suspicious Transaction Report and Supporting Documentation

A telecommunications company must maintain a record of any suspicious transaction report (STR) filed and the original or business record equivalent of any supporting documentation for a period of five years from the date of filing.

15. Currency Transaction Report

A telecommunications company must maintain a record of all Currency Transaction Reports (CTR) for a period of five years from the date of filing.

16. Customer Identification Programme

A telecommunications company must maintain a record of all information it obtains under its procedures for implementing its customer identification programme (CIP). At a minimum, these records must include the following:

(i) All identifying information about a customer (e.g., name, date of birth, address and TIN).

(ii) A description of the document that the telecommunications company relied upon to identity of the customer.

(iii) A description of the non-documentary methods and results of any measures the telecommunications company took to verify the identity of the customer.

(iv) A description of the telecommunications company's resolution of any substantive discrepancy discovered when verifying the identifying information obtained.

A telecommunications company must retain the identifying information about a customer for a period of five years after the date the account is closed or in the case of credit card accounts, five years after the account becomes closed or dormant.

A telecommunications company must retain the information relied on, methods used to verify identity and resolution of discrepancies for a period of five years after the record is made.

These AML/CFT record-keeping requirements are independent of and in addition to requirements to file and retain reports imposed by other laws.[132]

3.4. REPORTING MEASURES

Reporting measures are key to anti-money laundering/countering the financing of terrorism (AML/CFT) efforts and support law enforcement investigations.[133] These measures can be used by telecommunications companies to curb money laundering. The transaction record of a payment or funds transfer should be used to monitor the activities of the customer's account for suspicious activities. If a telecommunications company suspects or has reasonable grounds to suspect that funds are being paid to the wrong person, it should report promptly its suspicions to the police. This measure is in line with the **Financial Action Task Force Recommendations (Recommendation 20)** and the **Nigerian Money Laundering Prohibition Act 2011 (as amended) (Section 6).**

3.4.1 WHAT TO FILE

A telecommunications company is required to report any suspicious transaction relating to money laundering and terrorist financing.[134] A transaction is deemed to be suspicious if it involves

---

[132] Central Bank of Nigeria (2011), 'Central Bank of Nigeria's Anti-Money Laundering/Combating the Financing of Terrorism (AML/CFT) Risk Based Supervision (RBS) Framework, 2011', Available at: https://www.cbn.gov.ng/out/2012/ccd/cbn%20approved%20framework.pdf (accessed 16th April, 2019).

[133] Financial Action Task Force (2013), 'GUIDANCE FOR A RISK BASED-APPROACH: PREPAID CARDS, MOBILE PAYMENTS AND INTERNET-BASED PAYMENT SERVICES', Available at: http://www.fatf-gafi.org/media/fatf/documents/recommendations/Guidance-RBA-NPPS.pdf (accessed 12 January 2017).

[134] Money Laundering Prohibition Act 2011 (as amended), s. 6(2).

a frequency which is unjustifiable or unreasonable[135] or is surrounded by conditions of unusual or unjustified complexity.[136] It is also deemed suspicious if it appears to have no economic justification or lawful objective[137] or in the opinion of the telecommunications company involves terrorist financing or is inconsistent with the known transaction pattern of the account or business relationship.[138] The report required to be filed is called a Suspicious Transaction Report (STR).[139]

In addition to reporting any suspicious transaction, a telecommunications company is also required to report a transfer to or from a foreign country of funds or securities by a person or body corporate including a money service business of a sum exceeding ten thousand US dollars or its equivalent.[140] The law also requires a telecommunications company to report in writing any single transaction, lodgement or transfer of funds in excess of five million naira or its equivalent in the case of an individual or ten million naira or its equivalent in the case of a body corporate.[141] The report required to be filed is called a Currency Transaction Report (CTR).[142]

---

[135] Money Laundering Prohibition Act 2011 (as amended), s. 6(1)(a).

[136] Money Laundering Prohibition Act 2011 (as amended), s. 6(1)(b).

[137] Money Laundering Prohibition Act 2011 (as amended), s. 6(1)(c).

[138] Money Laundering Prohibition Act 2011 (as amended), s. 6(1)(d), See also the CBN (Anti-Money Laundering and Combating the Financing of Terrorism in Banks and Other Financial Institutions in Nigeria) Regulations, 2013, regulation 31 (1) for the definition of a Suspicious Transaction.

[139] Nigerian Financial Intelligence Unit: Anti-Money Laundering/Combating the Financing of Terrorism (AML/CFT) Reporting Guidelines 2012, para. 2.

[140] Money Laundering Prohibition Act 2011 (as amended), s. 2 (1).

[141] Money Laundering Prohibition Act 2011 (as amended), s. 10(1).

[142] Nigerian Financial Intelligence Unit: Anti-Money Laundering/Combating the Financing of Terrorism (AML/CFT) Reporting Guidelines 2012, para. 2.

3.4.2 WHERE TO FILE

A telecommunications company is required to file a STR with the Nigerian Financial Intelligence Unit.[143]

A telecommunications company is also required to file a CTR with the Nigerian Financial Intelligence Unit in writing.[144]

The Nigerian Financial Intelligence Unit shall acknowledge receipt of any disclosure, report or information received and may demand such additional information as it may deem necessary.[145] The acknowledgement of receipt shall be sent to the telecommunications company within the time allowed for the transaction to be undertaken and it may be accompanied by a notice deferring the transaction for a period not exceeding 72 hours.[146] If the acknowledgment of receipt is not accompanied by a stop notice, or where the stop notice has expired and the order to block the transaction has not reached the Telecommunications Company, it may carry out the transaction.[147]

Notwithstanding the provisions above, the Nigerian Financial Intelligence Unit shall place a Stop Order not exceeding 72 hours, on any account or transaction if it is discovered in the course of their duties that such account or transaction is suspected to be involved in any crime.[148]

Where it is not possible to ascertain the origin of the funds within the period of stoppage of the transaction, the Federal High Court may, at the request of the Nigerian Financial Intelligence Unit,

143 Money Laundering Prohibition Act 2011 (as amended), s. 6(2)(c).
144 Money Laundering Prohibition Act 2011 (as amended), s. 2(1), s. 10(1).
145 Money Laundering Prohibition Act 2011 (as amended), s. 6(4).
146 Money Laundering Prohibition Act 2011 (as amended), s. 6(5)(a).
147 Money Laundering Prohibition Act 2011 (as amended), s. 6(6).
148 Money Laundering Prohibition Act 2011 (as amended), s. 6(5)(b).

order that the funds, accounts or securities referred to in the report be blocked.[149]

A telecommunications company who receives a place no debit (PND) order from the Nigerian Financial Intelligence Unit must immediately freeze the suspect's account. There have been cases in the past where bank officials deliberately ignore the Nigerian Financial Intelligence Unit order of PND on suspects account or inform suspect about the PND to enable them make withdrawals using their ATM cards. The Nigerian Financial Intelligence Unit has stated that it would no longer condone such behaviour.[150]

3.4.3 WHEN TO FILE

A telecommunications company that suspects or has reason to suspect that funds are the proceeds of a criminal activity or are related to terrorist financing, is required to report its suspicions **immediately and without delay.[151]** The report is expected to be filed not later than within 24 hours.[152]

All suspicious transactions, including attempted transactions are to be reported regardless of the amount involved.[153]

The CTR on the other hand is to be filed within 7 days from the date of the transaction.[154]

---

[149] Money Laundering Prohibition Act 2011 (as amended), s. 6(7).
[150] Economic and Financial Crimes Commission (2017), 'Anti-Graft War: EFCC Sensitizes Compliance Officers of Banks', Available at: https://efccnigeria.org/efcc/news/2654-anti-graft-war-efcc-sensitizes-compliance-officers-of-banks (accessed 10 October 2017).
[151] Money Laundering Prohibition Act 2011 (as amended), s. 6(2).
[152] CBN (Anti-Money Laundering and Combating the Financing of Terrorism in Banks and Other Financial Institutions in Nigeria) Regulations, 2013, regulation 31(3).
[153] CBN (Anti-Money Laundering and Combating the Financing of Terrorism in Banks and Other Financial Institutions in Nigeria) Regulations, 2013, regulation 32 (7).
[154] Money Laundering Prohibition Act 2011 (as amended), s. 2(1), s. 10(1).

3.4.4 CONFIDENTIALITY OF STRS/TIPPING OFF (GENERAL RULE)

Telecommunications companies, their directors, officers and employees (permanent and temporary) are prohibited from disclosing the fact that a report is required to be filed with the competent authorities.[155]

3.4.5 CONFIDENTIALITY OF STRS/TIPPING OFF (EXCEPTION)

There are no exceptions to the general rule.[156]

3.4.6 PENALTIES

A person who discloses the fact that a report is required to be filed is liable on conviction to imprisonment for a term of not less than two years or a fine of not less than ten million naira.[157]

A person who fails to file a STR or CTR would be liable to imprisonment for a term of not less than 3 years or a fine of ten million naira or to both, in the case of an individual and twenty-five million naira in the case of a body corporate.[158]

3.5. TRAINING FOR ANTI-MONEY LAUNDERING COMPLIANCE

Telecommunications companies are recommended to train all appropriate personnel with respect to their responsibilities to comply with the requirements of due diligence, record keeping and reporting. Sufficient training will need to be given to all relevant employees to enable them to recognise when a transaction is

155 Money Laundering Prohibition Act 2011 (as amended), s. 16(1)(a).
156 Money Laundering Prohibition Act 2011 (as amended), s. 16(1) which provides for no exception to the General Rule.
157 Money Laundering Prohibition Act 2011 (as amended), s. 16(2)(a).
158 Money Laundering Prohibition Act 2011 (as amended), s. 16(2)(b).

unusual or suspicious, or when they should have reasonable grounds to know or suspect that fraud or money laundering is taking place.[159] A telecommunications company's training programs should provide relevant examples of fraud/money laundering in the mobile banking scheme and should discuss AML/CFT policies and procedures, liability issues and regulatory requirements. In addition, the training program should provide for regular updates to ensure employees are kept current in Anti-Fraud/Money Laundering policies and regulatory changes. This measure is in line with the **Financial Action Task Force Recommendations (Recommendation 18)** and the **Nigerian Money Laundering Prohibition Act 2011 (as amended) (Section 9 (1) (b)).**

The CCO shall ensure adequate training of staff on AML/CFT compliance issues and act as a contact point within the telecommunications company to provide answers to compliance queries from respondent telecommunications companies and staff members. The Office shall also help in establishing written guidance for staff on the appropriate compliance with laws, rules and standards through policies and procedures and other documents such as compliance manuals, codes of conduct and practice guidelines.

At a minimum, all new employees must receive formal training within 60 days of their joining the Telecommunications Company. This training should cover local anti-money laundering laws, Anti- Money Laundering Policy and Procedures, and recognizing and reporting Suspicious Transactions (employee responsibilities and examples of suspicious activity, "red flags").

---

[159] The Joint Money Laundering Steering Group JMLSG, *Prevention of Money Laundering/ Combating Terrorist Financing* (2017) revised version, Guidance for the United Kingdom Financial Sector Part I, June 2017 [Amended December 2017], para. 7.32.

AML/CFT Compliance Office must maintain a record of all formal training, to include the names and positions of the participants, for at least 5 years. Annually all staff are targeted to attend AML refresher training to update them of all new developments including information on current. Money Laundering ML/ FT techniques, methods and trends; ML red flags; KYC requirements; customer transaction monitoring and suspicious transaction reporting; new changes in the Global AML world and local regulations.[160]

There is no single solution when determining how to deliver training; a mix of training techniques may be appropriate. On-line learning systems can often provide an adequate solution for many employees, but there will be classes of employees for whom such an approach is not suitable. Focused classroom training for higher risk or minority areas can be more effective. Relevant videos always stimulate interest, but continually re-showing the same video may produce diminishing returns.[161]

3.6. AUDIT FOR COMPLIANCE WITH ANTI-MONEY LAUNDERING MEASURES

An important component of an AML Program is an independent test or audit of the program. The independent test requirement must be performed, either internally or externally, by parties independent of the creation of the business' AML procedures. In most cases, this testing is performed by Internal Audit Department. To supplement this independent test, there are several other internal controls to be performed by AML/CFT Compliance

[160] Central Bank of Nigeria' Anti-Money Laundering/Combating the Financing of Terrorism (AML/CFT) Policy and Procedure Manual' 2018, para. 32.0.

[161] The Joint Money Laundering Steering Group JMLSG, *Prevention of Money Laundering/ Combating Terrorist Financing* (2017) revised version, Guidance for the United Kingdom Financial Sector Part I, June 2017 [Amended December 2017], para. 7.42.

Office. The scope and breadth of the activities of the AML/CFT compliance function shall be subject to periodic review by the internal audit function. An audit programme which covers the adequacy and effectiveness of the telecommunications company's compliance function should be established, including testing of controls commensurate with the perceived level of risk.[162]

Telecommunications companies must have an independent testing or audit function for Anti-Money Laundering compliance, including Suspicious Activity Reporting. Audit programs should focus on high-risk accounts and should include comprehensive transaction testing. This measure is in line with the **Financial Action Task Force Recommendations (Recommendation 18)** and the **Nigerian Money Laundering Prohibition Act 2011 (as amended) (Section 9 (1) (d)).**

Senior management will need to have a means of independently validating the development and operation of the risk assessment and management processes and related internal controls, and obtaining appropriate comfort that the adopted risk-based methodology reflects the risk profile of the telecommunications company. This independent testing and reporting should be conducted by, for example, the internal audit department, external auditors, specialist consultants or other qualified parties who are not involved in the implementation or operation of the telecommunications company's AML/CFT compliance programme. The testing should be risk-based (focusing attention on higher-risk customers, products and services); should evaluate the adequacy of the telecommunications company's overall AML/CFT programme and the quality of risk management for the telecommunications company's operations, departments and

---

[162] Central Bank of Nigeria' Anti-Money Laundering/Combating the Financing of Terrorism (AML/CFT) Policy and Procedure Manual' 2018, para. 33.0.

subsidiaries; include comprehensive procedures and testing; and cover all activities.

While the frequency of audit is not specifically defined in any statute, a sound practice is for the telecommunications company to conduct independent testing generally every 12 to 18 months or commensurate with the Money Laundering/Financing of Terrorism ML/FT risk profile of the institution.

Telecommunications companies that do not employ outside auditors, consultants or have internal audit departments may comply with this requirement by using qualified persons who are not involved in the function that is tested.

The persons conducting the AML/CFT testing should report directly to the board of directors or to a designated board committee consisting primarily or completely of outside directors.

Those persons responsible for conducting an objective independent evaluation of the written AML/CFT Compliance Programme should perform testing for specific compliance with the FATF Recommendations (Recommendation 1). They are required to also evaluate pertinent management information systems (MIS). The audit has to be risk-based and must evaluate the quality of risk management for all the telecommunications company's operations, departments and subsidiaries.

Risk-based Audit Programmes will vary depending on the institution's size, complexity, scope of activities, risk profile, quality of control functions, geographic diversity and use of technology. An effective risk-based auditing Programme will cover all of the institution's activities. The frequency and depth of each audit activity will vary according to the activity's risk assessment.

It should be noted that the risk-based auditing will enable the board of directors and auditors to use the institution's risk assessment to focus its scope of audit on the areas of greatest concern. The testing should assist the board of directors and management in identifying areas of weakness or areas where there is a need for enhancements or stronger controls.

Independent testing should (at a minimum) include:

- **The evaluation of the overall adequacy and effectiveness of the AML/CFT Compliance Programme, including policies, procedures and processes.** This evaluation will contain an explicit statement about the AML/CFT compliance programme's overall adequacy and effectiveness and compliance with applicable regulatory requirements. At the very least, the audit should contain sufficient information for the reviewer (e.g. an Examiner, review auditor or Financial Intelligence Unit officer) to reach a conclusion about the overall quality of the AML/CFT Compliance Programme;
- A review of the telecommunications company's risk assessment for reasonableness given the institution's risk profile (products, services, customers, entities and geographic locations);
- Appropriate risk-based transaction testing to verify the telecommunications company's adherence to the Financial Action Task Force record keeping and rendition of returns requirements on Politically Exposed Persons (PEPs), STRs and CTRs information sharing requests;
- An evaluation of management's efforts to resolve violations and deficiencies noted in previous audits and regulatory examinations, including progress in addressing outstanding supervisory actions (if applicable);

- A review of staff training for adequacy, accuracy and completeness;
- A review of the effectiveness of the suspicious transaction monitoring systems (are they manual, automated or a combination?) used for AML/CFT compliance. Related reports may include, but are not limited to:
  - Suspicious transaction monitoring reports;
  - Large currency aggregation reports;
  - Monetary instrument records;
  - Funds transfer records;
  - Non-sufficient funds (NSF) reports;
  - Large balance fluctuation reports;
  - Account relationship reports;
- An assessment of the overall process for identifying and reporting suspicious transaction, including a review of filed or prepared STRs to determine their accuracy, timeliness, completeness and effectiveness of the institution's policy; and
- An assessment of the integrity and accuracy of MIS used in the AML/CFT Compliance Programme. MIS includes reports used to identify and extract data on the large currency transactions, aggregate daily currency transactions, funds-transfer transactions, monetary instrument sales transactions and analytical and trend reports.

The auditors' reports should include their documentation on the scope of the audit, procedures performed, transaction testing completed and findings of the review.

All audit documentation and work-papers should be made available for the Examiner to review. Any violations, policy and/or procedures exceptions or other deficiencies noted during the audit should be included in the audit report and reported to the board of directors or its designated committee in a timely manner.

The board or designated committee and the audit staff are required to track the deficiencies observed in the auditors' report and document the corrective actions recommended and taken.[163]

3.7. KNOW YOUR EMPLOYEE PROGRAM

Knowing your employees is as important as knowing your customers. An insider can pose the same fraud/money laundering threat as a customer and a criminally co-opted telecommunications employee might facilitate fraud and money laundering.[164]

A Know Your Employee (KYE) program means that the telecommunications company has a program in place that allows it to understand an employee's background, conflicts of interest and susceptibility to fraud/money laundering complicity. Policies, procedures, internal controls, job descriptions, code of conduct/ethics, levels of authority, compliance with personnel laws and regulations, accountability, dual control, and other deterrents should be firmly in place.

The **Central Bank of Nigeria (Anti-Money Laundering and Combating the Financing of Terrorism in Banks and other Financial Institutions in Nigeria) Regulations 2013** requires:

---

[163]Central Bank of Nigeria's Anti-Money Laundering/Combating the Financing of Terrorism (AML/CFT) Risk Based Supervision (RBS) Framework, 2011, para. 5.1.
[164] SSA ZAIDI (2015), 'Banks need to follow Know Your Employees norms for robust internal AML control systems', Available at: https://www.moneylife.in/article/banks-need-to-follow-know-your-employees-norms-for-robust-internal-aml-control-systems/44095.html (accessed 15 February 2018).

i. That financial institutions put in place adequate policies, procedures, and controls including appropriate compliance management arrangement and adequate screening procedures to ensure high standards when hiring employees; and

ii. That every Employee's accounts be monitored for potential signs of Money laundering and be subjected to the same anti-money laundering and combating the financing of terrorism (AML/CFT) Procedures as applicable to other customers' accounts. This is required to be performed under the supervision of the Chief Compliance Officer.[165]

3.7.1 BACKGROUND SCREENING OF PROSPECTIVE AND CURRENT EMPLOYEES

Background screening of prospective and current employees, especially for criminal history, is essential to keeping out unwanted employees and identifying those to be removed. While some foresee legal requirements for mandatory background screening by employers, it is still a matter of employer discretion in most industries.

KYE information such as background information should be obtained prior to job interview, during job interview and just before offer of employment. Any serious gap observed must be documented and should form part of the basis for offer of employment. After acceptance of offer, but before confirmation; background screening checks must be conducted to verify the identity of employees. All information supplied by prospective employees must be verified during probation. Any change in such information, including marital status and additional qualifications

[165] Central Bank of Nigeria (CBN) (Anti-Money Laundering and Combating the Financing of Terrorism in Banks and other Financial Institutions in Nigeria) Regulations 2013, regulation 38.

obtained during the period must be verified against appropriate documents and issuing institutions.[166]

The pre-employment background screening process can be an effective risk-management tool by providing management with a degree of certainty that the information provided by the applicant is true and correct, and that the potential employee does not have a criminal record. Used effectively, the pre-employment background screening process may reduce turnover by verifying that the potential employee has the requisite skills, certification, license or degree for the position; deter theft and embezzlement; and prevent litigation over hiring practices. Telecommunications companies should verify that contractors are subject to screening procedures similar to those used by financial institutions in Nigeria.

There are costs associated with developing and implementing an effective screening process. However, absent an effective screening process, a telecommunications company may incur significant expenses from recruiting, hiring and training unqualified individuals based upon their skill sets or backgrounds. These individuals may have to be replaced due to an inability to perform assigned duties or for other reasons.

The Federal Deposit Insurance Corporation (FDIC), a U.S. regulator, has provided guidance on employee screening in its paper "Pre-Employment Background Screening: Guidance on Developing an Effective Pre-Employment Background Screening Process".

---

166 FCMB (2013), 'FCMB Enterprise Risk Management (Compliance Risk Management) Know Your Customer, Anti-Money Laundering and Countering Financing of Terrorism and Proliferation Manual', Available at: http://www.fcmb.com/sites/default/files/NEW-AML-POLICY-1.pdf (accessed 15 February 2018).

According to the FDIC, Management should develop a risk-focused approach to determining when pre-employment background screening is considered appropriate or when the level of screening should be increased, based upon the position and responsibilities associated with a particular position. The sensitivity of the position or the access level of an individual staff member may warrant additional background screening, which should include verification of references, experience, education and professional qualifications. Furthermore, management should verify the applicant's identity. An on-going approach to screening should be considered for specific positions, as circumstances change, or for a comprehensive review of departmental staff over a period of time. Management should also have a policy that addresses appropriate actions when a pre-employment or subsequent screening detects information contrary to what the applicant or employee provided.

Section 19 of the Federal Deposit Insurance Act prohibits any person who has been convicted of any criminal offence involving dishonesty or a breach of trust or money laundering, or has agreed to enter into a pretrial diversion or similar program in connection with a prosecution, from becoming or continuing as an institution-affiliated party; owning or controlling, directly or indirectly, an insured institution; or otherwise participating, directly or indirectly, in the conduct of the affairs of an insured institution without the prior written consent of the FDIC. Note that consultants who participate in the conduct of the affairs of an insured institution may be subject to Section 19. Therefore, a pre-employment background screening process should be established by all Telecommunications Companies that, at a minimum, uncovers information regarding a job applicant's convictions and program entries to ensure that only appropriate persons are employed.

3.7.2 MONITORING OF EMPLOYEES

Once a business relationship has been established with an employee, telecommunications companies must conduct ongoing monitoring of the business relationship in accordance with the assessed level of risk. Telecommunications companies must ensure that employees are subject to effective systems for monitoring. Tools like modern employee monitoring software are a new implementation.

Telecommunications companies may monitor their employees for suspicious activity. The following examples are red flags that, when encountered, may warrant additional scrutiny. The mere presence of a red flag is not by itself evidence of criminal activity. Closer scrutiny should help to determine whether the activity is suspicious or one for which there does not appear to be a reasonable business or legal purpose:

i. Employee exhibits a lavish lifestyle that cannot be supported by his or her salary;

ii. Employee fails to conform to recognized policies, procedures and processes, particularly in private banking;

iii. Employee is reluctant to take a vacation;

iv. Employee exaggerates the credentials, background or financial ability and resources of a customer in written reports the bank requires;

v. Employee frequently overrides internal controls or established approval authority or circumvents policy;

vi. Employee uses company resources to further private interests;

vii. Employee assists transactions where the identity of the ultimate beneficiary or counter party is undisclosed.[167]

3.8 DISCUSSION

Nigeria has a centralized biometric identification system for the banking industry tagged Bank Verification Number (BVN), while the UK and US do not have this kind of system in place.

This system was launched by the **Central Bank of Nigeria** (the apex financial regulator in Nigeria) through the Bankers' Committee and in collaboration with all banks in Nigeria on February 14, 2014. The BVN project, which involved capturing biometrics of customers, was intended to protect bank customers and further strengthen the Nigerian banking system. It was also expected to minimise the incidences of fraud and money laundering in the banking industry. Every account holder is expected to do the BVN biometrics registration because it gives each bank depositor a unique identity, which can be verified at any bank where the customer has accounts.[168]

The biometric identification system has helped curb payroll fraud in the Nigerian civil service. A 2016 Punch Report revealed that 43,000 ghost workers were discovered through the use of the Bank Verification Number. According to the Honourable Minister of Finance, Mrs. Kemi Adeosun, the use of BVN exposed the links of some individuals in the civil service to multiple accounts, while, in

[167] Esoimeme, E.E. (2015), 'The Risk-Based Approach to Combating Money Laundering and Terrorist Financing', Eric Press; Available on Amazon: https://www.amazon.co.uk/Risk-Based-Combating-Laundering-Terrorist-Financing/dp/9789486030/ref=sr_1_2?ie=UTF8&qid=1437508453&sr=8-2&keywords=ehi+eric+esoimeme

[168] Central Bank of Nigeria (2018), 'Bank Verification Number', Available at: https://www.cbn.gov.ng/Paymentsystem/BVN.asp (accessed 6 April 2018).

other instances, the name on the BVN was inconsistent with that on the payroll.[169]

The Bank Verification Number also helped to expose how a former Chief of Defence Staff, Air Chief Marshal Alex Badeh (retd.), was linked to two hundred and forty-million-naira worth of property in Abuja.[170]

The biometric identification system has also helped to curb money laundering. On October 17, 2017, a Federal High Court in Abuja ordered the forfeiture of all monies in bank accounts owned by corporate organisations, government agencies and individuals without the BVN. It is believed that most of these accounts are owned by corrupt public officials who used fictitious names to open accounts for the purpose of laundering their ill-gotten wealth.

The forfeiture order, which was issued by Justice Dimgba Igwe, while ruling on an ex parte application filed by the Federal Government through the Office of the Attorney General of the Federation, is not final yet.[171]

Despite the successes being recorded by the Bank Verification Number project as noted above, a recent report by the **Economic and Financial Crimes Commission** revealed that some banks are helping corrupt government officials to operate secret accounts without Bank Verification Numbers. The report accused banks of not reporting suspicious transactions in line with statutory

---

[169] Awoyinfa, S. (2016), 'FG uncovers over 43,000 ghost workers', Available at: http://punchng.com/fg-uncovers-43000-ghost-workers/ (accessed 8 April 2018).
[170] Adesomoju, A. (2017), 'BVN exposed Badeh's link to N240m house, says witness', Available at: http://punchng.com/bvn-exposed-badehs-link-to-n240m-house-says-witness/ (accessed 8 April 2018).
[171] The Punch (2017), 'BVN: Banks move to stop deposit forfeiture, lobby AGF', Available at: https://punchng.com/bvn-banks-move-to-stop-deposit-forfeiture-lobby-agf/ (accessed 5 May 2019).

regulations.[172] This revelation epitomises systemic failure aggravated by the Central Bank of Nigeria's weak regulation.

It is worth noting that the **Financial Crimes Enforcement Network** (the delegated administrator of the **United States Bank Secrecy Act**) and the **Financial Conduct Authority** (the conduct regulator for 56,000 financial services firms and financial markets in the UK and the prudential regulator for over 18,000 of those firms) have all brought enforcement actions against a number of financial institutions for violations of the reporting, recordkeeping, or other requirements of the **Financial Action Task Force Recommendations 2012.**

For example, the **Financial Conduct Authority** (FCA) had on the 31st of January, 2017, fined Deutsche Bank AG (Deutsche Bank) £163,076,224 for failing to maintain an adequate anti-money laundering (AML) control framework during the period between 1 January 2012 and 31 December 2015. This is the largest financial penalty for AML controls failings ever imposed by the FCA, or its predecessor, the Financial Services Authority (FSA).

According to the FCA, "Deutsche Bank exposed the UK financial system to the risks of financial crime by failing to properly oversee the formation of new customer relationships and the booking of global business in the UK. As a consequence of its inadequate AML control framework, Deutsche Bank was used by unidentified customers to transfer approximately $10 billion, of unknown origin, from Russia to offshore bank accounts in a manner that is highly suggestive of financial crime."[173]

---

[172] Akinkuotu, E. (2017), 'Govt officials diverting money to accounts without BVN – EFCC', Available at: http://punchng.com/govt-officials-diverting-money-to-accounts-without-bvn-efcc/ (accessed 5 April 2018).

[173] Financial Conduct Authority (2017), 'FCA fines Deutsche Bank £163 million for serious anti-money laundering controls failings', Available at: https://www.fca.org.uk/news/press-releases/fca-fines-deutsche-bank-163-million-anti-money-laundering-controls-failure (accessed 9 April 2018).

On or about February 2017, the Financial Crimes Enforcement Network (FinCEN) had determined that grounds exist to assess a civil money penalty against Merchants Bank of California, N.A. (Merchants or the Bank), pursuant to the **Bank Secrecy Act (BSA)** and regulations issued pursuant to that Act.

According to FinCEN, "Merchants willfully violated the BSA's program and reporting requirements from March 2012 to September 2016. As described below, Merchants failed to (a) establish and implement an adequate AML program; (b) conduct required due diligence on its foreign correspondent accounts; and (c) detect and report suspicious activity. Merchants's failures allowed billions of dollars in transactions to flow through the U.S. financial system without effective monitoring to adequately detect and report suspicious activity. Many of these transactions were conducted on behalf of money services businesses (MSBs) that were owned or managed by Bank insiders who encouraged staff to process these transactions without question or face potential dismissal or retaliation."

In view of the above stated facts, FinCEN determined that the penalty in this matter would be $7 million. The penalty will run concurrent with the Office of the Comptroller of the Currency, OCC's $1 million penalty.[174]

The Central Bank of Nigeria, on the other hand, has brought no enforcement action against any financial institution in Nigeria despite disturbing revelations from the EFCC and the media.

It is worth noting that telecommunications companies are required to submit a formal application for the grant of a Payment Service Bank license addressed to the Governor of the

[174] Financial Crimes Enforcement Network (2017), 'FinCEN Penalizes California Bank for Egregious Violations of Anti-Money Laundering Laws', Available at: https://www.fincen.gov/news/news-releases/fincen-penalizes-california-bank-egregious-violations-anti-money-laundering-laws (accessed 5 May 2019).

Central Bank of Nigeria.[175] The application is to be accompanied with a detailed business plan or feasibility report which shall, at a minimum, include, among others, the Bank Verification Number (BVN) and Tax Clearance Certificate of each member of the Board and significant shareholders.[176] A significant shareholder is a person with a shareholding of 5% and above.[177]

While the above measure is very good, the business plan fails to capture shareholders who own less than 5 percent of the shares in the company. This loophole can allow corrupt individuals who intend to own up to 5 percent of the company's shares to circulate the shares among their friends or family members to bring the aggregate to 5 percent.

3.9. CONCLUSION

To reduce the money laundering risks associated with High Risk Accounts, telecommunications companies must apply a risk-based approach to their compliance programs.

Adopting a risk-based approach implies the adoption of a risk management process for dealing with fraud and money laundering. This process encompasses recognising the existence of the risk(s) at the Standard Due Diligence stage, undertaking an assessment of the risk(s) at the Enhanced Due Diligence stage and developing strategies to manage and mitigate the identified risks at the Enhanced on-going monitoring stage.[178]

175 The Central Bank of Nigeria Guidelines for Licensing and Regulation of Payment Service Banks 2018, para. 6.0.

176 The Central Bank of Nigeria Guidelines for Licensing and Regulation of Payment Service Banks 2018, para. 6.1.

177 The Central Bank of Nigeria' Revised Assessment Criteria for Approved Persons' Regime for Financial Institutions 2015, para. 7.0.

178 Esoimeme, E.E. (2015), 'The Risk-Based Approach to Combating Money Laundering and Terrorist Financing', Eric Press; Available on Amazon: https://www.amazon.co.uk/Risk-Based-Combating-Laundering-Terrorist-Financing/dp/9789486030/ref=sr_1_2?ie=UTF8&qid=1437508453&sr=8-2&keywords=ehi+eric+esoimeme

Risk Assessment will be conducted along the lines of our customers, products, geographic locations and delivery channels. It will ensure that identified lower and higher risks are properly mitigated. The telecommunications company shall adopt risk-based approaches that are commensurate with the specific risks of money laundering and terrorist financing.

Higher money laundering risks demand stronger controls than warranted by individuals or countries deemed to be of lower risk. However, all categories of risks whether low or high must be mitigated by the application of appropriate controls as provided in the telecommunications company's AML/CFT Manual, such as verification of customer identification, Know Your Customer (KYC) policies, and so on.[179]

Risk management is an ongoing process throughout the life of the relationship and as such reassessments must be carried out on a periodic basis. The period is determined by the initial risk assessment given to the customer at account opening. The customer's information should be updated as follows: High risk clients 2-year cycle; Medium risk clients 4-year cycle; and Low risk clients 5-year cycle.[180]

However, it is to be noted that an event can trigger a risk re-assessment review outside the aforementioned cycle i.e. "Event Driven Review" e.g. where there is a sudden change in the leadership or account signatories of the customer.[181]

The **Financial Action Task Force (FATF) Recommendations** support the development and implementation of a risk-based

---

[179] Central Bank of Nigeria' Anti-Money Laundering/Combating the Financing of Terrorism (AML/CFT) Policy and Procedure Manual' 2018, para. 12.0.

[180] Central Bank of Nigeria' Anti-Money Laundering/Combating the Financing of Terrorism (AML/CFT) Policy and Procedure Manual' 2018, para. 26.0.

[181] Central Bank of Nigeria' Anti-Money Laundering/Combating the Financing of Terrorism (AML/CFT) Policy and Procedure Manual' 2018, para. 26.0.

approach to anti-money laundering and countering the financing of terrorism measures. This risk-based approach allows countries, within the framework of the FATF requirements, to adopt a more flexible set of measures, in order to target their resources more effectively and apply preventive measures that are commensurate to the nature of risks, in order to focus their efforts in the most effective way.[182]

Independent testing (audit) should review a telecommunications company's risk assessment for reasonableness. Additionally, management should consider the staffing resources and the level of training necessary to promote adherence with these policies, procedures, and processes. For those telecommunications companies that assume a higher-risk Fraud profile, management should provide a more robust anti-fraud compliance program that specifically monitors and controls the higher risks that management and the board have accepted.[183]

Telecommunications companies are advised not to use the Employee Profiling methodology, to assess the risk posed by potential employees. Employee profiling, being a one-size-fits-all assessment methodology, may not be the best option. This chapter recommends a flexible approach that can adapt as risks evolve. Since the approach used to combat money laundering is more like a flexible approach, the methodology used to assess employee risk should also be flexible. Telecommunications companies should

---

182 Financial Action Task Force (2007), 'FATF Guidance on the Risk-Based Approach to Combating Money Laundering and Terrorist Financing - High Level Principles and Procedures', Available at: http://www.fatf-gafi.org/media/fatf/documents/reports/High%20Level%20Principles%20and%20Procedures.pdf (accessed 5 December, 2018).

183 Federal Financial Institutions Examination Council (2014), 'Bank Secrecy Act/Anti-Money Laundering Examination Manual', Available at: https://www.occ.treas.gov/publications/publications-by-type/other-publications-reports/ffiec-bsa-aml-examination-manual.pdf (accessed 10 January 2017).

label employees in sensitive positions as high risk, just as how they label customers. Telecommunications companies would need to apply enhanced scrutiny to such employees. Chief Compliance Officers, for example, should be labeled high-risk. Measures would have to be put in place to mitigate the risk (s) associated with high-risk employees.

Paragraph 6.1 of **the Central Bank of Nigeria Guidelines for Licensing and Regulation of Payment Service Banks** should be modified to mandate that the detailed business plan or feasibility report of the telecommunications company must include the Bank Verification Number of all the shareholders of the Payment Service Bank. This measure will help to prevent a situation where a corrupt individual with just 2 percent of the company's shares connives with other friends and family to own 5 percent of the company's shares.

CHAPTER 4

WHISTLE-BLOWING POLICY

By virtue of **paragraph 7.1 of the Central Bank of Nigeria Guidelines for Licensing and Regulation of Payment Service Banks**, the provisions of the **Central Bank of Nigeria Code of Corporate Governance for banks** will now apply to telecommunications companies also. For the purpose of this chapter, the focus will be on **paragraph 5.3** of the **Central Bank of Nigeria Code of Corporate Governance for Banks and Discount Houses in Nigeria, 2014**.

Paragraph 5.3 of the Central Bank of Nigeria Code of Corporate Governance for Banks and Discount Houses in Nigeria mandates Banks to have a whistle-blowing policy made known to employees and other stakeholders.

The policy is required to contain mechanisms, including assurance of confidentiality, that encourage all stakeholders to report any unethical activity to the bank and/or the **Central Bank of Nigeria.**

What this means is that telecommunications companies are required to put in place a whistle-blowing policy for the grant of a Payment Service Bank licence. The Management of the telecommunications company has a duty to conduct the company's affairs in a responsible and transparent manner and to take into account legal and regulatory requirements under which the company operates. The Board of the telecommunication company should also be committed to the principle of sound corporate governance and behavior as enunciated in the CBN Code of Corporate Governance for Banks in Nigeria. One of the several ways a breach of regulatory requirements and staff misconduct can be addressed is through a whistle blowing programme. As such, the whistle-blowing policy and procedures of the telecommunications company are designed to encourage stakeholders to bring unethical conduct and illegal violations to the attention of an internal and or external authority so that action can be taken to resolve the problem.

The whistle-blowing policy will indeed strengthen the fight against money laundering in telecommunications companies as employees of telecommunications companies can inform the Central Bank of Nigeria of wrongdoing where a Senior staff of the company conspires with fraudulent clients to evade Currency Transaction and Suspicious Activity reporting requirements.

Whistle-blowing Reports filed by an employee of a telecommunications company would assist tremendously in tracing and identifying illicit assets.

The **Central Bank of Nigeria** has provided guidelines for Whistle-Blowing for telecommunications companies in Nigeria. These Guidelines are designed to enable stakeholders of telecommunications companies to report acts of impropriety to appropriate authorities. This may include any of the following:

I. All forms of financial malpractice or impropriety or fraud;
II. Failure to comply with a legal obligation or Statutes;
III. Actions detrimental to Health & Safety or the environment;
IV. Any form of criminal activity;
V. Improper conduct or unethical behaviour;
VI. Failure to comply with regulatory directives;
VII. Other forms of corporate governance breaches;
VIII. Connected transactions;
IX. Insider abuses
X. Non-disclosure of interest;

XI. Attempts to conceal any of these, etc.[184]

This chapter will review the whistle-blowing procedures of the **Central Bank of Nigeria Guidelines for Whistle-Blowing for Banks and Other Financial Institutions in Nigeria** to determine the level of its effectiveness.

4.1 WHISTLE-BLOWING PROCEDURES

Telecommunications companies are required to have a whistle–blowing policy which shall be made known to employees, management, directors and other stakeholders such as contractors, shareholders, job applicants and the general public. The policy should be disclosed in their web sites.[185] It is the responsibility of the board to implement such a policy and to establish a whistle-blowing mechanism for reporting any illegal or unethical behavior.[186] The whistle-blowing mechanism shall include a dedicated "hot–line" or e–mail address and other electronic devices that could be used anonymously to report unethical practices.[187]

The Head of Internal Audit shall review reported cases and recommend appropriate action to the Managing Director (MD)/Chief Executive Officer (CEO) and where issues affect Executive Management, such issues should be referred to the Board. The Board or CEO shall take appropriate action to redress the situation within a reasonable time.[188] The Head of Internal Audit shall provide the Chairman of the Board Audit Committee

---

[184] Central Bank of Nigeria Guidelines for Whistle-Blowing for Banks and other Financial Institutions in Nigeria 2014, para. 2.0.

[185] Central Bank of Nigeria Guidelines for Whistle-Blowing for Banks and other Financial Institutions in Nigeria 2014, para. 3.1.

[186] Central Bank of Nigeria Guidelines for Whistle-Blowing for Banks and other Financial Institutions in Nigeria 2014, para. 3.2.

[187] Central Bank of Nigeria Guidelines for Whistle-Blowing for Banks and other Financial Institutions in Nigeria 2014, para. 3.4.

[188] Central Bank of Nigeria Guidelines for Whistle-Blowing for Banks and other Financial Institutions in Nigeria 2014, para. 3.5.

with a summary of cases reported and the result of the investigation.[189]

A whistle–blower shall disclose any information connected with the activities of the telecommunications company which indicates any of the following:

(i) that an infraction has been committed;

(ii) that a person has failed to comply with banking laws, internal policies and procedures, etc; and

(iii) that someone has concealed matters falling within (i) or (ii) above.[190]

A disclosure is deemed to have been made in accordance with **paragraph 3.8** of the **Central Bank of Nigeria Guidelines for Whistle-Blowing** if the whistle-blower discloses to the telecommunications company, CBN, and/or other appropriate agencies or exercise any other lawful option provided that such disclosure is:

(i) true; and

(ii) reasonable.[191]

Telecommunications companies may follow the whistle-blowing procedures as laid down in the FCMB Enterprise Risk Management AML/CFT Manual:

"i. All stakeholders will be provided with details of KPMG Ethics Line facilities via the bank's website. The KPMG Ethics Line facilities provide avenues for employees and any other person to confidentially and anonymously report all incidents relating to various categories of

[189] Central Bank of Nigeria Guidelines for Whistle-Blowing for Banks and other Financial Institutions in Nigeria 2014, para. 3.6.

[190] Central Bank of Nigeria Guidelines for Whistle-Blowing for Banks and other Financial Institutions in Nigeria 2014, para. 3.7.

[191] Central Bank of Nigeria Guidelines for Whistle-Blowing for Banks and other Financial Institutions in Nigeria 2014, para. 3.8.

unethical and criminal conduct including cases relating to social and environmental risk crystallization associated with projects the bank has financed.

ii. A disclosure is deemed to have been made through the KPMG Ethics Line facilities or to the CBN and/or any other Government agency provided that such disclosure is true and reasonable.

iii. The Bank shall not subject a Whistle-blower to any detriment whatsoever on the grounds that s/he has made a disclosure in accordance with the provisions of this policy.

iv. An employee who has suffered any detriment by reason of disclosure made pursuant to the provision of these guidelines shall be entitled to compensation and/or reinstatement provided that in the case of compensation, the employee's entitlement shall be computed as if he had attained the maximum age of retirement or had completed the maximum period of service, in accordance with his condition of service. For stakeholders, the whistle- blower shall be adequately compensated.

v. Whistle-blowers are encouraged but not required or obliged to disclose their identities to FCMB and/or KPMG when reporting incidents through KPMG Ethics Line facilities. In the event of the whistle-blower willfully disclosing his/her identity, it shall remain undisclosed to FCMB until the complainant provides written consent to KPMG. These measures are necessary in order to maintain the confidentiality and anonymity of the whistle-blowers.

vi. All reports received via the KPMG Ethics Line facilities will be transcribed unto call sheet memoranda and transmitted to designated officers within FCMB for further action.

vii. Reports of any allegation relating to fraud, theft of company asset and human resource related matters (e.g. sexual harassment) shall be submitted to the Managing Director, Company Secretary/ Group Legal Counsel, Chief Compliance Officer and Chief Inspector/ Head of Internal Audit.

viii. Whistle blowing matters relating to breach of the Code of Corporate Governance for Banks in Nigeria and other types of unethical conducts shall be reported to the Chairman of the Board, Managing Director, Group Head, Enterprise Management and Chief Compliance Officer.

ix. Where the matter relates to a report against a Director (excluding the Managing Director), irrespective of the type of incident, it shall be reported to the Chairman of the Board, Managing Director and Company Secretary/ Group Legal Counsel.

x. If the allegation is against the Managing Director, irrespective of the type of incident, it shall be conveyed to the Chairman of the Board and the Company Secretary/ Group Legal Counsel.

xi. In general, every call sheet memorandum is copied to the Chief Compliance Officer and Head of Internal Audit /Chief Inspector for report rendition purposes.

xii. The Head of Internal Audit shall provide the Chairman of the Board Audit and Risk Management Committee with a summary of cases reported and the result of the investigation. Provided the allegation has been made lawfully without malice, the employment position of the person making it will not be adversely affected. It is the responsibility of Executive Management to ensure that Whistle blowers are protected from victimization.

xiii. The person or persons against whom the allegation is made shall be informed of the allegation and the evidence supporting it and must be allowed to comment in writing before investigation is concluded.

xiv. If on preliminary investigation, the allegation is judged to be wholly without substance or merit, the allegation may be dismissed and the person making the allegation will be so informed through the Ethics Line service.

xv. Where an allegation is found to be valid, Executive management shall constitute Disciplinary Committee to review the matter and apply appropriate sanctions on the erring staff.

xvi. As may be required by extant regulations and guidelines, whistle blowing incidences shall be reported to Law Enforcement Agencies or appropriate Regulatory Bodies for any further action or prosecution.

xvii. All allegations, including those dismissed after preliminary examination, and the results of their investigation must be reported to the Board Audit and Risk Management Committee.

xviii. If someone who has made a whistle blowing allegation remains dissatisfied with the outcome of the investigation, the issue should be escalated to the Chairman of the Board of Directors who shall constitute a special panel to review the allegation.

xix. Where a Whistle-blower believes that s/he has been subjected to any detriment in contravention of the above, s/he may present a complaint to the Central Bank of Nigeria."

4.2 PROTECTION OF THE WHISTLE-BLOWER

The **Central Bank of Nigeria Guidelines for Whistle-Blowing for Banks and Other Financial Institutions in Nigeria** is designed to offer protection to whistleblower(s) who disclose such concerns provided the disclosure is made:

a) in the reasonable belief that it is intended to show malpractice or impropriety; and

b) to an appropriate person or authority.[192]

[192] Central Bank of Nigeria Guidelines for Whistle-Blowing for Banks and other Financial Institutions in Nigeria 2014, para. 4.1.

Telecommunications companies shall treat all disclosures resulting from whistle-blowing in a confidential manner. The identity of the whistle-blower shall be kept confidential.[193]

Stakeholders are encouraged to disclose their name when filing reports to make their reports more credible. However, anonymous disclosures may be considered on discretionary basis taking into account the following factors:

a) the seriousness of the issues;

b) the significance and credibility of the concern; and

c) the possibility of confirming the allegation.[194]

In making a disclosure through whistle-blowing, the individual should exercise due care in reporting his concern. If, however, an individual makes malicious allegations, and particularly if he or she persists with making them, no action shall be taken.[195]

By virtue of paragraph 4.5 of the **Central Bank of Nigeria Guidelines for Whistle-Blowing for Banks and Other Financial Institutions in Nigeria,** no telecommunications company shall subject a whistleblower to any detriment whatsoever on the grounds that s/he has made a disclosure in accordance with the provisions of these Guidelines.[196] For the purpose of these Guidelines, the word "detriment includes dismissal, termination, redundancy, undue influence, duress, withholding of benefits

[193] Central Bank of Nigeria Guidelines for Whistle-Blowing for Banks and other Financial Institutions in Nigeria 2014, para. 4.2.

[194] Central Bank of Nigeria Guidelines for Whistle-Blowing for Banks and other Financial Institutions in Nigeria 2014, para. 4.3.

[195] Central Bank of Nigeria Guidelines for Whistle-Blowing for Banks and other Financial Institutions in Nigeria 2014, para. 4.4.

[196] Central Bank of Nigeria Guidelines for Whistle-Blowing for Banks and other Financial Institutions in Nigeria 2014, para. 4.5.

and/or entitlements and any other act that has negative impact on the whistle-blower.[197]

Where a whistle-blower has been subjected to any detriment in contravention of the above, he or she may present a complaint to the CBN. This is without prejudice to the right of the whistleblower to take appropriate legal action.[198]

An employee who has suffered any detriment by reason of disclosure made pursuant to the provision of the **Central Bank of Nigeria Guidelines for Whistle-Blowing** shall be entitled to compensation and/or reinstatement provided that in the case of compensation, the employee's entitlement shall be computed as if he had attained the maximum age of retirement or had completed the maximum period of service, in accordance with his condition of service. For other stakeholders, the whistle-blower shall be adequately compensated.[199]

In addition to the above, telecommunications companies are also required to:

i. Make quarterly returns to the Central Bank of Nigeria and the Nigeria Deposit Insurance Corporation on all whistle-blowing reports and corporate governance related breaches.[200]
ii. Include a whistleblowing compliance status report in their audited financial statements.[201]

---

[197] Central Bank of Nigeria Guidelines for Whistle-Blowing for Banks and other Financial Institutions in Nigeria 2014, para. 4.9.
[198] Central Bank of Nigeria Guidelines for Whistle-Blowing for Banks and other Financial Institutions in Nigeria 2014, para. 4.6.
[199] Central Bank of Nigeria Guidelines for Whistle-Blowing for Banks and other Financial Institutions in Nigeria 2014, para. 4.7.
[200] Central Bank of Nigeria Guidelines for Whistle-Blowing for Banks and other Financial Institutions in Nigeria 2014, para. 4.10.
[201] Central Bank of Nigeria Guidelines for Whistle-Blowing for Banks and other Financial Institutions in Nigeria 2014, para. 4.11.

iii. Review their whistle-blowing policies every three (3) years and notify the regulatory authorities of all such reviews.[202]

By virtue of paragraph 4.8 of the **Central Bank of Nigeria Guidelines for Whistle-Blowing for Banks and Other Financial Institutions in Nigeria,** any telecommunications company which contravenes the provision of this section of the Guidelines will be sanctioned in line with section 60 of the Banks and Other Financial Institutions Act 1991 (as amended).

4.3 DISCUSSION

The Federal Executive Council had on the 21st day of December 2016 approved the Ministry of Finance Whistleblowing Programme that may see individuals, who voluntarily volunteers credible information on stolen or concealed funds, smiling home with between 2.5 per cent and five per cent of the funds when recovered.

The programme was designed to encourage anyone with information about a violation, misconduct or improper activity that impacted negatively on Nigerians and government, to report such.[203]

The policy has been very successful in achieving its main objectives.

On the 8th day of April 2017, the Economic and Financial Crimes Commission (EFCC) recovered four hundred and forty-nine million, eight hundred and sixty thousand naira hidden in an abandoned shop in Lagos following a tip-off.[204]

---

202 Central Bank of Nigeria Guidelines for Whistle-Blowing for Banks and other Financial Institutions in Nigeria 2014, para. 4.12.

203 Adetayo, O. (2016), 'FG okays 5% of recovered loot for whistleblowers', Available at: http://punchng.com/fg-okays-5-recovered-loot-whistleblowers/ (accessed 6 June 2017).

204 Akinkuotu, E. (2017), 'EFCC recovers N449m in abandoned Lagos shop', Available at: http://punchng.com/efcc-recovers-n449m-in-abandoned-lagos-shop/ (accessed 6 June 2017).

On the 10th day of April, 2017, the EFCC again recovered five hundred and forty-seven thousand, seven hundred and thirty euros and twenty-one thousand and ninety pounds as well as five million six hundred forty-eight thousand five hundred naira from a Bureau de Change operator in Balogun Market, Lagos. The figure sums up to two hundred fifty million five hundred fifty-eight thousand six hundred seventy naira when converted to naira, according to the EFCC.[205]

On the 12th day of April, 2017, the EFCC raided a house in Ikoyi, Lagos recovering about forty-three million dollars, twenty-three million naira and twenty-seven thousand pounds in cash. The operation followed a whistle-blower confidential alert received by the EFCC office in Lagos in the early hours of April, 11 2017.[206]

In total, the EFCC has recovered at least seventeen billion naira since the Federal Government introduced the whistle-blower policy on December 21, 2016.[207]

While the Ministry of Finance' Whistleblowing Programme could positively impact on the Whistle-Blowing policy of the Central Bank of Nigeria as staff of telecommunications companies may be encouraged to make external reports in view of the financial incentives involved, many Telecom employees may feel discouraged to make that report in view of the structure that is currently in place with regards to the filing of suspicious transaction reports and currency transaction reports. Employees who believe that a suspicious transaction report ought to have

205 The Punch (2017), 'EFCC intercepts N250m cash haul at Balogun market', Available at: http://punchng.com/efcc-intercepts-n250m-cash-haul-at-balogun-market/ (accessed 4 June 2017).
206 Akinkuotu, E. (2017), 'How EFCC recovered $43m, £27,000, N23m during house raid', Available at: http://punchng.com/efcc-recovers-43m-27000-n23m-during-house-raid/ (accessed 5 June 2017).
207 Akinkuotu, E. (2017), 'EFCC recovers N17bn in four months', Available at: http://punchng.com/efcc-recovers-n17bn-in-four-months/ (accessed 6 June 2017).

been filed may decide not to blow the whistle so as to avoid giving out false information and then going to prison for it.

For example, a situation may occur where an employee of a financial institution/telecommunications company to whom information or other matter comes in the course of business as a result of which they know or suspect, or have reasonable grounds for knowing or suspecting, that a person is engaged in money laundering or terrorist financing makes an internal report to the Compliance Officer as soon as it is reasonably practicable after the information or other matter comes to him, and then the Compliance Officer who the report is made to concludes that the internal report does not give rise to knowledge or suspicion of money laundering or terrorist financing but the employee who made that report to the Compliance Officer strongly believes that the report does give rise to knowledge or suspicion of money laundering or terrorist financing having reviewed the financial circumstances of the customer involved or beneficial owner, or any person on whose behalf the customer has been or is acting; the features of the transactions, including, where appropriate, the jurisdiction in which the transaction took place, which the firm entered into with or for the customer (or that person); and the underlying CDD information, and copies of the actual source documentation in respect of the customer; The employee may be discouraged from blowing the whistle to avoid being charged for conspiracy and giving false information to mislead the police, contrary to sections 125 and 125A of the Criminal Code Act and sections 97(1) and 140 of the Penal Code Law as the employee may be afraid that the Nigerian Financial Intelligence Unit may arrive at similar conclusions with the Compliance Officer or the Compliance Officer himself may decide to eliminate evidence that shows that the transaction was indeed suspicious.

Another example is a real-life case study which occurred at about 8 am on a Friday. On **May 26, 2017**, men of the Nigeria Police Force from the Inspector General of Police Special Squad raided the official guest house of the Deputy President of the Senate, Senator Ike Ekweremadu, located at No. 10 Ganges Street, Maitama, Abuja following a tip-off from a whistleblower. The raid was done without a search warrant. The police, however, stated at the end of the search that nothing incriminating was found.[208] Although the whistleblower was later arraigned before an Upper Area Court sitting at the Gudu District of Abuja on a one-count charge of criminal conspiracy and giving false information to mislead the police, contrary to section 97(1) and 140 of the Penal Code Law,[209] the search that was conducted on the premises of the Deputy President of the Senate, Senator Ike Ekweremadu without a warrant is unlawful and unconstitutional because the said act amounts to an infraction of the Constitutional right to privacy of Senator Ike Ekweremadu as provided by Section 37 of the Constitution of the Federal Republic of Nigeria 1999 (as amended).[210]

Also, on the 16th of May, 2017, the Economic and Financial Crimes Commission arraigned two self-acclaimed whistleblowers, Buhari Fannami and Ba-Kura Abdullahi on two separate charges before Justice M. T Salihu of the Federal High Court Maiduguri, for allegedly giving false information to the agency.

The EFCC said in a statement by its spokesman, Mr. Wilson Uwujaren, that Fannamit had misled the commission with the information about illegally acquired monies purportedly buried at

---

208 UMORU, H. and KUMOLU, C. (2017), 'My house was raided by Police, nothing was found – Ekweremadu', Available at: http://www.vanguardngr.com/2017/05/house-raided-police-nothing-found-ekweremadu/ (accessed 4 June 2017).

209 Umoru, H. and Nnochiri, I. (2017), 'Ekweremadu: Police dock whistleblower over false information', Available at: http://www.vanguardngr.com/2017/05/ekweremadu-police-dock-whistleblower-false-information/ (accessed 10 June 2017).

210 Hassan v. E.F.C.C. (2014) I NWLR (Pt. 1389) 607 at 625

the residence of one Ba'a Lawan but the information turned out to be false after the execution of a search warrant.[211]

The actions taken by the Police and the EFCC are bound to discourage opportunists from giving out false information to the relevant authorities, and also discourage bank employees from filing external reports to the NFIU in a situation where they strongly believe that the Compliance Officer was wrong in his decision.

Also, the Whistle-Blower protection provisions in the **Central Bank of Nigeria Guidelines for Whistle-Blowing for Banks and Other Financial Institutions in Nigeria** may not be enough to protect Telecom employees from retaliation by employers. The telecommunications company may still decide to go after the employee involved by terminating the employee's appointment and giving detailed reasons for that.

4.4 CONCLUSION

This chapter critically analysed the Central Bank of Nigeria Guidelines for Whistle-Blowing for Banks and Other Financial Institutions in Nigeria to determine that the Whistle-Blowing policy could achieve its desired objective of a balanced approach to financial inclusion and anti-money laundering measures if the following recommendations are implemented:

I. A Bank must require that anyone in the firm who makes a report to the Compliance Officer about information or other matter that comes to him or her in the course of business as a result of which they know or suspect, or have reasonable grounds for knowing or suspecting, that a person is engaged in money laundering or terrorist financing (this

[211] The Daily Times (2017), 'EFCC arraigns 2 whistleblowers over false information', Available at: https://dailytimes.ng/news/efcc-arraigns-2-whistleblowers-false-information/ (accessed 10 June 2017).

includes staff having an obligation to make an internal report to the Compliance Officer as soon as is reasonably practicable after the information or other matter comes to them) to directly file a report with the Nigerian Financial Intelligence Unit if the person is not satisfied with the decision of the Compliance Officer not to file that report.

II. The whistleblower policy of the Central Bank of Nigeria is likely to be more effective when the **Public Interest Disclosure and Witness Protection Bill, 2017 becomes law**. The Bill expressly prohibits retaliation by employers against whistleblowers and provides them with a private cause of action in the event that they are discharged or discriminated against by their employers in violation of the Act.[212] The Bill also protects whistleblowers from any criminal or civil action.[213] The Bill makes it unlawful for employers to retaliate against any employee who makes or intends to make a public interest disclosure on fraud, corruption and theft in relation to public funds or any Government property whatsoever.[214] Criminal penalties apply, with fines up to five hundred thousand naira or imprisonment for a term of not less than two years or to both.[215] This measure is in line with the **Hawaii Whistleblowers Protection Act.** The **Public Interest Disclosure and Witness Protection Bill, 2017** has been read the third time and passed into law by the Upper Legislative Chamber (The Senate) on June 8, 2017. It was sponsored by Isiaka Adeleke, the Osun West APC Senator who died in April, 2017. The bill must also be passed by

[212] Public Interest Disclosure and Witness Protection Bill, 2017, s. 44, s. 45
[213] Public Interest Disclosure and Witness Protection Bill, 2017, s. 42
[214] Public Interest Disclosure and Witness Protection Bill, 2017, s. 43, s. 52 (1)
[215] Public Interest Disclosure and Witness Protection Bill, 2017, s. 43

the House of Representatives and signed by the president to be law.[216] The **Public Interest Disclosure and Witness Protection Bill, 2017** should be given accelerated consideration in the House of Representatives based on its urgency and significance for the Federal Executive Council's whistleblowers Policy.

216 Hassan, A. (2017), 'Nigerian Senate passes bill to protect whistle-blowers', Available at: http://www.premiumtimesng.com/news/headlines/233385-breaking-nigerian-senate-passes-bill-to-protect-whistle-blowers.html (accessed 9 June 2017).

CHAPTER 5

THREE-TIERED KNOW YOUR CUSTOMER (KYC) REQUIREMENTS

Telecommunications companies are required to adopt a risk-based approach in the conduct of due diligence and ensure that every customer complies with the know your customer (KYC) requirements. All accounts shall be subjected to continuous suspicious transactions monitoring and any suspicious transactions shall be reported to the appropriate agency.[217]

The risk-based approach will require telecommunications companies to implement the three-tiered KYC requirements. The three-tiered KYC requirements was introduced by the **Central Bank of Nigeria** for compliance by banks and other financial institutions under its regulatory purview.[218]

The three-tiered KYC regime seeks to implement flexible account opening requirements for low-value and medium-value account holders subject to caps and transaction restrictions as the amount on the transactions increase. This means that account opening requirements will increase progressively with less restrictions on

---

[217] The Central Bank of Nigeria Guidelines for Licensing and Regulation of Payment Service Banks 2018, para. 11.1.

[218] CBN (Anti-Money Laundering and Combating the Financing of Terrorism in Banks and Other Financial Institutions in Nigeria) Regulations, 2013, regulation 45 (1); Central Bank of Nigeria (2013), 'Circular to all Banks and other Financial Institutions: Introduction of Three-Tiered Know Your Customer (KYC) Requirements', Available at: https://www.cbn.gov.ng/out/2013/ccd/3%20tiered%20kyc%20requirements.pdf (accessed 10 April 2018).

operations. However, the main objective of the approach is to promote and deepen financial inclusion.[219]

The structure ensures that the accounts remain attractive to customers of different socio-economic levels while close watch is kept on the risk involved.[220]

5.1 LOW VALUE ACCOUNTS

Low Value Accounts are subject to close monitoring by telecommunications companies and less scrutiny by Bank Examiners. The accounts can be opened at branches of telecommunications companies by the prospective customer or through banking agents. No amount is required for opening of accounts. Such accounts cover Mobile Banking products (issued in accordance with the Central Bank of Nigeria Regulatory Framework for Mobile Payments Services in Nigeria).

The main characteristics of the account are:

i. Deposits can be made by account holder and third parties while withdrawal is restricted to account holder only;

ii. It can be linked to mobile phone accounts;

iii. Operation is valid in Nigeria only;

iv. ATM transactions are allowed;

[219] CBN (Anti-Money Laundering and Combating the Financing of Terrorism in Banks and Other Financial Institutions in Nigeria) Regulations, 2013, regulation 45 (1); Central Bank of Nigeria (2013), 'Circular to all Banks and other Financial Institutions: Introduction of Three-Tiered Know Your Customer (KYC) Requirements', Available at: https://www.cbn.gov.ng/out/2013/ccd/3%20tiered%20kyc%20requirements.pdf (accessed 10 April 2018).

[220] Central Bank of Nigeria (2013), 'Circular to all Banks and other Financial Institutions: Introduction of Three-Tiered Know Your Customer (KYC) Requirements', Available at: https://www.cbn.gov.ng/out/2013/ccd/3%20tiered%20kyc%20requirements.pdf (accessed 10 April 2018).

v. International fund transfer is prohibited;

vi. Accounts are strictly savings.[221]

Low-value accounts are limited to a maximum single deposit of fifty thousand naira and maximum cumulative balance of three hundred thousand naira at any point in time.[222] Basic customer information required to be provided are:

i. Passport photograph;

ii. Name, place and date of birth;

iii. Gender, address, telephone number, e.t.c.[223]

The information may be sent electronically or submitted onsite in the institution's branches or agent's office.[224]

Evidence of information provided by a customer or verification of same is not required.[225]

Though Nigeria has a Centralized Biometric Identification system which requires every customer to undertake biometric capturing and generate a Bank Verification Number which they must provide to any Bank they intend to also bank with, Mobile Money

---

221 CBN (Anti-Money Laundering and Combating the Financing of Terrorism in Banks and Other Financial Institutions in Nigeria) Regulations, 2013, regulation 45 (2).

222 Central Bank of Nigeria (2016), 'Circular to Banks and Other Financial Institutions: Review of Restrictions and Limits on Levels I and II of the Tiered KYC Accounts', Available at: https://www.cbn.gov.ng/out/2016/fprd/july%202016%20circular%20tkyc%20review.pdf (accessed 6 May 2019).

223 CBN (Anti-Money Laundering and Combating the Financing of Terrorism in Banks and Other Financial Institutions in Nigeria) Regulations, 2013, regulation 45 (2).

224 CBN (Anti-Money Laundering and Combating the Financing of Terrorism in Banks and Other Financial Institutions in Nigeria) Regulations, 2013, regulation 45 (2).

225 CBN (Anti-Money Laundering and Combating the Financing of Terrorism in Banks and Other Financial Institutions in Nigeria) Regulations, 2013, regulation 45 (2).

wallet holders on Tiered KYC Level 1 are not required to provide Bank Verification Number as part of the KYC documentation.[226] This is very different from the United Kingdom's approach which makes it mandatory for a bank to verify the identity and address of an applicant even when it is a low risk account or a basic bank account.[227]

Non-verification of customer information at the account opening stage may negatively impact on information sharing mechanisms. For example, a customer who successfully opened a low value account at MTN may decide to open another low value account at Airtel, 9mobile, Ntel and Globacom for the purpose of circumventing the threshold mechanism. The customer could use different names and different addresses to open these new accounts. Since his information at MTN was not verified the customer can afford to open different accounts with different names in different telecommunication companies without being detected. With an account opened at 5 telecommunication companies, the customer would have attained a cumulative balance of one million five hundred thousand naira.

It is worth noting that the Central Bank of Nigeria (Anti-Money Laundering and Combating the Financing of Terrorism in Banks and Other Financial Institutions in Nigeria) Regulations, 2013 did not make it mandatory for a bank to verify whether a customer already holds an account with another bank before opening a low value account. This is different from the United Kingdom's approach where the United Kingdom's Payment Accounts Regulations 2015 mandates designated credit institutions to verify whether a consumer does not hold a

---

226 Central Bank of Nigeria (2017), 'Review of Daily Mobile Money Wallet Transaction and Balance Limit and Bank Verification Numbers (BVN) Requirement for Mobile Money Wallet Holders', Available at: https://www.cbn.gov.ng/out/2017/bpsd/review%20of%20daily%20mm%20wallet%20transaction%20&%20bvn%20requirement%20for%20mobile%20money%20wallet%20holders.pdf (accessed 6 May 2019).

227 United Kingdom Payment Accounts Regulations 2015, regulation 23 (3).

payment account with any United Kingdom credit institution, and in a situation where the bank determines that a customer does hold a payment account with another credit institution, the bank must not open a basic account for that customer.[228] This is not the case for Nigeria.

5.2 MEDIUM VALUE ACCOUNTS

Medium Value Accounts can be opened face to face at any branch of a telecommunications company by agents for enterprises (used for mass payroll) or by the account holder. Evidence of basic customer information is required at this level. ID verification and monitoring by telecommunications companies are required also.

The main characteristics of this account are:

i. Accounts can be contracted by phone or at the institution's website;

ii. Accounts may be linked to a mobile phone;

iii. They may be used for funds transfers within Nigeria only;

iv. The accounts are strictly savings;

v. No amount is required for opening of the accounts.[229]

---

[228] United Kingdom Payment Accounts Regulations 2015, regulation 23 (3). See also Santander (2018), 'Customer identification requirements for UK residents', Available at https://www.santander.co.uk/csdlvlr/BlobServer?blobtable=MungoBlobs&blobkey=id&blobcol=urldata&blobheader=application%2Fpdf&blobheadervalue1=inline%3Bfilename%3DCustomer+Identification+Requirements+do-ec-368.pdf&blobwhere=1314024309911&blobheadername1=Content-Disposition (accessed 3 April 2018); Barclays (2018), 'Identification for bank accounts: What ID do I need to open a bank account?', Available at: https://www.barclays.co.uk/current-accounts/what-do-i-need-to-open-a-bank-account/ (accessed 2 April 2018).

[229] CBN (Anti-Money Laundering and Combating the Financing of Terrorism in Banks and Other Financial Institutions in Nigeria) Regulations, 2013, regulation 45 (3).

Maximum single deposit of one hundred thousand naira and a maximum cumulative balance of five hundred thousand naira are allowed at any time for all accounts in this level[230] except for mobile money wallets which allows for a daily cumulative transaction limit of two hundred thousand naira and a cumulative balance limit of five hundred thousand naira.[231] Where cross-checking of client's ID information is not completed at the point of account opening, withdrawal should be denied.

Evidence of basic customer information (such as passport photograph, name, place and date of birth, gender, address, etc) is required. These may be forwarded electronically or submitted on-site in the institution's branches or agents' offices.

Customer information obtained are to be verified against similar information contained in the official data-bases e.g. National Identity Management Commission (NIMC), Independent National Electoral Commission (INEC) Voters Register, Federal Road Safety Commission (FSRC) etc.[232]

5.3 HIGH VALUE ACCOUNTS

For High Value Accounts, telecommunications companies are required to obtain, verify and maintain copies of all the required

[230] Central Bank of Nigeria (2016), 'Circular to Banks and Other Financial Institutions: Review of Restrictions and Limits on Levels I and II of the Tiered KYC Accounts', Available at: https://www.cbn.gov.ng/out/2016/fprd/july%202016%20circular%20tkyc%20review.pdf (accessed 6 May 2019).

[231] Central Bank of Nigeria (2017), 'Review of Daily Mobile Money Wallet Transaction and Balance Limit and Bank Verification Numbers (BVN) Requirement for Mobile Money Wallet Holders', Available at: https://www.cbn.gov.ng/out/2017/bpsd/review%20of%20daily%20mm%20wallet%20transaction%20&%20bvn%20requirement%20for%20mobile%20money%20wallet%20holders.pdf (accessed 6 May 2019).

[232] CBN (Anti-Money Laundering and Combating the Financing of Terrorism in Banks and Other Financial Institutions in Nigeria) Regulations, 2013, regulation 45 (3).

documents for opening of high value accounts. Account is to be opened at the institution's branches by physical presence of the prospective customer.

The main characteristics of the account are:

i. These accounts could be both savings and current;

ii. No amount is required for opening of accounts;

iii. Level Three Mobile Banking Products Are Allowed;

iv. No Limit is placed on the cumulative balance.[233]

The daily cumulative transaction limit for mobile money wallets is five million naira while the cumulative balance limit is unlimited, as provided in the three-tiered KYC requirements. Such products are subject to the Central Bank of Nigeria Regulatory Framework for Mobile Payments Services in Nigeria.[234]

It is important to note that maximum deposits and balances are specified only for the low-value and medium-value categories of accounts. In compliance with and in the spirit of the Central Bank of Nigeria monetary policy and financial inclusion, there is no minimum opening amount for accounts in all the levels.[235]

5.4. CONCLUSION

233 CBN (Anti-Money Laundering and Combating the Financing of Terrorism in Banks and Other Financial Institutions in Nigeria) Regulations, 2013, regulation 45 (4).

234 Central Bank of Nigeria (2017), 'Review of Daily Mobile Money Wallet Transaction and Balance Limit and Bank Verification Numbers (BVN) Requirement for Mobile Money Wallet Holders', Available at: https://www.cbn.gov.ng/out/2017/bpsd/review%20of%20daily%20mm%20wallet%20transaction%20&%20bvn%20requirement%20for%20mobile%20money%20wallet%20holders.pdf (accessed 6 May 2019).

235 CBN (Anti-Money Laundering and Combating the Financing of Terrorism in Banks and Other Financial Institutions in Nigeria) Regulations, 2013, regulation 45 (4).

The **Central Bank of Nigeria (Anti-Money Laundering and Combating the Financing of Terrorism in Banks and Other Financial Institutions in Nigeria) Regulations, 2013** should be amended to prohibit financial institutions/telecommunications companies from opening more than one low value account for Mobile Money wallet holders. In other words, financial institutions/telecommunications companies should be mandated to verify whether a customer already holds an account with another bank before opening a low value account, and in a situation where the bank/telecommunication company determines that a customer does hold a payment account with another credit institution, the bank/telecommunications company should not open a basic account for that customer.

Verification can be done by mandating all bank customers to provide their Bank Verification Number before an account can be opened. This is the approach being adopted by the United Kingdom's **Payment Accounts Regulations 2015.** This approach will positively impact on account monitoring procedures; customer identification and verification will reduce the risk of impersonation fraud and identity theft while still promoting financial inclusion.

CHAPTER 6

THE TELECOMMUNICATIONS REGULATORY FRAMEWORK AND ITS EFFECT ON FUNDAMENTAL HUMAN RIGHTS

Chapter Four of the Constitution of the Federal Republic of Nigeria secures the fundamental rights of Nigerians.

Fundamental Human rights are rights inherent to all human beings, whatever our nationality, place of residence, sex, national or ethnic origin, colour, religion, language, or any other status. We are all equally entitled to our human rights without discrimination. These rights are all interrelated, interdependent and indivisible.[236]

This chapter critically analyses the **Telecommunications Regulatory Framework** to determine if it interferes with the fundamental rights of Nigerians.

6.1 RIGHT TO RESPECT FOR PRIVATE AND FAMILY LIFE

Section 37 of the 1999 Constitution protects an interesting set of rights. According to Section 37, everyone has the right to respect for his private and family life.[237]

[236] United Nations Human Rights Office of the High Commissioner, (2016), 'What are human rights', Available at: http://www.ohchr.org/EN/Issues/Pages/WhatareHumanRights.aspx (accessed 29 February 2016).

[237] Constitution of the Federal Republic of Nigeria, 1999, s. 37.

Respect for private life comprises to a certain degree the right to establish and develop relationships with other human beings.[238] Family Life on the other hand encompasses marriage-based relationships and other de facto 'family ties' where parties are living together outside marriage. A child born out of such a relationship is ipso jure part of that 'family unit' from the moment of its birth and by the very fact of it.[239] Both rights can be violated where there is an interference with a person's relationship.[240] As regards private life, such interference could be with the relationship of a person with his lover while as regards family life, such interference could be with the relationship of a person with his wife or his child. Such interference may amount to a violation of a person's right when it is not justified.[241] An interference comes into play where a law that exists directly affects the private life of an individual, in such a way that such an individual would have to respect the law and be mandated to do something which may prevent him from developing his relationship with some people and if he does not do it, he could be liable to criminal prosecution.[242]

While **Regulation 10(2) of the Nigerian Communications Commission (Registration of Telephone Subscribers) Regulations, 2011** makes provision for Data Protection and Confidentiality by expressly stating that a Subscriber information shall not be released to a licensee, Security Agency or any other person, where such release of Subscriber Information would

---

238 Niemietz v. Germany (1993) 16 EHRR 97, para. 27. See also Evans V United Kingdom (2008) 46 EHRR 34, para. 71.

239 Kroon and Others v. the Netherlands [1994] ECHR 18535/91, para. 30, See also Keegan V Ireland [1994] ECHR 16969/90, para. 44, See also Mikulic V Croatia [2002] ECHR 53176/99, para. 51

240 Dudgeon v. United Kingdom (1982) 4 EHRR 149, para. 43.

241 Dudgeon v. United Kingdom (1982) 4 EHRR 149, para. 43 which is to the effect that an interference will not be justified unless it is in accordance with the law, has an aim or aims that is or are legitimate and is necessary in a democratic society for the aforesaid aim or aims.

242 See Dudgeon v. United Kingdom (1982) 4 EHRR 149, para. 41.

constitute a breach of the Constitution or any other Act of the National Assembly, for the time being in force in Nigeria or where such release of subscriber information would constitute a threat to national security, the same **Nigerian Communications Commission (Registration of Telephone Subscribers) Regulations, 2011** provides in **Regulation 8(1)** that Notwithstanding the provisions of these Regulations restricting access to Subscriber Information on the Central Database and subject to the provisions of any Act of the National Assembly, subscriber information on the Central Database shall be provided only to Security Agencies; provided that a prior written request is received by the Commission from an official of the requesting Security Agency who is not below the rank of an Assistant Commissioner of Police or a co-ordinate rank in any other Security Agency.

Regulation 8(1) of the Nigerian Communications Commission (Registration of Telephone Subscribers) Regulations, 2011 could be justified to the extent that such interference is in the interest of the general public as the intention of that proviso is to support investigations against terrorism and money laundering. But the purported violation does not come with a Court Order.

This provision is not in line with Section 13 of the **Nigerian Money Laundering Prohibition Act 2011 (as amended)** which provides as follows:

"The Commission, Agency, Central Bank of Nigeria or other regulatory authorities **pursuant to an order of the Federal High Court obtained upon an ex-parte application supported by a sworn declaration made by the Chairman of the Commission or an authorized officer of the Central Bank of Nigeria or other regulatory authorities justifying the request, may in order to identify and locate proceeds, properties, objects or other things related to the commission of an offence under this Act, the**

Economic and Financial Crimes Commission (Establishment) Act or any other law—

(a) place any bank account or any other account comparable to a bank account under surveillance;

(b) obtain access to any suspected computer system;

(c) obtain communication of any authentic instrument or private contract, together with all bank, financial and commercial records, when the account, the telephone line or computer system is used by any person suspected of taking part in a transaction involving the proceeds of a financial or other crime."

The absence of judicial review of customer information requests in **Regulation 8(1) of the Nigerian Communications Commission (Registration of Telephone Subscribers) Regulations, 2011** could leave room for abuse.

Security Agencies may request for information, even when the individual concerned is not the subject of an intelligence inquiry.

The above may lead to an unnecessary interference with a person's right to a private life, and such interference cannot be justified.[243]

6.2 DIRECT DISCRIMINATION

Section 42 (1) of the 1999 Constitution provides that:

A citizen of Nigeria of a particular community, ethnic group, place of origin, sex, religion or political opinion shall not, by reason only that he is such a person:

[243] The privacy of citizens, their homes, correspondence, telephone conversations and telegraphic communications is guaranteed and protected by s. 37 of the Constitution of the Federal Republic of Nigeria, 1999. For more on this, see Niemietz v. Germany (1993) 16 EHRR 97, para. 27, see also Evans v. United Kingdom (2008) 46 EHRR 34, para. 71. See Dudgeon v. United Kingdom (1982) 4 EHRR 149, para. 43, see also Pretty v. UK (2002) 35 EHRR 1 para. 61.

(a) be subjected either expressly by, or in the practical application of, any law in force in Nigeria or any executive or administrative action of the government, to disabilities or restrictions to which citizens of Nigeria of other communities, ethnic groups, places of origin, sex, religion or political opinions are not made subject; or

(b) be accorded either expressly by, or in the practical application of, any law in force in Nigeria or any such executive or administrative action, any privilege or advantage that is not accorded to citizens of Nigeria of other communities, ethnic groups, places of origin, sex, religion or political opinions.

This section will determine if the **Guidelines for Licensing and Regulation of Payment Service Banks issued by the Central Bank of Nigeria** directly discriminates against Small telecommunications Companies. It will determine this by looking into the conditions that must be cumulatively met in order for direct discrimination to be considered to have occurred. These conditions include differential treatment, prohibited grounds, without objective and reasonable justification and no reasonable relationship of proportionality.[244]

6.2.1 DIFFERENTIAL TREATMENT

One of the conditions that must exist before direct discrimination can occur is that there must be a given difference in treatment, which may concern the exercise of any right set forth by law.[245]

---

[244] Asika v. Atuanya (2008) 17 NWLR (Pt. 1117) 484 at 513, see also Timothy v. Oforka (2008) 9 NWLR (Pt. 1091) 204, see Belgian Linguistic Case, (1979 -80) 1 EHRR 252, para. 10, see also Swedish Engine Driver's Union v. Sweden (1979-80) 1 EHRR, 617, paras. 45, 47, 48, see National Union of Belgian Police v. Belgium (1979 -80) 1 EHRR 578, paras. 44, 46, see also Engel and Others v. The Netherlands (No.1) (1979-80) 1 EHRR 647, para. 72, See also The Republic of Ireland v. The United Kingdom (1979-80) 2 EHRR 25, para. 226.

[245] Belgian Linguistic Case (1979 -80) 1 EHRR 252, Para 10, see also National Union of Belgian Police v. Belgium (1979 -80) 1 EHRR 578 paras. 44, 46.

The Central Bank of Nigeria Guidelines for Licensing and Regulation of Payment Service Banks does create a difference in treatment.

In the **Guidelines for Licensing and Regulation of Payment Service Banks** issued by the Central Bank of Nigeria (CBN), the apex bank had pegged the minimum capital deposit for telecommunications companies with intent to deepen financial inclusion in Nigeria through mobile money services at N5 billion.[246]

While mandating that an evidence of the payment of N5 billion must be provided when applying for an Approval in Principle, the CBN granted the telecommunications companies a provisional approval to apply for a Payment Service Bank license through a subsidiary company.[247]

The telecommunications companies that have indicated interest in driving the financial inclusion plans of the Federal Government are MTN, Airtel, 9mobile, Ntel, and Globacom.[248] This are large telecommunications companies.[249] Smaller institutions are yet to indicate interest in the Payment Services Scheme for the likely reason that they may not be able to afford the N5 billion minimum capital deposit. This may negatively impact on financial inclusion but the impact will not be huge since the big telecommunications

---

246 The Central Bank of Nigeria Guidelines for Licensing and Regulation of Payment Service Banks 2018, para. 6.6.

247 The Central Bank of Nigeria Guidelines for Licensing and Regulation of Payment Service Banks 2018, para. 10.2.

248 The Punch (2018), 'Mobile money: CBN requests N5bn capital investment from telcos', Available at: https://punchng.com/mobile-money-cbn-requests-n5bn-capital-investment-from-telcos/ (accessed 5th of April, 2019).

249 Presently, the major telecommunication companies operating in Nigeria are Airtel, 9mobile, Globacom and MTN. Airtel has 44,970,973 subscribers in Nigeria, 9mobile has 16,385,317 subscribers, Globacom has 45,603,638 subscribers and MTN has 66,665,378 subscribers.

companies as mentioned above cover majority of Nigerians living at home.

6.2.2 PROHIBITED GROUNDS

Discrimination could be on the ground of sex, race, colour, national or social origin, property, birth or other status.[250]

Paragraph 6.6 of the **Central Bank of Nigeria Guidelines for Licensing and Regulation of Payment Service Banks** does discriminate on the ground of a person's financial status.

6.2.3 NO OBJECTIVE AND REASONABLE JUSTIFICATION

The third condition for a direct discrimination to occur is that the distinction or difference in treatment would have no objective and reasonable justification. The existence of such a justification must be assessed in relation to the aim and effects of the measure under consideration.[251] This means that the aims and objectives of **paragraph 6.6 of the Central Bank of Nigeria Guidelines for Licensing and Regulation of Payment Service Banks.**

The Central Bank of Nigeria (CBN) has explained the rationale behind the 5-billion-naira minimum cash deposit. According to the CBN, the aim and objective of **paragraph 6.6 of the Central Bank of Nigeria Guidelines for Licensing and Regulation of Payment Service Banks** is to further deepen financial inclusion.

The above reason given by the CBN for the 5-billion-naira minimum cash deposit requirement is not reasonable as financial inclusion could be more enhanced if more telecommunications companies had access to the payment service license.

---

[250] Constitution of the Federal Republic of Nigeria, 1999, s. 42 (1).

[251] Belgian Linguistic Case (1979 -80) 1 EHRR 252, para. 10, see also National Union of Belgian Police v. Belgium (1979 -80) 1 EHRR 578, para. 46.

6.2.4 NO REASONABLE RELATIONSHIP OF PROPORTIONALITY

An individual's right to equality is likewise violated when it is clearly established that there is no reasonable relationship of proportionality between the means employed and the aim.[252] In other words, the State must strike a fair balance between the protection of the interests of the community, and respect for the rights and freedoms safeguarded by the Constitution.[253] Hence, if the measure in question creates no impediment to the exercise of the individual rights enshrined in the Constitution, then it would be a fair balance.[254]

Paragraph 6.6 of the **Central Bank of Nigeria Guidelines for Licensing and Regulation of Payment Service Banks** does interfere with an individual's right to respect for private and family life. In other words, its measures directly discriminate against companies who cannot afford the minimum cash deposit of 5 billion naira.

Therefore, Paragraph 6.6 of the **Central Bank of Nigeria Guidelines for Licensing and Regulation of Payment Service Banks** does not strike a fair balance between the protection of the interests of the community and respect for the rights and freedoms safeguarded by the Constitution of the Federal Republic of Nigeria.

6.3 CONCLUSION

---

[252] Constitution of the Federal Republic of Nigeria, 1999, s. 42 (1), see Belgian Linguistic Case (1979 -80) 1 EHRR 252, para. 10, see also National Union of Belgian Police v. Belgium (1979 -80) 1 EHRR 578, para. 46.

[253] Constitution of the Federal Republic of Nigeria, 1999, s. 42 (1), see Belgian Linguistic Case (1979 -80) 1 EHRR 252, para. 7.

[254] See Belgian Linguistic Case (1979 -80) 1 EHRR 252, para. 13.

This chapter critically analysed the Telecommunications Regulatory Framework to determine that Regulation 10(2) of the Nigerian Communications Commission (Registration of Telephone Subscribers) Regulations, 2011 and Paragraph 6.6 of the Central Bank of Nigeria Guidelines for Licensing and Regulation of Payment Service Banks interferes with the fundamental rights of Nigerians.

In view of the above findings, this chapter makes the following recommendations:

i. A request for customer information, by Security Agents, should be made pursuant to an order of the Federal High Court obtained upon an ex-parte application supported by a sworn declaration by an authorized officer of the centre, justifying the request for customer information.
ii. The Central Bank of Nigeria should reduce the minimum cash deposit from 5 billion naira to 500 million naira. This will allow for fair competition amongst telecommunications companies and eliminate any form of differential treatment that could lead to a possible violation of a company's right to equality.

APPENDIX 1

CENTRAL BANK OF NIGERIA

GUIDELINES FOR LICENSING AND REGULATION OF PAYMENT SERVICE BANKS IN NIGERIA

1 INTRODUCTION

The Central Bank of Nigeria (CBN), in furtherance of its mandate to promoting a sound financial system in Nigeria and the need to enhance access to financial services for low income earners and unbanked segments of the society, continues to be innovative in deepening the financial services sector.

The National Financial Inclusion Strategy (NFIS) seeks to ensure that over 80% of the bankable adults in Nigeria have access to financial services by 2020. The Central Bank of Nigeria in collaboration with stakeholders launched the NFIS on 23rd October, 2012 with a view to reducing the exclusion rate to 20% by 2020.

Despite several initiatives including the Introduction of Microfinance banking, Agent Banking, Tiered Know-Your-Customer Requirements and Mobile Money Operation (MMO) in pursuit of this objective, the inclusion rate remains below expectation.

The CBN, in the circumstance and in collaboration with critical stakeholders in the digital financial ecosystem, such as the Nigerian Communication Commission, Commercial Banks, Mobile Money Operators and Telecommunication companies have conducted several study tours of other jurisdictions that have made significant progress in driving financial inclusion.

In view of the challenges to effective outreach to rural communities as well as the need to complement the services provided by other licensed entities, the CBN issues this draft regulation to provide for the licensing and operations of Payment Service Banks (PSBs) in Nigeria. PSBs are expected to leverage on mobile and digital services to enhance financial inclusion and stimulate economic activities at the grassroots through the provision of financial services. PSBs will also enable high-volume low-value transactions in remittance services, micro-savings and withdrawal services in a secured technology-driven environment.

Accordingly, PSBs are envisioned to facilitate high-volume low-value transactions in remittance services, micro-savings and withdrawal services in a secured technology-driven environment to further deepen financial inclusion and help in attaining the policy of 20% exclusion rate by 2020

This draft Guidelines is being issued in pursuant to the CBN Act 2007 and BOFIA 1991 (as amended). It covers the definition; objectives; eligible promoters; licensing requirements; corporate governance; business conduct; and permissible activities. The requirements for prudential regulation; supervision; Know Your Customer (KYC) as well as Risk Management of the proposed Payment Service Banks in Nigeria are also covered.

2. OBJECTIVES OF PAYMENT SERVICE BANKS

The key objective of setting up Payment Service Banks is to enhance financial inclusion in rural areas by increasing access to deposit products and payment/remittance services to small businesses, low-income households and other entities through high-volume low-value transactions in a secured technology-driven environment.

3. STRUCTURE OF PAYMENT SERVICE BANKS

Payment Service Banks shall:

i. Operate mostly in the rural centres and unbanked locations, with not less than 50% physical access points in 'rural areas' as defined by the CBN from time to time;

ii. Establish ATMs in some of these areas;

iii. Be at liberty to operate through banking agents (in line with the CBN's Guidelines for the Regulation of Agent Banking and Agent Banking Relationships in Nigeria);

iv. Use other channels including electronic platforms to reach-out to its customers;

v. Establish coordinating centres in clusters of outlets to superintend and control the activities of the various access points and banking agents;

vi. Be technology-driven and shall conform to best practices on data storage; security and integrity;

vii. Set up consumer help desks at its main office and coordinating centres to attend to consumer-related issues.

4. PERMISSIBLE AND NON-PERMISSIBLE ACTIVITIES

4.1 Permissible Activities

Payment Service Banks shall carry out the following activities:

i. Maintain savings accounts and accept deposits from individuals and small businesses, which shall be covered by the deposit insurance scheme;

ii. Carry out payments and remittance (including inbound cross-border personal remittances) services through various channels within Nigeria;

iii. Issue debit and pre-paid cards;

iv. Operate electronic purse;

v. Invest in FGN and CBN securities; and

vi. Carry out such other activities as may be prescribed by the CBN from time to time.

4.2 Non-Permissible Activities

Payment Service Banks shall not carry out the following activities;

i. Grant any form of loans, advances and guarantees;

ii. Trade in the foreign exchange market except as in 4.1 (ii) above;

iii. Insurance underwriting;

iv. Undertake any other transaction which is not prescribed by this Payment Service Bank guidelines;

v. Establish any subsidiary except as prescribed in the CBN Regulation on the Scope of Banking and Ancillary Matters, No 3, 2010

The Payment Service Banks shall use the words "Payment Service Bank" in its name to differentiate it from other banks.

5. ELIGIBLE PROMOTERS

i. Banking Agents

ii. Telecommunications companies (Telcos), through subsidiaries

iii. Retail chains (Supermarkets)

iv. Mobile Money Operators (MMOs that desire to convert to Payment Service Banks shall comply with the requirement of this Guideline)

The CBN may from time to time, consider any other entity as the above list is not exhaustive.

6. LICENSING REQUIREMENTS

The promoters of Payment Service Banks shall be required to submit a formal application for the grant of a Payment Service Bank licence addressed to the Governor of the Central Bank of Nigeria.

The application for a licence shall be preceded by a formal presentation of the proposal to the CBN's management.

6.1 Requirements for grant of Approval-In-Principle (AIP)

A) The application shall be accompanied with the following:

i. A non-refundable application fee of N500,000 (Five Hundred Thousand Naira Only) in bank draft, payable to the Central Bank of Nigeria or such other amount that may be specified by the CBN from time to time;

ii. Evidence of minimum capital deposit in line with Section 6.6 of this Regulation, to be verified by the CBN;

iii. Evidence of name reservation with the Corporate Affairs Commission (CAC);

iv. Detailed business plan or feasibility report which shall, at a minimum, include:

a) Objectives of the Payment Service Bank;

b) Justification for the application;

c) Ownership structure in a tabular form indicating the name of proposed investor(s), profession/business and percentage shareholdings;

d) Detailed bio-data/resume of proposed shareholders;

e) Sources of funding of the proposed equity contribution for each investor;

f) Where the source of funding the equity contribution is a loan, such shall be a long-term facility of at least 7-year tenor and shall not be taken from the Nigerian banking system;

g) Board and board committee charters stating the roles and responsibilities of the board and sub-committees;

h) Criteria for selecting board members;

i) Board composition and directors' detailed resumes. Note - the total number of directors shall be between 5 and 7, including at least two independent directors.

j) Completed Fitness and Propriety Questionnaire; and sworn declaration of net worth executed by the proposed shareholders, directors and management personnel;

k) Organizational structure, showing functional units, responsibilities, reporting relationships and grade of heads of departments/units;

I) List of proposed top management staff (AGM and above) and detailed curriculum vitae stating their qualification (including photocopies of academic and professional credentials), experience, records of accomplishments;

m) Schedule of services to be rendered;

n) Five-year financial projection of the proposed bank indicating expected growth, profitability and the underlying assumptions.

o) Details of information technology requirements and facilities; and

p) Bank Verification Number (BVN) and Tax Clearance Certificate of each member of the Board and significant shareholders.

v. For corporate investors, promoters shall forward the following additional documents:

a) Certificate of Incorporation and certified true copies of other incorporation documents.

b) Board resolution supporting the company's decision to invest in the equity shares of the proposed bank;

c) Names and addresses (business and residential) of owners, directors and their related companies, if any;

d) Audited financial statements & reports of the company and Tax Clearance Certificate for the immediate past 3 years; and

vi. Draft copy of the company's Memorandum and Articles of Association (MEMART). At a minimum, the MEMART shall contain the following information:

a) Proposed name of the bank

b) Objects clause

c) Subscribers to the MEMART

d) Procedure for amendment

e) Procedure for share transfer/disposal

f) Appointment of directors

vii. A written and duly executed undertaking by the promoters that the bank will be adequately capitalized for the volume and character of its business at all times, and that the CBN shall have powers to supervise and regulate its operations;

viii. For regulated foreign institutional investors, an approval or a 'no objection letter' from the regulatory authority in the country of domicile;

ix. Shareholders' agreement providing for disposal/transfer of shares as well as authorization, amendments, waivers, reimbursement of expenses;

x. Statement of intent to invest in the bank by each investor;

xi. Technical Services Agreement;

xii. Detailed Manuals and Policies, particularly:

a) Manual of Operations;

b) Asset/Liability Management Policy (ALM Policy) that highlights the bank's permissible assets and liabilities, sets the standards for managing its interest rate, duration risk and liquidity risk, and delineates the composition, duties, and operational procedures for the bank's Asset/Liability Management Committee;

c) Financial Management Policy that highlights the bank's financial management policies and procedures, and system of internal controls. The Policy should include, at a minimum:

i. Accounting policies and principles;

ii. Roles and responsibilities of the senior management officials responsible for financial management;

iii. Treasury operations, including funds management, vouchers, payroll and procurement;

iv. Financial record keeping and reporting; and

v. Auditing and periodic testing of internal controls.

d) Anti-Money Laundering and Combating Financing of Terrorism (AML/CFT) Policy;

e) Enterprise-Wide Risk Management Framework;

f) Code of Ethics and Business Conduct that specifies high standards for honesty, integrity, and impartiality for the bank's employees, officers, and directors and provides guidance on avoiding conflicts of interest, self-dealing, and other types of impropriety as specified in the BOFIA or by the Bank. Every director and officer of the bank shall be required to sign the Code of Ethics and Business Conduct;

xiii) Any other information that the CBN may require from time to time.

C) Following the receipt of an application with complete and satisfactory documentation, the CBN shall communicate its decision to the applicant within 90 days. Where the CBN is satisfied with the application, it shall issue an Approval-in-Principle (AIP) to the applicant.

D) The proposed bank shall not incorporate/register its name with the CAC until an AIP has been obtained from the CBN in writing, a copy of which shall be presented to the CAC for registration.

6.2 Requirements for Granting of Final License

Not later than six (6) months after obtaining the A.I.P, the promoters of a proposed Payment Service Bank shall submit application for the grant of a final licence to the CBN. The application shall be accompanied by the following:

i. Non-refundable licensing fee of N2,000,000.00 (Two Million Naira Only) in a bank draft payable to the Central Bank of Nigeria;

ii. Evidence of capital contribution made by each shareholder;

iii. Certified true copy (CTC) of Certificate of Incorporation of the bank;

iv. CTC of MEMART;

v. CTC of Form CAC 1.1;

vi. Evidence of location of Head Office (rented or owned) for the take-off of the business;

vii. Schedule of changes, if any, in the Board, Management and Shareholding after the grant of AIP;

viii. Evidence of ability to meet technical requirements and modern infrastructural facilities such as office equipment, computers, telecommunications, to perform the bank's operations and meet CBN and other regulatory requirements;

ix. Copies of letters of offer and acceptance of employment in respect of the management team;

x. Comprehensive plan on the commencement of the bank's operations with milestones and timelines for roll-out of key payment channels; and

xi. Board and staff training programme.

6.3 Conduct of Pre-Licencing Inspection

As a requirement to the grant of final licence, the CBN shall conduct an inspection of the premises and facilities of the proposed bank to, amongst others:

a. Check the physical structure of the office building and infrastructure provided for take-off of the PSB;

b. Sight the original copies of the documents submitted in support of the application for license;

c. Meet with the Board and Management team whose CVs had earlier been submitted to the CBN;

d. Verify the capital contributions of the promoters; and

e. Verify the integration of its infrastructure with the National Payments System.

6.4 Requirements for commencement of operations

The bank shall, through a letter, inform the CBN of its readiness to commence operations and such information shall be accompanied by one copy each of the following:

i. Shareholders' Register;

ii. Share certificate issued to each investor;

iii. Opening statement of affairs signed by directors and auditors;

iv. Enterprise Risk Management Framework (ERMF);

v. Internal control policy;

vi. Minutes of pre-commencement board meeting; and

vii. Evidence of integration of their infrastructure with the National Payments System.

6.5 Post-commencement Requirements

A Payment Service Bank shall:

i. Comply with all guidelines and regulations issued by the CBN and other sector regulators.

ii. Maintain adequate accounting system and keep records that capture information which reflect the financial condition of the bank.

iii. Maintain an unimpaired minimum capital at all times.

iv. Always comply with the requirements incidental to the authorization to perform banking operations as stipulated by the CBN.

6.6 Financial Requirements

The financial requirements which may be varied as the CBN considers necessary are as follows:

Minimum capital	N5,000,000,000.00
Non-refundable application Fee	N500,000.00
Non-Refundable Licensing Fee	N2,000,000.00

Promoters should note that in compliance with BOFIA, the investment of the Share Capital Deposit shall be subject to availability of investment instruments and upon the grant of license or otherwise, the Bank shall refund the sum deposited to the applicant, together with the investment income, if any, after deducting administrative expenses and tax on the income.

7. CORPORATE GOVERNANCE

7.1 The provisions of the CBN code of corporate governance for banks shall be applicable to PSBs.

7.2 The provisions of the Revised Assessment Criteria for Approved Persons' Regime for Financial Institutions shall be applicable to PSBs.

7.3 Where a PSB is a related company to an existing infrastructure provider which provides services to other financial institutions, the PSB shall ensure that its dealings with the infrastructure provider are at arms-length.

8. BUSINESS CONDUCT (FAIR COMPETITION)

The following conditions shall guide business conduct between PSBs and their Parent companies (where applicable)

i. Parent companies of a PSB, which render services to its PSB shall be open to extend similar services to other PSBs that so desire at the same terms and conditions.

ii. Parent companies of PSBs are prohibited from offering any preferential treatment, which negate fair competition, to its subsidiary.

iii. Preferential treatment by a Parent company shall, among others, include:

a. Precluding its subsidiary's competitor from using its infrastructure or services.

b. Offering lower quality of service to its subsidiary's competitors.

c. Offering such infrastructure or services at differential pricing

d. Precluding any specific infrastructure or service as may be prescribed by the CBN from time to time.

e. Failure of Parent companies to abide by this fair competition clause may lead to revocation of license of the PSB.

9. PRUDENTIAL REGULATION

9.1 Minimum Paid-Up Capital and Capital Reserves

i. The Minimum Paid-up Capital of PSBs shall be N5,000,000,000.00 (Five Billion Naira Only) or such other amount that may be prescribed by the CBN from time to time.

ii. Maintenance of Statutory Reserves by PSBs shall be as applicable to DMBs and in line with Section 16 of BOFIA or as may be prescribed by the CBN from time to time.

iii. The CBN may require a PSB to maintain additional capital as appropriate in respect of specific risks faced by the bank.

9.2 Payment of Dividend

A PSB shall not declare or pay dividend on its shares until it has:

i. Completely written-off all its preliminary and pre-operational expenses;

ii. Made adequate provisions to the satisfaction of the CBN for actual and contingent losses;

iii. Satisfied the minimum Capital Adequacy Ratio requirement as stipulated in 6.3 of this Regulation;

iv. Met all matured obligations;

v. Obtained the approval of the CBN in respect thereof; and

vi. Comply with all relevant CBN regulations on dividend payments.

9.3 Capital Adequacy Ratio

i. The capital adequacy ratio of a PSB shall be measured as a percentage of the shareholders' funds unimpaired by losses to its risk weighted assets. The minimum Capital Adequacy Ratio (Capital/Risk Weighted Assets Ratio) for PSBs shall be 10 per cent or as may be prescribed by the CBN from time to time.

ii. Capital measurement approach for PSBs shall be as applicable to Deposit Money Banks (DMBs) or as may be prescribed by the CBN from time to time.

9.4 Investment of Deposit Liabilities

i. PSBs shall be required to maintain not less than 75% of their deposit liabilities in Treasury Bills (TBs) and other short-term federal government debt instruments at any point in time.

ii. PSBs shall have the privilege to make their investments from the CBN window

iii. All funds in excess of the PSBs' operational float should be placed with any DMB.

9.5 Participation in Payment and Settlement System

Payment Service Banks shall participate in the payment and settlement system and have access to the inter-bank and the CBN collateralised repo window for its temporary liquidity management.

9.6 Cash Reserve Requirement

Cash Reserve Requirement shall be prescribed by the CBN from time to time.

9.7 Limit of Investment in Fixed Assets (Including Branch Expansion)

Investments in fixed assets by PSBs shall be as applicable to DMBs or as may be prescribed by the CBN from time to time.

9.8 Revaluation of Fixed Assets

Requirement for revaluation of fixed asset shall be in line with the Prudential Guidelines for DMBs or as may be prescribed by the CBN from time to time.

10. SUPERVISION OF PAYMENT SERVICE BANKS

10.1 Payment Service Banks shall be supervised by the Central Bank of Nigeria.

10.2 Where a Payment Service Bank is a subsidiary or associate of a legal entity, the entity shall be required to comply with all extant CBN Guidelines and circulars.

10.3 Payment Service Banks shall be required to render returns to the Banking Supervision Department in a format and frequency as may be prescribed by the CBN from time to time.

11. KNOW YOUR CUSTOMER (KYC) REQUIREMENTS

PSBs shall comply with relevant provisions of the Money Laundering (Prohibition) Act, 2011 (as amended). Terrorism Prevention Act, 2011 (as amended), CBN AML/CFT Regulations for Banks and Other Financial Institutions 2013, other extant laws and regulations on KYC issued by the CBN.

11.1 PSBs shall adopt risk-based approach in the conduct of KYC and ensure that every customer complies with the KYC requirements. All accounts shall be subjected to continuous suspicious transactions monitoring and any suspicious transactions shall be reported to the appropriate agency.

11.2 PSBs shall maintain robust, effective and efficient AML/CFT software solutions to monitor thresholds as may be prescribed by the Bank from time to time. They shall also designate and dedicate officers to monitor compliance.

12. RISK MANAGEMENT

12.1 Credit Risk Management (Including credit concentration risk)

In accordance with Section 4.2 (i) of this Regulation, PSBs are not permitted to grant any form of loans and advances, as such, the provision of credit risk management for DMBs shall not apply.

12.2 Capital Measurement Approach for Credit Risk

Without prejudice to sub-section 9.1 above, Capital measurement approach for credit risk for PSBs shall be as applicable to Deposit Money Banks (DMBs) or as may be prescribed by the CBN from time to time.

12.3 Management of other Risks

Management of other Risks (e.g. Market, Operational, Liquidity, Strategic, and Reputational Risks) shall be as applicable to DMBs or as may be prescribed by the CBN from time to time.

12.4 Internal Controls

The provisions regarding internal controls, audit and compliance by the PSBs shall be as applicable to DMBs, with appropriate enhancements to take care of the Information System related aspects and operations through agents.

13. REVOCATION OF LICENSE

This shall be in line with the provision of BOFIA or through voluntary liquidation subject to the approval of the CBN.

FINANCIAL POLICY AND REGULATION DEPARTMENT
OCTOBER 2018

APPENDIX 2

CENTRAL BANK OF NIGERIA

REGULATORY FRAMEWORK FOR MOBILE MONEY SERVICES IN NIGERIA

Table of Content

16. Consumer Protection and Dispute Resolution

1.0 Introduction

A robust payments system is vital for effective monetary policy implementation and the promotion of economic efficiency. The introduction of mobile telephony in Nigeria, its rapid growth and adoption and the identification of person to person payments as a practical strategy for financial inclusion, has made it imperative to adopt the mobile channel as a means of driving financial inclusion of the unbanked. These factors underscore the decision of the Central Bank of Nigeria to issue this regulatory framework to create an enabling environment for the orderly introduction and management of mobile payment services in Nigeria. The framework defines the regulatory environment as a policy path towards achieving availability, acceptance and usage of mobile payment services.

Mobile payment has evolved as a veritable channel for facilitating the growth of commerce. The use of the mobile phone for the initiation, authorization and confirmation of the transfer of value out of a current, savings or stored value account has been recognized as a development that is expanding the growth of commerce among both the financially included and non-included units in the economy.

This regulatory framework addresses business rules governing the operation of mobile payment services, and specifies basic functionalities expected of any mobile payment service and solution in Nigeria. It identifies the participants and defines their expected roles and responsibilities in providing mobile payment services in the system. In addition, it sets the basis for the regulation of services offered at different levels and by the participants.

The overriding vision of achieving a nationally utilized and internationally recognized payments system necessitates strategies to bring informal payment transactions into the formal system.

This framework has identified two models for the implementation of mobile money services namely;

A. Bank Led – Financial Institution(s) and/or its Consortium as Lead Initiator

B. Non-Bank Led- A corporate organisation duly licensed by the CBN as Lead Initiator

The CBN recognizes the importance of Mobile Network Operator (MNOs) in the operations of mobile money and appreciates the criticality of the infrastructure they provide. However, the telco-led model (where the lead initiator is an MNO), shall not be operational in Nigeria.

Its exclusion will enable the CBN have full control of monetary policy operations, minimise risks and ensure that the offering of financial services are driven by organizations that have been licensed by CBN to do so.

2.0 Objectives

The objectives of the regulatory framework are as follows:

A. Provision of an enabling environment for the adoption of mobile payment services in reducing cash dominance in the Nigeria economy.

B. Ensure a structured and orderly development of mobile payment services in Nigeria, with clear definition of various participants and their expected roles and responsibilities.

C. Specification of the minimum technical and business requirements for the various participants recognized for the mobile money services industry in Nigeria.

D. Provision of the basis for broad guidelines for the implementation of processes and flow of mobile payment transactions, from initiation to completion.

E. Promoting safety and effectiveness of mobile money services and thereby enhance user confidence in the services.

3.0 Scope

To achieve the above stated objectives, two types of mobile payment services are identified for operation in Nigeria:

1. The Bank-led Model: This is a model where a bank either alone or a consortium of banks, whether or not partnering with other approved organizations seek to deliver banking services leveraging on the mobile money system. This model shall be applicable in a scenario where the bank operates on stand-alone basis or in collaboration with other bank(s) and any other CBN approved organization. The Lead Initiator must be a bank or consortium of banks, and shall be legally responsible and accountable to the Central Bank of Nigeria and the end users.

2. The Non Bank-led Model: This model allows a corporate organization that has been duly licensed by the CBN to deliver mobile payment services to subscribers. The Lead Initiator must be a corporate organization (other than a deposit money bank or a telecommunication company) specifically licensed by the Central Bank of Nigeria to provide mobile payment services in Nigeria.

4.0 Participants in the Mobile Money System

This framework shall guide the activities of Participants in the provision of mobile money services.

Participants are grouped into six (6) categories:

A. Regulators

B. Mobile Money Operators

C. Infrastructure providers

D. Other Service Providers

E. Consumers

F. Mobile Money Agents

A. Regulators

The Regulators for this purpose are the Central Bank of Nigeria (CBN), Nigerian Communications Commission (NCC).

B. Mobile Money Operators

These are organizations that are licensed by the Central Bank of Nigeria to provide the system for the mobile money services. The organizations approved to perform the role of Mobile Money Operations are Banks and Corporate Organizations.

All approved Mobile Money Operators are required to provide:

1. The infrastructure (hardware, software, switching and security) for mobile payment services;

2. Business continuity and disaster recovery plans, to ensure services are always available at all times.

3. 99.99% system availability and ensure all signed on participating institutions follow same rule

Mobile Money Operators are required to connect to the National Central Switch (NCS) for the purpose of ensuring interoperability of all schemes in the system. A scheme operator can either be a bank or a licensed corporate organization.

The Mobile Money Operators are the Lead initiators for the mobile scheme and shall be responsible for ensuring that the various solutions and services within an approved mobile payment scheme meets the entire regulatory requirements as defined in this framework and as may be specified from time to time.

The Lead initiator (as an entity and as representative of other partners) shall be legally responsible and accountable to the Central Bank of Nigeria and the end user. All advertisements and public pronouncements on their scheme shall emanate and be issued by the Lead Initiator only.

b (i). Bank

The roles of the bank as a MMO include:

a. Provision of all financial services for the operation of the mobile money service.

b. Verification, approval and accountability for the credibility and integrity of their partner organizations, and recommending same to the CBN for approval.

b (ii) Licensed Corporate Organizations

The roles of Licensed Corporate Organizations include:

a. The provision and management of the technology required to deliver mobile payment services to the subscriber.

b. The provision of the agent network required to extend all the proposed services to the market place.

C. Infrastructure Providers

These are organizations providing infrastructure that enable switching, processing and settlement facilities for mobile money services. Settlement here refers to Inter-Scheme Settlement.

1. Telecommunications: Telecommunication companies play the important role of providing the infrastructure to drive the exchange of messages for mobile payments.

2. Inter -Scheme Settlement: The role of Inter-Scheme Settlement Provider shall be to provide net positions of transactions across schemes to the inter-bank settlement system to affect the finality of payment for services consummated across two different Schemes by various participants.

D. Other Service Providers:

The CBN recognizes that, with the evolution of the mobile money system, spin-off services would be identified by MMOs which can be outsourced to entities with specialized skills and resources to support such services in a more efficient and effective manner.

The service providers may employ the infrastructures of the MMOs to provide services to the end users.

E. Consumers

These are end users of mobile money services.

F. Mobile Money Agents

The activities of Mobile Money Agents shall be guided by the provisions of the Guidelines on Agent Banking and Agent Banking Relationship in Nigeria.

5.0 The Nigerian Mobile Money System

Mobile money system in Nigeria refers to the various components required to deliver mobile money to the banking and non-banking community. The providers of these services and solutions shall be required to operate within the defined regulatory framework specified in this document and any other regulation/guideline issued by the CBN.

The CBN is responsible for defining and monitoring the mobile money systems in Nigeria.

6.0 Mobile Money Scenarios

The following scenarios are the methods through which mobile money can be carried out in Nigeria:

1. Bank Account Based
2. Card Account Based
3. Stored Value (e-Wallet) Account Based

6.1 Bank Account Based

This is a scenario where the mobile money system drives transactions through the bank accounts of customers. These accounts include current, savings, domiciliary etc.

6.1.1 Types of Bank Account Based

The types of Bank Account Based scenario shall include, but not limited to Pull based account transactions (debits through a mobile payment solution) and Push based account transactions (credits through a mobile money solution). A pull based transaction shall be authorized by the account holder via a verifiable mode before the transaction is consummated.

6.1.2 Card Account Based

This is a scenario where a payment card is linked to a mobile phone for the purpose of initiating and concluding payment transactions

6.2.1 Types of Card – Driven Payments

The types of card – driven payments recognized by this framework are:

A. Credit

B. Debit, and

C. Pre-Paid

6.3 Stored Value Account Based

This is a scenario where a mobile money system drives transactions through a system-based account that shall comply with the standards defined within this framework.

6.3.1 Types of Stored Value Account

The various options recognized by this framework include Re-loadable Stored Value Account, Pre-paid Account, etc.

7.0 Mobile Money Processes

The Mobile Money Operators shall provide a detailed payments management process that covers the entire solution delivery, from user registration and management, Agent recruitment and management, Consumer protection/dispute resolution procedures, Risk management process to transaction settlement. These processes shall cover the scope of the value chain across all the participants in the mobile money ecosystem.

8.0 Infrastructure

The core infrastructure for providing a National mobile payment system comprises of transaction processing, clearing and settlement platforms and agent network. The responsibility for the provision and management of these platforms is shared amongst the various stakeholders/service providers.

9.0 Settlement

The settlement finality for mobile money shall leverage the NIBSS Infrastructure and the CBN Inter-Bank Funds Transfer System (CIFTS). The Infrastructure shall facilitate instant payment to the end users and settlement of the Scheme providers on a T+1 cycle for the mobile money system.

10.0 Scheme Dispute Resolution

NIBSS shall provide the dispute resolution platform for the mobile payment systems for the use of participants in resolving inter scheme transaction disputes. The dispute resolution process will be aligned with the global best practices for arbitration.

11.0 Risk Management

In view of the peculiarity of the operations of other licensed providers and the unique risks associated with their operations, the regulatory framework hereby specifies the following requirements to mitigate risks arising from their activities.

The MMOs must ensure that risk mitigation techniques are in place to minimize operational, liquidity, technical, fraud, financial and money laundering risks. The mobile payment system should not be susceptible to sustained operational failures as a result of system outages. A risk compliance officer must be assigned by the MMOs, who are to provide internal risk management oversight. The CBN will review the risk management program, including all of the controls that are in place to manage the risks on a periodic basis

12.0 Technology

The technology implemented for mobile payment services is to comply with the standards and requirements on international best practice on mobile payment services. The technology to be deployed is expected to be reliable, user friendly, safe and secure. All MMO are to interconnect through NIBSS to ensure interoperability.

13.0 User Interface

13.1 The user interface shall at the minimum, be menu-driven.

13.2 The user interface shall not provide access to confidential information.

13.3 PIN shall be encrypted at the point of entry.

14.0 Know Your Customer (KYC) and Customer Due Diligence (CDD) Requirements

All MMOs shall comply with the provisions of the Circular on "Three – Tiered Know Your Customer Requirements".

15.0 Anti-Money Laundering Regulation

In addition to the provisions of the requirements prescribed in the KYC Guidelines, the CBN AML document shall also apply to mobile money service

The regulatory authorities reserve the right to change the criteria for suspicious transactions reporting in respect of mobile money as it deemed fit. Such amendments shall be communicated by appropriate channels to the mobile money operators and other stakeholders.

16.0 Consumer Protection and Dispute Resolution

To build confidence in the mobile money system, a dispute resolution mechanism needs to be put in place.

APPENDIX 3

CENTRAL BANK OF NIGERIA

GUIDELINES ON MOBILE MONEY SERVICES IN NIGERIA

Table of Content

17. Consumer Protection and Dispute Resolution

18. Cessation of Mobile Payments Service

19. Statutory Returns

20. Remedial Measures

21. Sanctions

22. Review of Guidelines

22. Glossary of Terms

1.0 PREAMBLE

In exercise of the powers conferred on the Central Bank of Nigeria (CBN) by Section 47(2) of the CBN Act, 2007, to promote and facilitate the development of efficient and effective system for the settlement of transactions, including the development of electronic payment systems; and

Pursuant to its mandate of promoting a sound financial system in Nigeria, the CBN hereby issues the following guidelines for Mobile Money Services in Nigeria

2.0 INTRODUCTION

The introduction of mobile telephony in Nigeria, its rapid growth and adoption, and the identification of person to person payments as a practical strategy for financial inclusion, has made it imperative to adopt the mobile channel as a means of driving financial inclusion of the unbanked. These factors underscore the decision of the Central Bank of Nigeria to issue these guidelines, to create an enabling environment for the orderly introduction and management of mobile money services in Nigeria.

This guideline addresses business rules governing the operation of mobile money services, and specifies basic functionalities expected of any mobile payment service and solution in Nigeria. It identifies the participants, and defines their expected roles and responsibilities in providing mobile money services in the system. In addition, it sets the basis for the regulation of services offered at different levels and by the participants.

These guidelines have identified two models for the implementation of mobile money services namely;

A. Bank Led – Bank and/or its Consortium as Lead Initiator

B. Non-Bank Led- A corporate organisation duly licensed by the CBN as Lead Initiator

3.0 OBJECTIVES

The objectives of the guidelines are as follows:

a. To ensure a structured and orderly development of mobile money services in Nigeria, with clear definition of various participants and their expected roles and responsibilities.

b. Specification of the minimum technical and business requirements for the various participants recognized for the mobile money services industry in Nigeria.

c. To promote safety and effectiveness of mobile money services and thereby enhance user confidence in the services.

4.0 SCOPE

To achieve the above stated objectives, this Guideline covers models, agent network, business rules, roles and responsibilities of participants under mobile money services in Nigeria.

5.0 MODELS

Two models of mobile money services are identified for operation in Nigeria:

a. The Bank-led Model: This is a model where a bank either alone or a consortium of banks, whether or not partnering with other approved organizations, seek to deliver banking services, leveraging on the mobile payments system. This model shall be applicable in a scenario where the bank operates on stand-alone basis or in collaboration with other bank(s) and any other approved organization. The Lead Initiator shall be a bank or a consortium of banks.

b. The Non-Bank led Model: This model allows a corporate organization that has been duly licensed by the CBN to deliver mobile money services to customers. The Lead Initiator shall be a corporate organization (other than a deposit money bank or a telecommunication company) specifically licensed by the CBN to provide mobile money services in Nigeria.

6.0 AGENCY NETWORK

The provisions of the Guidelines for the Regulation of Agent banking and Agent banking relationships in Nigeria shall apply to Mobile Money Agent Network.

7.0 BUSINESS RULES

7.1 Licensing

All Mobile Money Operators (MMOs) shall:

(a) Be licensed by the CBN on such terms and conditions as contained in "Appendix I" in this document, and may be reviewed from time to time.

(b) Be issued a unique Scheme Code by the NIBSS for managing interoperability.

(c) Be issued unique short codes by the NCC.

(d) Ensure that all telecommunication equipment are type approved by the NCC.

(e) Register users of its scheme based on technology standards and the requirements of

these Guidelines.

(f) Ensure that the registration processes within its mobile money scheme shall fulfil

the entire KYC requirements specified in these Guidelines.

7.2 Activation

(a) The Mobile Money System shall require a registered user to activate the service

before the commencement of transactions with a security code (e.g. PIN/Password etc).

(b) The Mobile Money Operators shall ensure that the activation process is not compromised or altered within its infrastructure.

7.3 Transactions

(a) All transactions initiated and concluded within the mobile payment system shall have a unique transaction reference issued by the system

(b) All transactions shall have the following elements: Transaction reference number, payer and payee phone numbers, transaction amount, transaction date and time stamps, and other relevant transaction details and unique identifiers.

(c) Where transaction involves merchants, the following details shall be provided in addition to (b) above merchant category, merchant addresses and codes.

(d) Each transaction detail logged within the payment system shall contain a valid description as in 7.3. (b).

(e) No airtime deductions shall be made in respect of charges on any transaction.

(f) MMOs shall appoint and notify CBN of their settlement banks.

(g) All obligations arising from mobile payment transactions shall be settled into settlement accounts held with Deposit Money Banks. MMOs shall maintain separate accounts for their other business activities.

7.4 Rules of Operations for bank account based Transactions

(a) Transactions shall be originated via a bank's banking application into the mobile wallet.

(b) The bank account based relationships shall comply with the existing account opening standards and practice in the Nigerian banking system.

(c) The transaction activities generated shall be traceable, monitored and logged within the mobile payments system.

(d) Access to the account through the Mobile Payments System shall be via a secured channel that meets the defined standards, as specified in these guidelines.

(f) Authorization of transactions originating from or terminating on these accounts shall be based on standards defined by the ISSUING bank.

7.5 Card Account Based

This is a scenario where a payment card is issued and linked to a mobile phone account subject to the appropriate KYC and Card Issuance Rules (Please, see the Guidelines on the Issuance and Usage of Cards in Nigeria)

(a) Types of Card – Driven Payments

The types of card – driven payments recognized by these guidelines are:

i. Credit

ii. Debit, and

iii. Pre-Paid

(b) Rules of Operations for Card Based Transactions

a. The Card Account based transactions shall be based on an infrastructure that relies on the global 3DES secure architecture at the minimum.

b. The card shall be issued by a CBN approved Card issuing Organization.

c. The card system shall comply with the existing regulation and standard for cards.

d. All Card Account based transactions must be authenticated against the originating Card Management System.

(c) Types of Stored Value Account

The various options recognized by these guidelines include Re-loadable Stored Value Account, Pre-paid Account, etc.

(d) Rules of the Operations for Stored Value Account

a. All system based accounts shall have an identification system that generates unique identifier per user account within the Mobile Payments System.

b. These accounts shall only be accessible through the Mobile Payments System.

c. The user may specifically request for other means of access to his/her system based account other than as specified in 7.5(f)(ii) above. However, the liability of the user shall be clearly stated before granting such request

d. All accounts and transaction details shall comply with PCI DSS standards.

e. The Mobile Payments System account unit shall comply with all the standards and requirements defined in these guidelines

f. All system based account shall be tied to a settlement account with a licensed deposit- taking institution. The settlement account shall be funded to the tune of the total amount of the system based accounts on the scheme.

7.6 Mobile Payments Processes

The MMOs shall put in place detailed processes that cover the entire solution delivery, from user registration and management, agent recruitment and management, Consumer protection, dispute resolution procedures, Risk management processes, to transaction settlement.

These processes shall cover the scope of the value chain across all the participants in the mobile payments ecosystem.

8.0 ROLES AND RESPONSIBILITIES OF PARTICIPANTS

8.1 BANKS

The role/responsibilities of banks as Scheme Operators shall include:

(a) Provision of all financial services for the operation of the mobile payments service.

(b) Verification, approval and accountability for the credibility and integrity of their partner organizations.

(c) Seeking and obtaining necessary approvals from relevant regulatory authorities.

(d) The deployment and delivery of the mobile payment services to the customer.

(e) Ensuring that the mobile payment service meets all specified mobile payment standards as provided in this Guidelines.

(f) Putting in place adequate measures to mitigate all the risks that could arise, following the deployment and use of its mobile payment service.

(g) Facilitating remittances to both scheme and non–scheme recipients.

(h) Providing financial, clearing and settlement services to the mobile payments system.

(i) Educating the customers on the appropriate use of the service and ensuring the deployment of adequate channels for enquiries and complaints.

8.2 LICENSED CORPORATE ORGANIZATIONS

The roles/responsibilities of Licensed Corporate Organizations shall include:

(a) The provision and management of the solution required to deliver mobile payment services to the subscriber.

(b) Ensuring that the proposed services meet all the regulatory standards and requirements specified in the mobile payments Guidelines; the deployment and delivery of the mobile payment solutions to the customer;

(c) Educating the customers on appropriate use of the solution and ensuring the deployment of adequate channels for enquiries and complaints. ensuring that international inflow messages shall at a minimum be conveyed to the recipients by secure SMS.

(d) Ensuring that the mobile payments system provides transaction monitoring and reporting in compliance with this Guideline.

(e) Providing access for on-the-spot assessment and verification of its transactions by the Central Bank of Nigeria on demand basis.

(f) Providing a monthly assessment report on the performance in prescribed format, and the submission of same to the Banking and Payment Systems Department of the Central Bank of Nigeria.

(g) Keeping records of transactions emanating from the organization's mobile payment system for a minimum of seven (7) years.

(h) Ensuring that the mobile payment services comply with specified standards as stated in this guidelines.

(i) Putting in place adequate measures to mitigate all the risks that could arise from the deployment and use of its mobile payment services.

8.3 INFRASTRUCTURE PROVIDERS

These are organizations providing infrastructure that enable switching, processing and settlement facilities for mobile money services. Settlement here refers to Inter-Scheme Settlement.

8.4 Mobile Network Operators (MNOs):

Their role shall be guided by the following provisions:

(a) Providing telecommunication network infrastructure for the use of Mobile Money Operators;

(b) Ensuring that a secure communication channel based on the minimum technology standard stipulated in this Guidelines are implemented;

(c) That MNOs shall not give preferential treatment to any MMO over another in terms of traffic and price.

(d) Ensuring that its customers are free to use any mobile payments scheme service of their choice;

(e) Shall not receive deposits from the public, except in respect of the airtime billing of their customers;

(f) Shall not allow the use of the airtime value loaded by their customers for purposes of payments or to transfer monetary value;

(g) Shall ensure seamless interconnection between MMOs; and

(h) Shall not engage in any conduct which has a purpose or effect of anti-competition in any aspect of mobile money services.

8.5 CONSUMERS

They shall have rights/responsibilities as follows:

(a) Ease of enrolment

(b) Ease of use (SMS, USSD, STK, IVR, etc)

(c) Privacy, Trust and Security of transaction

(d) Convenience

(e) Accessibility to funds on completion of transaction process

(f) Real time transfer of value

(g) Easy and prompt access to dispute resolution process

(h) Ensure the protection of PIN / Password

(i) Ensure prompt reporting of fraud cases, errors and complaints

(j) Ensure proper confirmation of transaction details and recipients' mobile phone numbers at all times before authorizing transactions.

(k) Comply with all security rules as provided by the scheme operator

(l) Escalate complaints to the Consumer Protection Departments of the Central Bank of Nigeria, if resolution of complaints is unduly delayed.

9. NOMINEE/SETTLEMENT ACCOUNT

(a) MMOs shall appoint and notify CBN of their settlement banks.

(b) All obligations arising from mobile money transactions shall be settled into settlement accounts held with Deposit Money Banks. MMOs shall maintain separate accounts for their other business activities.

(c) The settlement accounts with the deposit money banks shall be opened as Nominee Accounts on behalf of the customers of the Mobile Money Operators. The operations of the account shall be guided by the following conditions:

i. the account shall be non-interest bearing,

ii. no right of set-off,

iii. debit transactions into the account shall only be for settlement related transactions

iv. No charges of any form shall apply to the account

(d) The settlement account shall not be used, under any guise or purpose, as collateral for negotiation of loans by the organisation.

(e) The balance on the settlement account shall always be equal to the total outstanding (un-spent) balance of all holders of the e-money.

(f) Mobile Money Operators shall be required to reconcile on a daily basis, the balances in their pool accounts and make weekly returns to the Director, Banking & Payments System Department of the CBN.

(g) All customer transactions shall be traceable; auditable and can be validated.

(h) Remittance inflow messages shall, at a minimum, be conveyed to the recipient through SMS.

10. SETTLEMENT

a. The settlement process to be deployed by Mobile Money Operators shall ensure compliance with the settlement standards and requirements defined in these Guidelines.

b. The MMO shall ensure that its mobile payment infrastructure fully complies with the clearing and settlement rules for finality of settlement.

c. The scheme operator shall, on a daily basis request for its settlement positions from its bankers for reconciliation of transactions.

d. All inter scheme settlements shall be routed through the inter-bank settlement system.

e. The scheme operator shall ensure that all settlement information details are preserved for reference for a minimum period of seven (7) years.

f. The Scheme Operator shall maintain a minimum Shareholders' Fund unimpaired by losses of N2 billion, with effect from 1st June, 2016.

10.1 Operating Rules for Scheme Settlement Operator

Nigeria Inter-bank Settlement System Plc (NIBSS) shall:

(a) Provide net settlement positions of all Inter-Scheme service providers and effect final settlement using the CBN Inter-Bank Funds Transfer System (CIFTS) on (T+1) cycle.

(b) Provide statistical reports to the regulatory bodies and participants as may be prescribed from time to time

(c) Maintain audit trail and transaction log of all transactions consummated on the scheme.

(d) Provide the infrastructure (hardware, software, switching and security) to link all inter scheme providers.

(e) Provide business continuity/disaster recovery plans to ensure services are available at all times.

(f) Provide 99.99% system availability and ensure that all signed-on participating institutions follow same rules.

(g) Ensure MMOs are connected to the National Central Switch (NCS) for the purpose of interoperability

(h) Ensure that the mobile payments system is interoperable with the network infrastructure of different MNOs, solution providers, MMOs and the NCS

10.2 Inter -Scheme Settlement

The role of NIBSS as Inter-Scheme Settlement Provider shall be to provide net positions of transactions across schemes to the inter-bank settlement system to affect the finality of payment for services consummated across two different Schemes by various participants.

10.3 Forms of Settlement

There are two transaction scenarios that come into play. These scenarios On-us and Not on-us transactions:

(a) On-Us Transactions

i. These are payment transactions in which all parties involved in the transaction cycle are of the same scheme i.e. Issuer, Acquirer, Merchant and Consumer.

ii. Transactions are not routed through a switch except where an external processor is involved e.g. Airtime Recharge Transactions, Bills payment.

iii. These set of transactions do not require settlement.

(b) Not-on-Us/Remote-on-Us Transactions

i. These are payment transactions where an Acquirer Terminal is used by other Issuers.

ii. The role of the Inter-Scheme Settlement Providers shall be to provide a net position of all participants, the acquirer and the issuer, which consummate services across schemes to the inter-bank settlement system to affect the finality of payment.

10.4 Final Settlement

For finality of settlement between participating institutions, settlement providers shall provide settlement information of their participants to the final settlement system. Final Settlement shall be done through the CBN Inter-Bank Funds Transfer System (CIFTS) by effecting the net positions provided by the national central switch and the inter-bank settlement system.

11 TRANSACTION SECURITY STANDARDS

11.1 Mobile Payments solutions deployed shall adhere to the following minimum standards:

(a) The minimum encryption standard is 3DES encryption. Encryption shall be on an end-to-end basis.

(b) ISO 8583

(c) EMV standards in the case of Card payment related transactions.

(d) PCIDSS

(e) All subsequent routing of messages to the Mobile Money Operators' servers must be with the highest level of security with dedicated connectivity like leased lines (E1 links) / VPNs;

(f) That any sensitive information stored in third party systems is restricted with appropriate encryption and hardware security standards as contained in this guidelines;

(g) All transactions on an account shall be allowed only after authentication of the mobile number and the PIN associated with it;

(h) That mobile payments application shall not allow the option of saving the PIN either on the handset or on the application;

(i) All accounts activated by the consumer on the mobile application are linked to the mobile phone number. This mobile phone number shall be used as the second factor authentication for mobile transactions;

(j) The PIN shall not travel in plain text during the transaction;

(k) That proper system of verification of the phone number shall be implemented;

(l) The payment authorisation message from the user's mobile phone shall, at the minimum, be 3DES encrypted and checked for tampering by the scheme operator. It shall not be possible for any interceptor to change the contents of the message;

(m) There shall exist, a security policy duly approved by the Board of Directors of the organisation providing the service;

(n) Segregation of duty of Security Officer / Group dealing exclusively with information systems security and Information Technology Division which actually implements the computer systems;

(o) The Information Systems Auditor shall conduct periodic audit of the system to ensure adherence to the specified security standards;

(p) Logical access controls to data, systems, application software, utilities, telecommunication lines, libraries, system software, etc. exists;

(q) At the minimum, there shall be in place, the use of proxy server type of firewall so that there is no direct connection between the Internet and the Mobile Money Operators' systems. For sensitive systems, an inspection firewall shall be implemented to thoroughly inspect all packets of information, compare past and present transactions and enable a real time security alert;

12. INFRASTRUCTURE

The core infrastructure for providing a national mobile payment system comprises of transaction processing, clearing and settlement platforms. The responsibility for the provision and management of these platforms shall be that of the Lead Initiator

13. RISK MANAGEMENT

13.1 In view of the peculiarity of the operations of the MMOs and the unique risks associated with their operations, this guidelines hereby specifies the following requirements to mitigate risks arising from their activities.

(a) The MMOs shall ensure that risk mitigation techniques are in place to minimize operational, liquidity, technical, fraud, financial and money laundering risks.

(b) The mobile payments system shall not be susceptible to sustained operational failures, as a result of system outages.

(c) A risk management officer shall be assigned by the MMOs, who is to provide internal risk management oversight.

(d) The CBN will review the risk management program, including all the controls that are in place to manage the risks from time to time.

13.2 Credit and Settlement Risk

The central role of the settlement infrastructure requires that MMOs shall:

(a) Ensure that the mobile payment settlement platform automatically generates transaction settlement information/records.

(b) Adopt standard messaging formats as provided by NIBSS, for all schemes for settlement purposes.

(c) Maintain audit trail and settlement log for a minimum of seven (7) years.

(d) Fulfill other conditions that may be reviewed by the regulatory authorities from time to time.

13.3 Business Continuity Risk

MMOs shall:

(a) Maintain proper backup infrastructure.

(b) Implement a disaster recovery and business continuity plan.

(c) Periodically test the effectiveness of the backup infrastructure and business continuity plan.

13.4 Business Continuity Plan (BCP)

MMOs shall:

(a) Ensure that BCP is approved by their board.

(b) Comply with laid down minimum technology standards as specified in this document.

(c) Ensure proper/adequate back up of data as may be required by their operations.

(d) Ensure that the BCP is tested through a fail-over process, at least twice a year.

(e) Have, well documented and tested business continuity plans approved by the board, that address all aspects of the mobile payment business, to take care of business disruptions and ensure system availability and recoverability:

i. Both data and software should be backed up periodically

ii. Recovery and business continuity measures, based on the criticality of the systems, shall be in place and a documented plan with the organization and assignment of responsibilities of the key decision making personnel shall exist.

iii. An off-site back up is required for recovery from major failures / disasters to ensure business continuity. Depending on criticality, different technologies based on backup, hot sites, warm sites or cold sites should be available for business continuity.

iv. Develop and implement comprehensive risk management framework to identify, monitor and control risks. This should provide the strategy to resolve potential problems that may result from internal and external interdependencies.

13.5 The BCP shall be:

(a) Based on a comprehensive Business Impact Analysis and Risk Assessment;

(b) Documented in a written program;

(c) Reviewed and approved by the board and senior management, at least annually;

(d) Disseminated to employees;

(e) The responsibility of the MMO, where it is outsourced to a third-party;

(f) Flexible to respond to unanticipated threat scenarios and changing internal conditions;

(g) Focused on the impact of various threats that could potentially disrupt operations rather than on specific events;

(h) Developed based on valid assumptions and an analysis of interdependencies; and

(i) Effective in minimizing service disruptions and financial loss through the implementation of mitigation strategies.

(j) Ensure that processing priorities can be adequately implemented and that business operations can be resumed in a timely manner.

(k) Monitor closely mobile traffic and system capacity to ensure that any service degradation due to capacity problems are addressed promptly.

(l) Ensure that the BCP is reviewed by external auditors at least annually, and forwarded to CBN;

(m) Ensure employees are trained and aware of their roles in the implementation of the BCP;

(n) Ensure the BCP is tested, at least quarterly, on an enterprise-wide basis;

(o) Review the BCP testing program and test results on a regular basis;

(p) Ensure the BCP is continually updated to reflect the current operating environment.

14.0 TECHNOLOGY

The technology implemented for mobile money services shall comply with the following standards and other requirements outlined in the provisions of these Guidelines.

14.1 Standards

(a) Modularity of Technologies

i. The MMOs shall ensure that the minimum technology standards for communication are met (Interoperability and Interconnectivity).

ii. Only secure channels shall be used in providing mobile money services.

iii. The mobile money services shall ensure non-repudiation.

(b) Reliability

i. Payment instruction shall be consistently executed. In the event of failure, reversal shall be immediate and automatic.

ii. Consumers shall get immediate value for every successful transaction.

(c) User Interface

i. The user interface shall, at the minimum, adhere to the security requirements as stated in the guideline.

ii. The user interface shall not provide access to confidential information.

iii. PIN shall be encrypted at the point of entry.

15.0 KNOW YOUR CUSTOMER (KYC) AND CUSTOMER DUE DILIGENCE (CDD) REQUIREMENTS

All MMOs shall comply with the provisions of the KYC Guidelines (CBN AML/CFT Regulation 2009

16.0 CERTAINTY OF MOBILE TRANSACTIONS

For the purpose of establishing certainty of transactions through mobile payments, MMOs shall ensure the following:

a. Summary of transaction requested must be displayed to the user for confirmation. The transaction summary shall include, the phone numbers of the paying user and receiving user, transaction description, the transaction amount, date and time and a unique transaction identifier. By confirming the summary, the user commits to the transaction.

b. Option for the user to save such transaction summary.

c. Upon completion of the transaction, the user receives an electronic receipt which shall conform to the transaction summary earlier displayed and the option for saving the electronic receipt shall be available to the user.

d. The electronic summary of transaction and the electronic receipt should be securely logged and the log maintained online for a minimum period of three (3) months and subsequently archived for a minimum period of seven (7) years. However, if a complaint arises before the expiration of the seven (7) years, the log in respect of such pending complaints shall be maintained until the case is completely resolved or discharged.

e. Regulatory authorities, Law Enforcement Agencies or Arbiters are granted access to the log, when required, for the purpose of certifying a printed copy for evidential purposes.

17.0 CONSUMER PROTECTION MEASURES

MMOs shall comply with the following minimum requirements:

a. Ensure that customers understand the transactions they are entering and adequate disclosures are made.

b. Ensure that a channel of communication is in place 24/7 to entertain enquiries and complaints in a language understood by customers.

c. Clearly display charges for services through its agents.

d. Factor in the vulnerability of the lower end of the society in product and services design. There should be adequate consumer education activities to ensure that consumers are sensitized on the services.

e. Ensure that appropriate consumer protection mechanisms are put in place against loss of service, fraud and privacy of customer information to enhance confidence in the mobile money services.

f. Provide the leading role in dispute resolutions and take necessary steps to reach other agencies in the ecosystem that are relevant to resolving disputes.

g. Resolve customer complaints within a reasonable time and not later than 48 hours from the date of reporting or lodging the complaint with the MMO.

h. Be held responsible for the actions and inactions of their agents.

17.1 DISPUTE RESOLUTION MECHANISMS

Disputes arising between parties shall be settled as follows:

a. The parties shall settle disputes within 14 days.

b. Customers may escalate complaints to the Central Bank of Nigeria where they are dis-satisfied with item 1 above.

c. If resolution is not achieved, after 1 & 2 above, parties may thereafter settle the dispute in accordance with the provisions of the Arbitration and Conciliation Act, Cap A18, Laws of the Federation of Nigeria, 2004.

18.0 CESSATION OF MOBILE PAYMENT SERVICE

a. Any MMO wishing to exit from the mobile payments system shall notify the CBN in writing regarding the intention for the discontinuation, 120 days before ceasing its operations;

b. The CBN shall have powers to order any MMO exiting from the mobile payments system to meet its outstanding obligations.

19.0 STATUTORY RETURNS

a. MMOs shall, at the end of every month and not later than the 14th day of the next month, submit to the CBN, data and other information on mobile money operations including:

b. Nature, value and volume of transactions;

c. Incidents of fraud; and

d. Nature and number of customer complaints and remedial measures taken.

19.1 Annual Reporting

MMOs shall include in their annual reports and accounts, in the prescribed format all activities of its mobile money operations.

20.0 REMEDIAL MEASURES

If an MMO or its agent fails to comply with these Guidelines, the CBN may take any corrective action against the MMO as may be prescribed from time to time.

21.0 SANCTIONS

In addition to the use of remedial measures in Section 22, the Bank may impose any or all of the following sanctions against an MMO, its board of directors, officers or agents:

(a) Withholding Corporate approvals;

(b) Financial Penalties;

(c) Suspension from mobile money operation; and

(d) Revocation of the mobile money operation license.

22.0 REVIEW OF THE GUIDELINES

This Guideline shall be reviewed from time to time by the Central Bank of Nigeria.

23.0 GLOSSARY OF TERMS

CIFTS: The Real Time Gross Settlement (RTGS) System deployed by the Central Bank of Nigeria which effects settlement of transfer among banks on real time and gross basis. It is known as the CBN Inter-Bank Funds Transfer System (CIFTS).

Bank: A deposit taking institution duly licensed by the Central Bank of Nigeria.

Interoperability: a situation in which payment instruments belonging to a given scheme may be used in systems installed by other schemes.

Inter-Scheme Operation: Inter-Scheme operations are mobile payments consummated across two different schemes by various participants.

Intra-Scheme Operations: Intra-Scheme operations are mobile payments that are consummated within a particular service provider's scheme.

Issuer: the entity which receives payment in exchange for value distributed in the system and which is obligated to pay or redeem transactions or balances presented to it.

Mobile Money Operators: provide the infrastructure for the mobile payment systems for the use of participants that are signed-on to their scheme.

NCC: refers to the Nigeria Communications Commission with Regulatory powers over the telecommunication companies (Telcos)

Service Providers: employ the infrastructure of the scheme operator to provide services to end users.

Settlement Infrastructure Providers: Organizations providing infrastructure that enables message exchange, switching and settlement facilities for mobile money services.

NIBSS: Nigeria Inter-Bank Settlement System

3DES: Triple(3) Data Encryption Standard

Nominee Account: Account set up by a Nominee (MMO) for settlement of customer transactions held on behalf of the individual customers (the 'beneficial owner') under a custodial agreement.

Licensed Corporate Organizations: Companies licensed by the Corporate Affairs Commission (CAC) under the Companies and Allied Matters Act 2004 (CAMA), to carry business in Nigeria.

Infrastructure Providers: These are organizations providing infrastructure that enable switching, processing and settlement facilities for mobile money services. Settlement here refers to Inter-Scheme Settlement.

"APPENDIX I" OF THE GUIDELINES ON MOBILE BANKING SERVICES IN NIGERIA

REQUIREMENTS FOR MOBILE MONEY LICENCE

1. Evidence of the formation of the Consortium that will deploy the project (Certificate of Incorporation)

2. The Consortium's profile and functional contact e-mails and telephone numbers

3. Memorandum & Articles of Association

4. Shareholding structure of the Consortium

5. Forms C02 (Return on Allotment of shares) and C07 (Particulars of Directors)

6. CV's of Board and Management of the Company

7. Organogram of the company

8. Business Plan, to include:

a. Nature of the Business

b. Features of the scheme

c. Securities features that will be put in place

d. 3 years Financial projections for the company

e. Transaction and other charges that will be borne by customers

f. Profit sharing agreement among the parties

g. Diagrammatic illustration of transaction flows

9. Information Technology Policy of the Company including:

a. Privacy Policy

b. Information Ownership/Disclosure/Loss Policy

c. Backup and Restore Policy

d. Network Security Policy

e. Encryption Policy

f. Confidential Data Policy

g. Password Policy

h. Third Party Connection Policy

i. Incidence Response Policy

j. Physical Security Policy

10. Enterprise Risk Management Framework

11. Contingency and Disaster Recovery Plan (Business Continuity Programme)

12. Draft agreements with the following:

a. Technical Partners

b. Participating banks

c. Switching company/(s)

d. Merchants

e. Telcos

f. Any other party

13. Tax Clearance Certificate for three (3) years of each party in the Consortium

14. Project Deployment Plan (time, location, operation, etc.)

15. Payment of non-refundable Application fee of N100,000.00 (One hundred thousand naira) made payable to the CBN via the RTGS Third Party Transfer.

16. Evidence of Shareholders' Fund of N2 billion before a license is issued.

APPENDIX 4

CENTRAL BANK OF NIGERIA

GUIDELINES ON INTERNATIONAL MOBILE MONEY REMITTANCE SERVICE IN NIGERIA

1. Introduction

2. Objectives

3. Scope

4. Operations of International Mobile Money Remittance Services (IMMRS) in Nigeria.

5. Authority to Provide international Mobile Money Remittance Services in Nigeria.

6. Business Rules

7. Roles and Responsibilities of Participants

8. Nominee/Settlement Account

9. Settlement

10. Transaction Security Standards

11. Infrastructure

12. Risk Management

13. Know Your Customer (KYC) and Customer Due Diligence (CDD) Requirements

14. Anti-Money Laundering (AML) and Countering the Financing of Terrorism (CFT)

15. Consumer Protection Measures

16. Cessation of International Mobile Money Remittance Service

17. Statutory Returns

18. Remedial Measures

19. Sanctions

20. Review of Guidelines

21. Glossary of Terms

1.0 INTRODUCTION

Following the widespread use of mobile telephone as a means of communication in Nigeria, and in recognition of its potential as a tool for financial inclusion and efficient payments system, the Central Bank of Nigeria (CBN), pursuant to its powers under Section 47(2) of the CBN Act, 2007, issued the "Guidelines on Mobile Money Services in Nigeria" in 2009. The above guidelines, however, restricts users and operators of mobile payments services to local currency transactions within Nigeria. Also, the extant CBN "Guidelines on International Money Transfer Services in Nigeria" issued in June 2014 did not cover money remittances via mobile applications.

Consequent upon representations by some stakeholders on the need to facilitate foreign exchange transactions via a more convenient and flexible payment channel, the CBN has approved the inclusion of mobile money as part of international money transfer services in Nigeria. It is in this regard that the Bank hereby issues the "Guidelines on International Mobile Money Remittance Service (IMMRS) in Nigeria" to complement the existing guidelines.

These guidelines cover the business rules governing the operation of IMMRS and specify the infrastructural and risk management requirements for international mobile payments services in Nigeria. It also identifies the participants, and defines their expected roles and responsibilities in the system. In addition, it sets the basis for the regulation of services offered by the participants.

2.0 OBJECTIVES

The objectives of these guidelines are to:

i. Provide minimum standards and requirements for the operation of international funds remittance over mobile devices in Nigeria;

ii. Specify delivery channels for offering international funds remittance over mobile (inbound/outbound), in a cost effective manner;

iii. Provide an enabling environment for International funds remittance over mobile devices in the Nigerian economy;

iv. Specify minimum technical and business requirements for various participants in the International Funds Remittance over mobile devices in Nigeria; and

v. Provide broad guidelines for implementation of processes and flows of international money transfer services, from initiation to completion.

vi. Ensure a structured and orderly development of International Funds Remittance over mobile devices in Nigeria, with clear definition of various participants and their expected roles and responsibilities.

vii. Promote safety and effectiveness of mobile money services and thereby enhance user confidence.

3.0 SCOPE

To achieve the above stated objectives, these Guidelines cover business rules, agent network, roles and responsibilities of participants under the scheme.

4.0 OPERATIONS OF INTERNATIONAL MOBILE MONEY REMITTANCE SERVICE (1MMRS) IN NIGERIA

4.1 Permissible Activities

The permissible activities of International Mobile Money Remittance Service (IMMRS) shall consist of allowable inbound and outbound transactions as follows:

(A) Inbound Remittances

The transaction shall be limited to the receipt of monies transmitted via mobile phones and other hand held devices to persons resident in Nigeria and foreign visitors.

(B) Outbound Remittances

This includes all outbound Person-to-Person money remittances from Nigeria towards family maintenance. To safeguard against circumventing the statutory reporting threshold, the mobile money remittance service shall target individual customers only.

5.0 AUTHORITY TO PROVIDE INTERNATIONAL MOBILE MONEY REMITTANCE SERVICE IN NIGERIA

Institutions seeking to offer international mobile money remittance service in Nigeria shall apply and obtain a valid approval from the CBN subject to the following conditions;

a. Be a registered entity, licensed in its home country to carry on money transfer activities.

b. Have a minimum Net Worth of US$1 billion, as per the latest audited financial statement, or as may be determined by the CBN from time to time.

c. Should hold a valid Mobile Money Operator's license

d. The Institution should be well established (operate in at least twenty countries with at least 10 years' experience) in the money transfer business, with a track record of operations.

e. There should be an MOU that clearly delineates liabilities in the event of disputes and/or process failures.

For operation of this service there must be in partnership with at least an Authorised Dealer bank licensed in Nigeria shall be eligible for the grant of CBN approval under these guidelines.

5.1 RESERVE RIGHTS OF THE CENTRAL BANK OF NIGERIA

The Central Bank of Nigeria shall have the right to decline the issuance of any license without any reason.

6.0 BUSINESS RULES

6.1 Requirements

All financial institutions authorised to carry out international mobile money remittance service in Nigeria shall:

i. Be issued a unique Scheme Code by the NIBSS for managing interoperability.

ii. Be issued unique short codes by the NCC.

iii. Ensure that all telecommunication equipment is type approved by the NCC.

iv. Register users of its scheme based on technology standards and the requirements of these Guidelines.

v. Ensure that the registration processes within its International Funds Remittance scheme shall fulfil the entire KYC requirements specified in these Guidelines.

vi. Display the summary of transaction requested to the user for confirmation which shall include the phone numbers of the initiator and receiver, transaction description, the transaction amount, date and time and a unique transaction identifier.

vii. The user commits to the transaction by confirming the summary.

viii. Provide the user option to save transaction summary.

ix. Ensure upon completion of the transaction, that the user receives an electronic confirmation.

x. Regulatory authorities shall have access to the transaction log.

xi. Ensure that all transfers are subjected to the sanction screen platform

6.2 Activation

(a) All banks offering international funds remittance over mobile devices shall provide an Application, which shall require a registered user to activate the service before the commencement of transactions with a security code (e.g. PIN/Password, etc.).

(b) The bank shall ensure that the activation process is not compromised or altered within its infrastructure.

6.3 Transactions

(a) All transactions within the IMMRS shall have a unique reference issued by the system.

(b) All transactions shall have; reference number, payer and payee phone numbers, amount, unique identifier date and time and other relevant transaction details.

(c) IMMRS providers shall appoint and notify CBN of their settlement/correspondent banks.

6.4 International Mobile Money Remittance Payments Processes

The IMMRS shall put in place detailed processes that cover the entire solution delivery, from user registration and management, consumer protection, dispute resolution procedures, risk management processes, to transaction settlement.

7.0. ROLES AND RESPONSIBILITIES OF PARTICIPANTS

7.1 Banks

The role/responsibilities of banks as Scheme Operators shall include:

(a) Verification, approval and accountability for the credibility and integrity of their partner organizations.

(b) Seeking and obtaining necessary approvals from relevant regulatory authorities.

(c) The deployment and delivery of the International Funds Remittance over mobile payment services to the customer.

(d) Ensuring that the International Funds Remittance over mobile payment service meets all specified mobile payment standards as provided in this Guidelines.

(e) Putting in place adequate measures to mitigate all the risks that could arise in the use of its mobile payment service.

(f) Facilitating remittances to both scheme and non-scheme recipients.

(g) Providing financial clearing and settlement services to the mobile payments system.

(h) Educating the customers on the appropriate use of the service and ensuring the deployment of adequate channels for enquiries and complaints.

7.2 Infrastructure Providers

These are organizations providing infrastructure that enable switching, processing and settlement facilities for International Funds Remittance over mobile services. Settlement here refers to Foreign Exchange Settlement.

7.3 Mobile Network Operators (MNOs):

Their role shall be guided by the following provisions:

(a) Providing telecommunication network infrastructure for the use of International Funds Remittance over Mobile devices;

(b) Ensuring that a secure communication channel based on the minimum technology standard stipulated in these Guidelines are implemented;

(c) That MNOs shall not give preferential treatment to any mobile money operator over another in terms of traffic and price;

(d) Ensuring that its customers are free to use any mobile payments scheme service of their choice;

(e) Shall not receive deposits from the public, except in respect of the airtime billing of their customers;

(f) Shall not allow the use of the airtime value loaded by their customers for purposes of payments or to transfer monetary value;

(g) Shall ensure seamless interconnection between MMOs; and

(h) Shall not engage in any conduct which has a purpose or effect of anti-competition in any aspect of mobile money services.

7.4 Consumers

They shall have rights/responsibilities as follows;

(a) Ease of enrolment

(b) Ease of use (SMS, USSD, STK, IVR, etc.)

(c) Privacy, Trust and Security of transaction

(d) Convenience

(e) Accessibility to funds on completion of transaction process

(f) Real time transfer of value

(g) Easy and prompt access to dispute resolution process

(h) Ensure the protection of PIN / Password

(i) Ensure prompt reporting of fraud cases, errors and complaints

(j) Ensure proper confirmation of transaction details and recipients' mobile phone numbers at all times before authorizing transactions.

(k) Comply with all security rules as provided by the scheme operator

(I) Report complaints to the Consumer Protection Departments of the Central Bank of Nigeria, if resolution exceeds 14 working days.

8.0 NOMINEE/SETTLEMENT ACCOUNT

(a) IMMRS providers shall notify CBN of their settlement/correspondent banks.

(b) All obligations arising from mobile money transactions shall be settled into settlement accounts.

(c) The settlement accounts with the deposit money banks shall be opened as Nominee Accounts on behalf of the customers of the international Mobile Money Service providers. The operations of the account shall be guided by the following conditions:

i. no right of set-off,

ii. debit transactions into the account shall only be for settlement related transactions

iii. No charges of any form shall apply to the account

(d) The settlement account shall not be used, under any guise or purpose, as collateral for negotiation of loans by the bank.

(e) The balance on the settlement account shall always be equal to the total outstanding (un-spent) balance of all holders of the mobile money.

(f) International Mobile Money Service Providers shall be required to reconcile on a daily basis, the balances in their pool accounts and make monthly returns to the Director, Trade & Exchange Department of the CBN.

(g) All customer transactions shall be traceable; auditable and can be validated.

(h) Remittance inflow messages shall, at a minimum, be conveyed to the recipient through SMS.

9.0 SETTLEMENT

a. The settlement process to be deployed by International Mobile Money Remittance Service providers shall ensure compliance with the settlement standards and requirements defined in these Guidelines.

b. The IMMRS provider shall ensure that its mobile payment infrastructure fully complies with the clearing and settlement rules for finality of settlement.

c. The scheme operator shall, on a daily basis request for its settlement positions from its correspondent bankers for reconciliation of transactions.

d. The scheme operator shall ensure that all settlement information details are preserved for reference for a minimum period of seven (7) years.

9.1 Operating Rules for Scheme Settlement Operator

Nigeria Inter-bank Settlement System Pic (NIBSS) shall:

(a) Provide net settlement positions of all Inter-Scheme service providers and effect final settlement using the CBN Inter- Bank Funds Transfer System (CIFTS) on (T+l) cycle.

(b) Provide statistical reports to the regulatory bodies and participants as may be prescribed from time to time

(c) Maintain audit trail and transaction log of all transactions consummated on the scheme.

(d) Provide the infrastructure (hardware, software, switching and security) to link all inter scheme providers.

(e) Provide business continuity/disaster recovery plans to ensure services are available at all times.

(f) Provide 99.99% system availability and ensure that all signed-on participating institutions follow same rules.

(g) Ensure MMOs are connected to the National Central Switch (NCS) for the purpose of interoperability.

(h) Ensure that the mobile payments system is interoperable with the network infrastructure of different MNOs, solution providers, IMMRS and the NCC.

10.0 TRANSACTION SECURITY STANDARDS

10.1 Mobile Payments solutions deployed shall adhere to the following minimum standards:

(a) The Advanced Encryption Standard (AES). Encryption shall be on an end-to-end basis.

(b) ISO 8583

(c) All subsequent routing of messages to the Mobile Money Operators' servers must be with the highest level of security with dedicated connectivity;

(d) That any sensitive information stored in third party systems is restricted with appropriate encryption and hardware security standards as contained in this guidelines;

(e) All transactions on an account shall be allowed only after authentication of the mobile number and the PIN associated with it;

(f) That mobile payments application shall not allow the option of saving the PIN either on the handset or on the application;

(g) All accounts on the mobile application shall be activated using the customer on the mobile application linked to the mobile phone number. This mobile phone number shall be used as the second factor authentication for mobile transactions;

(h) The PIN shall not travel in plain text during the transaction;

(i) That proper system of verification of the phone number shall be implemented;

(j) The payment authorisation message from the user's mobile phone shall, at the minimum, be AES encrypted and checked for tampering by the scheme operator. It shall not be possible for any interceptor to change the contents of the message;

(k) There shall exist, a security policy duly approved by the Board of Directors of the organisation providing the service;

(I) Segregation of duty of Security Officer/Group dealing exclusively with information systems security and Information Technology Division which actually implements the computer systems;

(m) The Information Systems Auditor shall conduct periodic audit of the system to ensure adherence to the specified security standards half yearly;

(n) Logical access controls to data, systems, application software, utilities, telecommunication lines, libraries, system software, etc. exists;

(o) At the minimum, there shall be in place, the use of proxy server type of firewall so that there is no direct connection between the Internet and the Mobile Money Operators' systems. For sensitive systems, an inspection firewall shall be implemented to thoroughly inspect all packets of information, compare past and present transactions and enable a real time security alert;

11.0 INFRASTRUCTURE

The core infrastructure for providing an international mobile payment system shall comply with the following standards and other requirements outlined in these guidelines;

a. Standards

i. Transaction processing, clearing and settlement platforms. The responsibility for the provision and management of these platforms shall be that of the bank.

ii. The IMMRSs shall ensure that the minimum technology standards for communication are met (Interoperability and Interconnectivity).

iii. Only secure channels shall be used in providing mobile money services

iv. The mobile money services shall ensure non-repudiation.

b. Reliability

i. Payment instruction shall be consistently executed. In the event of failure, reversal shall be immediate and automatic.

ii. Consumers shall get immediate value for every successful transaction.

c. User interface

i. The user interface shall, at the minimum, adhere to the security requirements as stated in the guideline.

ii. The user interface shall not provide access to confidential information.

iii. PIN shall be encrypted at the point of entry.

12.0 RISK MANAGEMENT

12.1 In view of the peculiarity of the operations of the IMMRS and the unique risks associated with their operations, these guidelines hereby specifies the following minimum requirements to management of risks arising from their activities.

(a) The IMMRS shall ensure that risk management policies are in place to minimize operational, liquidity, settlement, fraud, financial and money laundering risks.

(b) The mobile payments system shall not be susceptible to sustained operational failures, as a result of system outages.

(c) A risk management officer shall be assigned by the IMMRS, who is to provide internal risk management oversight.

(d) The CBN will review the risk management policies, including all the controls that are in place to manage the risks from time to time.

(e) Without prejudice to the existing enterprise Risk management framework in the bank, emerging risks from the deployment of this service should be submitted to the Central Bank of Nigeria for review and approval as part of the licensing process

12.2 Credit and Settlement Risk

The central role of the settlement infrastructure requires that IMMRS shall:

(a) Ensure that the mobile payment settlement platform automatically generates transaction settlement information/records.

(b) Maintain audit trail and settlement log for a minimum of seven (7) years.

(c) Fulfill other conditions that may be reviewed by the regulatory authorities from time to time.

12.3 Business Continuity Plan (BCP)

IMMRS shall:

(a) Ensure that BCP is approved by their board.

(b) Comply with laid down minimum technology standards as specified in this document.

(c) Ensure proper/adequate back up of data as may be required by their operations.

(d) Ensure that the BCP is tested through a fail-over process, at least twice a year.

(e) Have, well documented and tested business continuity plans approved by the board, that address all aspects of the mobile payment business, to take care of business disruptions and ensure system availability and recoverability:

i. data should be backed up daily while software should be updated as appropriate

ii. Recovery and business continuity measures, based on the criticality of the systems, shall be in place and a documented plan with the organization and assignment of responsibilities of the key decision making personnel shall exist.

iii. An off-site back up is required for recovery from major failures / disasters to ensure business continuity. Different technologies based on backup, hot sites, warm sites or cold sites should be available for business continuity.

12.4 The BCP shall be:

(a) Based on a comprehensive Business Impact Analysis and Risk Assessment;

(b) Documented in a written format;

(c) Reviewed and approved by the board and senior management, at least annually;

(d) Disseminated to employees;

(e) The responsibility of the IMMRS, where it is outsourced to a third-party;

(f) Flexible to respond to unanticipated threat scenarios and changing internal conditions;

(g) Focused on the impact of various threats that could potentially disrupt operations rather than on specific events;

(h) Developed based on valid assumptions and an analysis of interdependencies;

(i) Effective in minimizing service disruptions and financial loss through the implementation of mitigation strategies

(j) Ensure that processing priorities can be adequately implemented and that business operations resumes within twenty-four (24) hours.

(k) Monitor closely mobile traffic and system capacity to ensure that any service degradation due to capacity problems are addressed promptly.

(l) Ensure that the BCP is reviewed by external auditors at least annually, and forwarded to CBN;

(m) Ensure employees are trained and aware of their roles in the implementation of the BCP;

(n) Ensure the BCP is tested, at least quarterly, on an enterprise-wide basis;

(o) Review the BCP testing program and test results on a quarterly basis;

(p) Ensure the BCP is continually updated to reflect the current operating environment.

13.0 KNOW YOUR CUSTOMER (KYC) AND CUSTOMER DUE DILIGENCE (CDD) REQUIREMENTS

All IMMRS shall comply with the provisions of the KYC Guidelines (CBN AM L/C FT Regulation 2013).

14.0 ANTI-MONEY LAUNDERING (AML) AND COUNTERING THE FINANCING OF TERRORISM (CFT)

The IMMRS providers shall have measures in place to prevent money laundering and terrorist financing. The mobile money IT system shall have inbuilt mechanisms to identify suspicious transactions. The following measures shall be in place:

(a) Adhere to international Know Your Customer (KYC) standards at account opening by carrying out Customer Due Diligence (CDD). The entity conducting customer verification should require at least one of the following documents to verify the identity of the customer: a valid international passport, National Identity card, permanent voter's card, driver's license.

(b) Allowable maximum limit of the outbound mobile money remittance per week shall be US$100 or its equivalent, subject to periodic review by the CBN.

(c) Suspicious transactions should be reported in line with the AML/CFT Act.

15.0 CONSUMER PROTECTION MEASURES

IMMRS shall comply with the following minimum requirements:

a. Ensure that customers understand the transactions they are entering and adequate disclosures are made.

b. Ensure that a channel of communication is in place twenty four (24) hours a day, seven (7) days a week to entertain enquiries and complaints in a language understood by customers.

c. Clearly display charges for services rendered.

d. Factor in the vulnerability of the lower end of the society in product and services design. There should be adequate consumer education activities to ensure that consumers are sensitized on the services.

e. Ensure that appropriate consumer protection mechanisms are put in place against loss of service, fraud and privacy of customer information to enhance confidence in the mobile money services.

f. Provide the leading role in dispute resolutions and take necessary steps to reach other agencies in the ecosystem that are relevant to resolving disputes.

g. Respond to customer complaints within a reasonable time and not later than 48 hours from the date of reporting or lodging the complaint with the IMMRS.

h. Be held responsible for the actions and inactions IMMRS.

15.1 DISPUTE RESOLUTION MECHANISMS

Disputes arising between parties shall be settled as follows:

a. The parties shall settle disputes within 14 working days.

b. Customers may report complaints addressed to the Director, Consumer Protection Department Central Bank of Nigeria where they are dis-satisfied with item a above.

c. If resolution is not achieved, after (a & b) above, parties may thereafter settle the dispute in accordance with the provisions of the Arbitration and Conciliation Act, Cap A18, Laws of the Federation of Nigeria, 2004 and other applicable legislations.

16.0 CESSATION OF MOBILE PAYMENT SERVICE

a. Any IMMRS wishing to exit from the mobile payments system shall notify the CBN in writing regarding the intention for the discontinuation, 120 days before ceasing its operations;

b. The CBN shall have powers to order any IMMRS exiting from the mobile payments system to meet its outstanding obligations.

17.0 STATUTORY RETURNS

IMMRS shall, at the end of every month and not later than the 10th day of the following month, submit to the CBN, data and other information on International mobile money operations including:

i. Nature, value and volume of transactions;

ii. Incidents of fraud; and

iii. Nature and number of customer complaints and remedial measures taken.

17.1 Annual Reporting

IMMRS shall include in their annual reports and accounts, in the prescribed format all activities of its mobile money operations.

18.0 REMEDIAL MEASURES

If an IMMRS or its agent fails to comply with these Guidelines, the CBN may take any corrective action against the IMMRS as may be prescribed from time to time.

19.0 SANCTIONS

In addition to the use of remedial measures, the Bank may impose any or all of the following sanctions against an IMMRS, its board of directors, officers or agents;

(a) Withholding Corporate approvals;

(b) Financial Penalties;

(c) Suspension from International mobile money operation; and

(d) Revocation of the mobile money operationlicense.

20.0 REVIEW OF THE GUIDELINES

These Guidelines shall be reviewed from time to time by the Central Bank of Nigeria.

21.0 GLOSSARY OF TERMS

Bank: A deposit taking institution duly licensed by the Central Bank of Nigeria.

EMV: Europay, Mastercard and Visa (Chip and PIN)

Infrastructure Providers: These are organizations providing infrastructure that enable switching, processing and settlement facilities for mobile money services. Settlement here refers to Inter-Scheme Settlement.

International Mobile Money Remittance Service Providers: provide the infrastructure for the mobile payment systems for the use of participants that are signed-on to their scheme.

Interoperability: a situation in which payment instruments belonging to a given scheme may be used in systems installed by other schemes.

Inter-Scheme Operation: Inter-Scheme operations are mobile payments consummated across two different schemes by various participants.

Intra-Scheme Operations: Intra-Scheme operations are mobile payments that are consummated within a particular service provider's scheme.

IS08583: International Organisation Standard 8583 (messaging format)

Issuer: the entity which receives payment in exchange for value distributed in the system and which is obligated to pay or redeem transactions or balances presented to it.

Non-scheme recipients:

Nominee Account: Account set up by a Nominee (MMO) for settlement of customer transactions held on behalf of the individual customers (the 'beneficial owner') under a custodial agreement.

PCIDSS: Payment Cards Industry Data Security Standard

Settlement Infrastructure Providers: Organizations providing infrastructure that enables message exchange, switching and settlement facilities for mobile money services.

Scheme recipients:

AES: Advanced Encryption Standard

"APPENDIX I" OF THE GUIDELINES ON INTERNATIONAL MOBILE MONEY REMITTANCE SERVICE IN NIGERIA

APPROVAL REQUIREMENTS FOR INTERNATIONAL MOBILE MQNEY_SERVICE PROVIDERS

1. Evidence of the formation of the Consortium that will deploy the project (Certificate of Incorporation]

2. The Consortium's profile and functional contact e-mails and telephone numbers

3. Memorandum & Articles of Association

4. Shareholding structure of the Consortium

5. Forms C02 (Return on Allotment of shares) and CO7 (Particulars of Directors)

6. CV's of Board and Management of the Company

7. Organogram of the company

8. Business Plan, to include:

   a. Nature of the Business

   b. Features of the scheme

   c. Securities features that will be put in place

   d. 3 years Financial projections for the company

   e. Transaction and other charges that will be borne by customers

   f. Profit sharing agreement among the parties

   g. Diagrammatic illustration of transaction flows

9. Information Technology Policy of the Company including:

   a. Privacy Policy

b. Information Ownership/Disclosure/Loss Policy

c. Backup and Restore Policy

d. Network Security Policy

e. Encryption Policy

f. Confidential Data Policy

g. Password Policy

h. Third Party Connection Policy

i. Incidence Response Policy

j. Physical Security Policy

10. Enterprise Risk Management Framework

11. Contingency and Disaster Recovery Plan (Business Continuity Programme)

12. Draft agreements with the following:

a. Technical Partners

b. Participating banks

c. Switching company/(s)

d. Merchants

e. Telcos

f. Any other party

13. Tax Clearance Certificate for three (3) years of each party in the Consortium

14. Project Deployment Plan (time, location, operation, etc.)

15. Payment of non-refundable Application fee of N 1,000,000.00 (One million naira) made payable to the CBN via the RTGS Third Party Transfer.

APPENDIX 5

GLOSSARY OF TERMINOLOGY

"Access" means the making available of communications facilities and communications services one licensee to another for the purpose of providing services, and includes the connection of equipment by wire or wireless means, access to physical infrastructure including but not limited to buildings, ducts and masts, access to mobile networks, in particular for roaming, and access to number translation or systems offering equivalent functionality;

"Account" means a facility or arrangement by which a Financial Institution—

(a) accepts deposits of currency;

(b) allows withdrawals of currency or transfers into or out of the account;

(c) pays cheques or payment orders drawn on a Financial Institution or cash dealer by a person or collect cheques or payment orders on behalf of a person; or

(d) supplies a facility or an arrangement for a safe deposit box;

"Activate" means to allow full access to a Licensee's Network Service, including the ability to make and receive calls, to send and receive short message services and other range of services usually provided by Mobile Telecommunication Service providers;

"Activation window" means the period of one month from the day a subscriber acquires a new line on the network of a licensee, within which a new subscriber is required to register with the relevant licensee and during which, the new subscriber will be granted limited Access;

"An Agent or Dealer" refers to an individual or firm authorized to act on behalf of a Network Service Provider regarding SIM Replacement. Commission" shall have the same meaning as in the Nigerian Communications Act 2003.

"Agreement" means an agreement, whether formal or informal, oral or written, express or implied;

"Applications service" means a service provided by means of, but not solely by means of one, or more network services;

"Applications service provider" means a person who provides an application service;

"Assignment" means the assignment by the Commission of rights to use the spectrum, numbers or electronic addresses and may include conditions to which the exercise of those rights shall be subject;

"Authorised interception" means interception by the licensee of any network facilities, network service or applications service permitted under section 148 of the Nigerian Communications Act, 2003;

"Bank" means a deposit taking institution duly licensed by the Central Bank of Nigeria.

"Basic information" means subscriber account information or details; call data which, in the context of this definition, shall include the data of any communication service subscribed to or used by a consumer; and such other information as the Commission may, from time to time, determine;

"BDC" means Bureau De Change;

"Beneficiary" includes a natural or legal person or any other form of legal arrangement identified by the originator as the receiver of the requested wire transfer;

"Beneficial owner" refers to—

(a) the natural person who ultimately owns or controls a customer;

(b) the natural person on whose behalf a transaction is being conducted; and

(c) a person who exercises ultimate effective control over a legal person or arrangement;

"Biometric information" refers to finger prints and facial image of a subscriber in accordance with the Registration Specifications (as may be amended from time to time) provided by the Commission for the registration of subscribers;

'Business Relationship' means any arrangement between the financial institution and the applicant for business the purpose of which is to facilitate the carrying out of transactions between the parties on a 'frequent, habitual or regular' basis and where the monetary value of dealings in the course of the arrangement is not known or capable of being ascertained at the outset;

"Central Bank" means the Central Bank of Nigeria;

"Central Database" means subscriber information database, containing the biometric and other registration information of all Subscribers;

"CIFTS" means the Real Time Gross Settlement (RTGS) System deployed by the Central Bank of Nigeria which effects settlement of transfer among banks on real time and gross basis. It is known as the CBN Inter-Bank Funds Transfer System (CIFTS).

"Class licence" means a licence for any or all persons to conduct a specified activity and may include conditions to which the conduct of that activity shall be subject;

"Commercial launch date" means the date on which a licensee commences in provision of commercial services;

"Commission" means the Nigerian Communications Commission established under section 3 of the Nigerian Communications Act, 2003;

"Communications licence" or "licence" means either an individual licence or a class licence issued by the Commission under Chapter IV;

"Communications" means any communication, whether between persons and persons, things and things, or persons and things, in the form of sound, data, text, visual images, signals or any other form or any combination of those forms;

"Communications sector" or "market" means an economic sector or market for a network service, or an applications service, or for goods or services used in conjunction with a network service or an applications service, or for access to facilities used in conjunction with· either a network service or an applications service;

"Consolidated Revenue Fund" means the Fund established by section 80 of the Constitution of the Federal Republic of Nigeria 1999;

"Constitution" means the Constitution of the Federal Republic of Nigeria, 1999;

"Consumer", "customer", or "subscriber" means any person who subscribes to and uses a communication service;

"Content" means any sound; text, still picture, moving picture or other audiovisual representation, tactile representation or any combination of the preceding which is capable of being created, manipulated, stored, retrieved or communicated electronically;

"Content applications service" means an applications service which provides content;

"Contravention" includes non-compliance with or the infringement of any of the provisions of the Nigerian Communications Act, 2003, the Nigerian Money Laundering Prohibition Act, 2011 (as amended) or any regulations made thereunder or of any license;

"Council" means the Federal Executive Council of the Federal Republic of Nigeria;

"Court" means a court of law of competent jurisdiction;

"Correspondent banking" means the provision of banking services by one bank (the correspondent bank) to another bank (the respondent bank);

"Cross-border transfer" means any wire transfer where the originator and beneficiary institutions are located in different jurisdictions. This term also refers to any chain of wire transfers that has at least one cross-border element:

"Customer equipment" means any equipment, whether hardware or software, or device, used on the customer side of the network boundary;

'Designated categories of offences' includes—

(a) participation in an organized criminal group and racketeering;

(b) terrorism, including terrorist financing;

(c) trafficking in human beings and migrant smuggling;

(d) sexual exploitation, including sexual exploitation of children;

(e) illicit trafficking in narcotic drugs and psychotropic substances;

(f) illicit arms trafficking;

(g) illicit trafficking in stolen and other goods;

(h) corruption and bribery;

(i) fraud;

(j) counterfeiting currency;

(k) counterfeiting and piracy of products;

(l) environmental crime;

(m) murder, grievous bodily injury;

(n) kidnapping, illegal restraint and hostage-taking;

(o) robbery or theft;

(p) smuggling (including in relation to customs and excise duties and taxes);

(q) tax crimes (related to direct taxes and indirect taxes);

(r) extortion;

(s) forgery;

(t) piracy;

(u) insider trading and market manipulation; and

(v) all other predicate offences as contained in section 15 of Money Laundering (Prohibition) Act, 2011 (as amended).

"Designated non-financial businesses and professions" includes any institution as designated by the Minister of Trade and Investment, MLPA, 2011 (as amended) and CBN AML/CFT Regulations, 2013;

'Domestic transfer' means any wire transfer where the originator and beneficiary institutions are both located in Nigeria. This term therefore, refers to any chain of wire transfers that takes place entirely within Nigeria's borders, even though the system used to effect the wire transfer may be located in another jurisdiction;

"Economic and Financial Crimes" means the non-violent criminal and illicit activity committed with the objectives of earning wealth illegally either individually or in a group or organized manner thereby violating existing legislation governing the economic activities of government and its administration and includes any form of fraud, narcotic drug trafficking, money laundering, embezzlement, bribery, looting and any form of corrupt malpractices, illegal arms deal, smuggling, human trafficking and child labour, illegal oil bunkering and illegal mining, tax evasion, foreign exchange malpractices including counterfeiting of currency, theft of intellectual property and piracy, open market abuse, dumping of toxic wastes and prohibited goods, etc.

"Enforcement" means any action or processes for securing compliance with any of the provisions of the Act, any regulations made thereunder or of any license including but not limited to suspension or revocation of license, criminal or civil proceedings against any person who committed the contravention and any administrative action by the Commission;

"Enforcement Regulations" means the Nigerian Communications (Enforcement Processes; etc) Regulations 2005, as may be amended from time to time.

"Equipment" means any equipment or apparatus used or intended to be used for communications and that is part of or connected to or comprises a communications system;

"False declaration or disclosure" means failing to declare or, to misrepresent the value of currency or bearer negotiable instruments being transported, or a misrepresentation of other relevant data requested for by the authorities;

"FATF" means Financial Action Task Force;

"FATF Recommendations" means the revised FATF Recommendations issued by the Financial Action Task Force;

"Federal Government" means the Federal Government of the Federal Republic of Nigeria;

"Financial Institution" include banks, body corporates, associations or group of persons, whether corporate or incorporate which carries on the business of investment and securities, a discount house, insurance institution, debt factorization and conversion firm, bureau de change, finance company, money brokerage firm whose principal business includes factoring, project financing, equipment leasing, debt administration, fund management, private ledger service, investment management, local purchase order financing, export finance, project consultancy, financial consultancy, pension funds management and such other business as the Central Bank or other appropriate regulatory authorities may from time to time designate;

"Financing of terrorism" extends to all acts so defined under the Terrorism (Prevention) Act, 2011 (as amended) and the Terrorism Prevention ((Freezing of International Terrorists Funds and other Related Measures) Regulations, 2013;

"Foreign Licensee" refers to a Network Service provider licensed by a telecommunications regulator other than the Commission, to provide telecommunication services in a country other than Nigeria;

"Funds" refers to assets of every kind whether tangible or intangible, movable or immovable, howsoever acquired and legal documents or instruments in any form, including electronic or digital, evidencing title to or interest in such assets, including bank credits, travellers cheques, bank cheques, money orders, shares, securities, bonds, drafts or letters of credit;

"Funds transfer" means any transaction carried out on behalf of an originator person, both natural and legal through a financial institution by electronic means with a view to making an amount of money available to a beneficiary person at another financial institution and the originator and the beneficiary may be the same person;

"General Consumer Code of Practice for Telecommunications Services" means the General Code (as amended from time to time) attached as Schedule 1 to the Nigerian Communications Commission Consumer Code of Practice Regulations, 2006 (as may be amended from time to time);

"Harmful interference" means interference which endangers the functioning of a radio-navigation service or of other safety services or seriously degrades, obstructs, or repeatedly interrupts a radiocommunication service operating in accordance with Radio Regulations;

"Independent Registration Agent" means a company contracted by the Commission for the registration of existing subscribers on such terms as may be agreed upon between the Commission and the company;

"Individual licence" means a licence for a specified person to conduct a specified activity and may include conditions to which the conduct of that activity shall be subject;

"Infrastructure Providers" are organizations providing infrastructure that enable switching, processing and settlement facilities for mobile money services. Settlement here refers to Inter-Scheme Settlement.

"Instrument" includes a direction, determination or declaration;

"Intercept" means the aural or other acquisition of the contents of any communications through the use of any electronic,' mechanical or other equipment, device or apparatus;

"Interception capability" means the capability of any network facilities or network service or applications service to intercept communications under section 147 of this Act;

"Interconnection" means the physical and logical linking and connection of communications systems used or operated by the same or different licensees in order to convey messages to and from the respective systems for the provision of services;

"Interference" means the effect of unwanted energy due to one or a combination of emissions, radiations, or inductions upon reception in a radiocommunication system, manifested by any performance degradation, misinterpretation, or loss of information which could be extracted in the absence of such unwanted energy;

"Inter-Scheme operations" are mobile payments consummated across two different schemes by various participants.

"Intra-Scheme operations" are mobile payments that are consummated within a particular service provider's scheme.

"Issuer" is the entity which receives payment in exchange for value distributed in the system and which is obligated to pay or redeem transactions or balances presented to it.

"ITU" means International Telecommunications Union;

"Legal arrangement" means express trusts or other similar legal arrangements;

"Legal persons" mean bodies corporate, foundations, partnerships, or associations, or any similar bodies that can establish a permanent customer relationship with a financial institution or otherwise own property;

"Licensee" means a provider of Mobile Telephone Services that utilises a subscription Medium in the Federal Republic of Nigeria;

"Licensee" means a person who either holds an individual licence or undertakes activities which are subject to a class licence granted under the Nigerian Communications Act, 2003;

"Licensed area" means the geographical area covered by the licence and within which area the licensee is authorised to provide the service;

"Licensed Corporate Organizations" are Companies licensed by the Corporate Affairs Commission (CAC) under the Companies and Allied Matters Act 2004 (CAMA), to carry business in Nigeria.

"Limited access" means the limitation by a licensee of services available to a subscriber to receive calls and short message services and making of calls to emergency centre numbers and the licensee's call centre only;

"Minister" means the Minister for the time being charged with the responsibility for Communications;

"Minister of Finance" means the Federal Minister for the time being charged with the responsibility for Finance;

"Ministry" means the Federal Ministry for the time being charged with the responsibility for Communications;

"Mobile Money Operators" provide the infrastructure for the mobile payment systems for the use of participants that are signed-on to their scheme;

"Mobile Telephone Services" mean telephone services that utilise a subscription medium;

"Money Laundering" is the act of directly or indirectly concealing or disguising any fund or property that is derived from the proceeds of an unlawful activity. Simply put, it is the process by which "dirty" money is made to look legitimate or "clean" so that the funds may be used freely without trace of its illicit source;

"Money or value transfer services (MVTS)" include financial services that involve the acceptance of cash, cheques, other monetary instruments or other stores of value and the payment of a corresponding sum in cash or other form to a beneficiary by means of a communication, message, transfer or through a clearing network to which the MVTS provider belongs and transactions performed by such services can involve one or more intermediaries and a final payment to a third party, and may include any new payment methods. Sometimes these services have ties to particular geographic regions and are described using a variety of specific terms, including hawala, hundi, and feichen;

"Money Service Business" includes currency dealers, money transmitters, cheque cashers, and issuers of travellers' cheques, money orders or stored value.

"Monitoring" refers to the powers of the Nigerian Communications Commission to monitor compliance with or infringement of any of the provisions of the Act, any regulations made thereunder or any licence;

"MSISDN" means Mobile Station International Subscriber Directory Number and is the telephone number assigned to a SIM.

"National Assembly" means the National Assembly of the Federal Republic of Nigeria;

"National Frequency Plan" means the frequency plan prepared under Part II of Chapter III and Part I of Chapter VIII for the management of any part or all of the national spectrum;

"**NCC"** refers to the Nigeria Communications Commission with Regulatory powers over the telecommunication companies (Telcos)

"Network facilities" means any element or combination of elements of physical infrastructure used principally for or in connection with the provision of services but does not include customer equipment;

"Network facilities provider" means a person who is an owner of any network facilities;

"Network service" means a service "for carrying communications by means of guided or unguided electromagnetic radiation;

"Network service provider" means a person who provides network services;

"**NFM Council"** means National Frequency Management Council;

"**NIBSS"** means the Nigeria Inter-Bank Settlement System;

"Nigerian Financial Intelligence Unit (NFIU)" refers to the central unit responsible for the receiving, requesting, analyzing and disseminating to the competent authorities disclosures of financial information concerning the suspected proceeds of crime and potential financing of terrorism;

"Nominee Account" is the Account set up by a Nominee (MMO) for settlement of customer transactions held on behalf of the individual customers (the 'beneficial owner') under a custodial agreement;

"Non-profit/non-governmental Organization" means a legal entity or organization that primarily engages in raising or disbursing funds for purposes such as charitable, religious, cultural, educational, social or fraternal purposes, or for the carrying out of other types of good works;

"Number" means a number, letter or symbol;

"One-off transaction" means any transaction carried out other than in the course of an established business relationship. It is important to determine whether an applicant for business is undertaking a one-off transaction or whether the transaction is or will be a part of a business relationship as this can affect the identification requirements;

"Online SIM Replacement" means the process by which a subscriber can replace its SIM online.

"Originator" means an account holder or where there is no account, the person natural or legal that places the order with the financial institution to perform the wire transfer;

"Owner" means the legal or beneficial owner;

"Payable through account" means correspondent accounts that are used directly by third parties to transact business on their own behalf;

"Person" includes a corporate body or partnership and where an individual is required to represent a corporate body or partnership in any circumstance pursuant to this Act or its subsidiary legislation it shall be sufficient if in the case of a—

(a) corporate body, it is represented by its competent officer; and

(b) partnership, it is represented by a partner in the partnership or a competent employee of the partnership;

"Personal information" refers to the full names (including mother's maiden name), gender, date of birth, residential address, nationality, state of origin, occupation and such other personal information and contact details of subscribers specified in the Registration Specifications;

"Photo Identification" This includes an International Passport, Drivers Licence or National Identity card or voter's identification card or Letter of Authentication by a traditional ruler/community leader affixed with passport photograph, Affidavit and declarations sworn to under oath.

"Physical Presence" in relation to shell banks, means having structure and management located within a country and not merely the existence of a local agent or low level staff;

"PIN" means Personal Identification Number

"Politically exposed persons ('PEPs')" includes—

(a) individuals who are or have been entrusted with prominent public functions by a foreign country, for example Heads of State or Government, senior politicians, senior government, judicial or military officials, senior executives of State owned corporations and important political party officials;

(b) individuals who are or have been entrusted domestically with prominent public functions, for example Heads of State or of Government, senior politicians, senior government, judicial or military officials, senior executives of State owned corporations and important political party officials; and

(c) persons who are or have been entrusted with a prominent function by an international organization and includes members of senior management such as directors, deputy directors and members of the board or equivalent functions other than middle ranking or more junior individuals;

"President" means the President of the Federal Republic of Nigeria;

"Proceeds" means property derived from or obtained, directly or indirectly through the commission of an offence;

"Property" means assets of every kind, whether corporeal or incorporeal, moveable or immoveable, tangible or intangible and legal documents or instruments evidencing title to or interest in such assets;

"Public Officers" means individuals who are or have been entrusted with prominent public function, both within and outside Nigeria and those associated with them;

"Registration of Telephone Subscribers Regulations" means the Registration of Telephone Subscribers Regulations 2011 as may be amended from time to time;

"Registration Specifications" mean the Data Dictionary, Guidelines on Fingerprint Quality, specifications for Digital Image Standards and Quality, the XML Schema, Transmission protocol and the Technical Interface specifications and such other specifications and amendments thereto that may be made or issued by the Commission, from time to time, to guide the registration of subscribers and the interaction of Licensees' or Independent Registration Agents' databases with the Central Database;

"Regulators" means competent regulatory authorities responsible for ensuring compliance of Financial Institutions and Designated Non-Financial Institutions with requirements to combat money laundering and terrorist financing;

"Relevant authority" means the Nigeria Police Force, National Intelligence Agency, State Security Services, Economic and Financial Crimes Commission, National Drug Law Enforcement Agency and any other organisation or agency as the Commission may from time to time specify and publish;

"Risk" means the risk of money laundering and/or terrorist financing;

"SCUML" means Special Control Unit against Money Laundering in the Federal Ministry of Trade and Investment;

"Security Agency" or "Security Agencies" refers to any or all of the following law enforcement and security agencies : (a) Nigerian Police Force (b) the Economic and Financial Crimes Commission (c) the State Security Service (d) the Federal Road Safety Corps (e) the National Intelligence Agency (f) the Office of the National Security Adviser ; and (g) any other law enforcement or Security Agency established by the Federal Government ;

"Service", except where the context otherwise requires, means applications, content, network or facilities services or any combination of these services;

"Service Providers" employ the infrastructure of the scheme operator to provide services to end users.

"Settlement Infrastructure Providers" are Organizations providing infrastructure that enables message exchange, switching and settlement facilities for mobile money services.

"Settlors" Settlors include persons or companies who transfer ownership of their assets to trustees by means of a trust deed and where the trustees have some discretion as to the investment and distribution of the trust's assets, the deed may be accompanied by a non-legally binding letter setting out what the settlor wishes to be done with the assets;

"Shell bank" means a bank that is not physically located in the country in which it is incorporated and licensed and which is unaffiliated with a regulated financial group that is subject to effective consolidated supervision;

"Shell company" generally refers to an entity without a physical presence in any country;

"SIM" means a Subscriber Identity Module, and includes Removable User Identity Module (RUIM).

"SIM Replacement" means the process by which a SIM is replaced by a Network Service Provider enabling the subscriber keep the same phone number being used on the faulty, damaged, stolen, or lost SIM;

"Spectrum" means the continuous range of electromagnetic wave frequencies up to and including a frequency of 420 terahertz;

"Subscriber" means a person who subscribes to data or Mobile Telecommunication Services by purchasing a subscription medium or entering into a subscription contract with a Network Service Provider.

"Subscriber Information" refers to the Biometrics and other Personal Information of a Subscriber recorded and stored by licensees or the Independent Registration Agents;

"Subscriber Registration Period" means the six months period from the effective date or such other date as the Commission may specify and any extensions thereto that may be announced by the Commission, within which existing subscribers are required to register their Subscription Mediums pursuant to these Regulations;

"Subscription Medium" means a Subscriber Identity Module (SIM) smart card, a Removable User Identity Module (R-UIM) smart card, a CDMA Subscriber Identity Module (CSIM) smart card, a Universal Subscriber Identity Module (USIM) smart card or any other mobile phone subscription medium marketed from time to time by licensees, containing the telephone number of a subscriber, encoded network identification details, the personal identification number and other user data normally provided by a licensee for the provision of Network Services;

"Suspicious" means a matter which is beyond mere speculations and is based on some foundation;

"Telecommunication" means any transmission, emission or reception of signs, signals, writing, images, sounds or intelligence of any nature by wire, radio, visual or other electro-magnetic systems;

"Terrorist Financing" is defined in the Central Bank of Nigeria AML/CFT Policy and Procedure manual to include both legitimate and illegitimate money characterized by concealment of the origin or intended criminal use of the funds. The techniques used to launder money are essentially the same as that used to disguise the origin of, and use, for terrorism financing.

"Terrorism Financing" means financial support, in any form, of terrorism or of those who encourage, plan or engage in terrorism;

"Those who finance terrorism" include any person, group, undertaking or other entity that provides or collects, by any means, directly or indirectly, funds or other assets that may be used, in full or in part, to facilitate the commission of terrorist acts, or to any persons or entities acting on behalf of, or at the direction of such persons, groups, undertakings or other entities and those who provide or collect funds or other assets with the intention that they should be used or in the knowledge that they are to be used, in full or in part, in order to carry out terrorist acts;

"Transmit" or "transmission" means to cause any emission of unguided electromagnetic energy in any part of the spectrum;

"Transaction" means—

(a) acceptance of deposit and other repayable funds from the public;

(b) lending;

(c) financial leasing;

(d) money transmission service;

(e) issuing and managing means of payment (for example, credit and debit cards, cheques, travellers' cheque and bankers' drafts etc.);

(f) financial guarantees and commitment;

(g) trading for account of costumer (spot-forward, swaps, future options, etc.) in—

(i) money market instruments (cheques, bills of exchange, etc.);

(ii) foreign exchange;

(iii) exchange interest rate and index instruments;

(iv) transferable securities; and (v) commodity futures trading;

(h) participation in capital markets activities and the provision of financial services related to such issues;

(i) individual and collective portfolio management;

(j) safekeeping and administration of cash or liquid securities on behalf of clients;

(k) life insurance and all other insurance related matters; and

(l) money changing;

"Trustees" include paid professionals or companies or unpaid persons who hold the assets in a trust fund separate from their own assets. They invest and dispose of them in accordance with the settlor's trust deed, taking account of any letter of wishes. There may also be a protector who may have power to veto the trustees' proposals or remove them, or a custodian trustee, who holds the assets to the order of the managing trustees;

"Unauthorised" means an act or omission not within the scope of operating licence, the Act or any subsidiary legislation;

"Unique identifier" means any unique combination of letters, numbers or symbols that refers to a specific originator;

"Unlawful" means any act or omission that is contrary to or against the Act or any regulations made thereunder or any other law governing the telecommunications industry; and

"Wire transfer" means any transaction carried out on behalf of a natural person or legal originator through a Financial Institution by electronic means with a view to making an amount of money available to a beneficiary person at another financial institution, irrespective of whether the originator and the beneficiary are the same person.

APPENDIX 6

EHI ERIC ESOIMEME'S PUBLICATIONS

BOOKS

- Esoimeme, E.E. (2018), 'Deterring and Detecting Money Laundering and Terrorist Financing: A Comparative Analysis of Anti–Money Laundering and Counterterrorism Financing Strategies', DSC Publications Ltd, Available on Amazon: https://www.amazon.co.uk/Deterring-Detecting-Laundering-Terrorist-Financing/dp/9782787795/ref=sr_1_1?ie=UTF8&qid=1520869556&sr=8-1&keywords=ehi+esoimeme

- Esoimeme, E.E. (2015), 'The Risk-Based Approach to Combating Money Laundering and Terrorist Financing', Eric Press; Available on Amazon: https://www.amazon.co.uk/Risk-Based-Combating-Laundering-Terrorist-Financing/dp/9789486030/ref=sr_1_2?ie=UTF8&qid=1437508453&sr=8-2&keywords=ehi+eric+esoimeme

- Esoimeme, E.E. (2014), 'A Comparative Study of the Money Laundering Laws/Regulations in Nigeria, the United States and the United Kingdom', Eric Press; Available on Amazon: https://www.amazon.co.uk/Comparative-Laundering-Regulations-Nigeria-Kingdomebook/dp/B00OC2X7HK/ref=sr_1_8?s=digital-text&ie=UTF8&qid=1413235091&sr=1-8&keywords=money+laundering

- Onwudiwe, C.C. and Esoimeme, E.E. (2016), 'Banker-Customer Relationship: A Practical Legal Guide', Bank Customers Association of Nigeria.

ARTICLES

- Esoimeme E.E. (2019), 'Enhancing Financial Inclusion: Telecoms and AML in Nigeria', KYC360 (the global financial crime and compliance knowledge hub powered by RiskScreen), https://www.riskscreen.com/kyc360/research-papers/enhancing-financial-inclusion-telecoms-and-aml-in-nigeria/

- Esoimeme E.E. (2019), 'Institutionalising the War Against Corruption: New Approaches to Assets Tracing and Recovery', Journal of Financial Crime, https://papers.ssrn.com/sol3/papers.cfm?abstract_id=3243108, forthcoming (this paper was presented by Ehi Eric Esoimeme at the just concluded Nigerian Bar Association Annual General Conference 2018 in a session titled: Institutionalising the War Against Corruption: New Approaches to Assets Tracing and Recovery).

- Esoimeme E.E. (2019), 'Using Anti-Money Laundering Measures to Curb Pension Fraud in Nigeria', Journal of Financial Crime, forthcoming. The Article version of this research paper has already been published on KYC360 (the global financial crime and compliance knowledge hub powered by RiskScreen), https://www.riskscreen.com/kyc360/research-papers/using-anti-money-laundering-measures-to-curb-pension-fraud-in-nigeria/

- Esoimeme, E.E. (2019), 'Using the Lie Detector Test to Curb Corruption in the Nigerian Police Force', Journal of Financial Crime, Vol. 26, Issue: 3 https://doi.org/10.1108/JFC-06-2018-0058. The Article version of this research paper has already been published on KYC360 (the global financial crime and compliance knowledge hub powered by RiskScreen), https://kyc360.com/article/using-lie-detector-test-curb-corruption-nigerian-police-force/

- Esoimeme, E.E. (2019), 'A Critical Analysis of the Anti-Corruption Policy of the Federal Executive Council of Nigeria', Journal of Money Laundering Control, Vol. 22, Issue: 2, https://www.emeraldinsight.com/doi/pdfplus/10.1108/JMLC-06-2017-0021

- Esoimeme, E.E. (2019), 'Balancing Anti-money laundering measures and Financial Inclusion: the example of the United Kingdom and Nigeria', Journal of Money Laundering Control, Forthcoming, https://papers.ssrn.com/sol3/papers.cfm?abstract_id=3172081

- Esoimeme, E.E. (2018), 'A Comparative Analysis of the Prepaid Card Laws/Regulations in Nigeria, the United Kingdom, the United States and India', Journal of Money Laundering Control, Vol. 21, Issue: 4, pp.481-493, https://doi.org/10.1108/JMLC-03-2017-0010

- Esoimeme, E.E. (2018), 'Banking: Curbing employee fraud and corruption with an effective KYE program', KYC360 (the global financial crime and compliance knowledge hub powered by RiskScreen), https://www.riskscreen.com/kyc360/article/banking-curbing-employee-fraud-and-corruption-with-an-effective-kye-program/

- Esoimeme E.E. (2018), 'Fighting Corruption? It's Worth Considering a Preventive Approach to Asset Recovery', KYC360 (the global financial crime and compliance knowledge hub powered by RiskScreen), https://kyc360.com/article/fighting-corruption-its-worth-considering-a-preventive-approach-to-asset-recovery/

- Esoimeme, E.E. (2018), 'A Critical Analysis of the Anti-Corruption Policy of the National Judicial Council of Nigeria', Journal of Money Laundering Control, Vol. 21, Issue: 3, https://www.emeraldinsight.com/doi/pdfplus/10.1108/JMLC-01-2017-0001

- Esoimeme, E.E. (2018), 'The money laundering risks and vulnerabilities associated with MMM Nigeria', Journal of Money Laundering Control, Vol. 21, Issue: 1, pp.112-119, http://www.emeraldinsight.com/doi/full/10.1108/JMLC-01-2017-0002

- Esoimeme, E.E. (2017), 'A critical analysis of the effects of the Central Bank of Nigeria foreign exchange policy on financial inclusion, anti-money laundering measures and fundamental rights', Journal of Money Laundering Control, Vol. 20, Issue: 4, pp.417-427, https://doi.org/10.1108/JMLC-05-2016-0020

- Esoimeme, E.E. (2017), "The Nigerian Money Laundering (Prevention and Prohibition) Bill, 2016: a critical appraisal", Journal of Money Laundering Control, Vol. 20, Issue: 1, pp.79-88, https://doi.org/10.1108/JMLC-07-2016-0025

- Esoimeme, E.E. (2016), 'Wealth Management, Tax Evasion and Money Laundering: The Panama Papers Case Study', Law Digest Issue 11 Autumn 2016. Available at Law Digest: https://issuu.com/nglawdigest/docs/law_digest_issue_11_autumn_2016

- Esoimeme, E.E. (2016), 'Balancing Anti-Money Laundering/Counter-Terrorist Financing Requirements and Financial Inclusion for Migrants: A Case Study of Germany', Available at SSRN: https://ssrn.com/abstract=2710097

- Esoimeme, E.E. (2015), 'A Critical Analysis of the Bank Verification Number Project Introduced by the Central Bank of Nigeria', Available at SSRN: https://ssrn.com/abstract=2544934 or http://dx.doi.org/10.2139/ssrn.2544934

- Esoimeme, E.E. (2015), 'A Comparative Study of the Money Laundering Laws/Regulations in Nigeria, the United States and the United Kingdom: Reporting Requirements', Professionals Center for Business Research Volume 2 – June 2015 (06). Available at SSRN: https://ssrn.com/abstract=2441086

- Esoimeme, E.E. (2015), 'The Death Penalty: An Effective Anti-Corruption Mechanism?', Available at SSRN: https://ssrn.com/abstract=2621268

- Esoimeme, E.E. (2015), 'A Critical Analysis of the Anti-Money Laundering Measures Adopted by BitGold Inc', Available at SSRN: https://ssrn.com/abstract=2604721 or http://dx.doi.org/10.2139/ssrn.2604721

- Esoimeme, E.E. (2014), 'Has the Concept of Plea Bargaining Been Abused in Nigeria's Criminal Justice System?', The Legal Aid Journal Volume 1. Available at SSRN: https://ssrn.com/abstract=2462307

- Esoimeme, E.E. (2014), 'A Comparative Study of the Money Laundering Laws/Regulations in Nigeria, the United States and the United Kingdom: Cash Couriers', The PUNCH, VOL 38 NO. 20,733, 20,739 PAGE 25, 29. Available at SSRN: https://ssrn.com/abstract=2476587

- Esoimeme, E.E. (2013), 'A Critical Analysis of the Effect of the Double Criminality Test on the Investigation Team and the Prosecution's Case', Available at SSRN: https://ssrn.com/abstract=2514719

- Esoimeme, E.E. (2013), 'A Critical Analysis of the Effect of the Double Criminality Test on Nominated Officers and Money Laundering Reporting Officers (MLRO) in the Regulated Sector', Available at SSRN: https://ssrn.com/abstract=2462952

- Esoimeme, E.E. (2013), 'The Importance of Why Firms Dealing with PEPs Must Adopt a Risk-Based Approach to Their Compliance Programmes', Available at SSRN: https://ssrn.com/abstract=2430972

EHI ERIC ESOIMEME HAS EDITED THE FOLLOWING PUBLICATIONS:

- Sasegbon's Judicial Dictionary of Nigerian Law (the first comprehensive judicial dictionary in Nigeria in 7 Volumes), DSC Publications Ltd., forthcoming.

- Sasegbon on Election Petitions, DSC Publications Ltd., Volume 3 Part III and 12 other volumes.

EHI ERIC ESOIMEME HAS ALSO PEER REVIEWED THE FOLLOWING PUBLICATIONS:

- Ross, I. (2015), 'Exposing Fraud: Skills, Process and Practicalities', Wiley Corporate F&A. Available on Amazon: https://www.amazon.co.uk/Exposing-Fraud-Process-Practicalities-Corporate-ebook/dp/B01CJK4Z8Q/ref=sr_1_fkmr0_2?ie=UTF8&qid=1493990138&sr=8-2-fkmr0&keywords=ian+ross+on+fraud

- Nwachukwu, E. (2015), 'Academic Excellence in 21 Days', Partridge Africa. Available on Amazon: https://www.amazon.co.uk/Academic-Excellence-Days-Eric-Nwachukwu/dp/1482826224/ref=sr_1_1?ie=UTF8&qid=1493990393&sr=8-1&keywords=eric+nwachukwu

INDEX

REFERENCES ARE TO PARAGRAPH NUMBERS

E

F

S

T

Made in United States
Orlando, FL
05 November 2026

90229824R00194